Feminism in Popular Culture

Feminism in Popular Culture

Edited by
JOANNE HOLLOWS
and
RACHEL MOSELEY

Oxford • New York

First published in 2006 by
Berg
Editorial offices:
1st Floor, Angel Court, 81 St Clements Street, Oxford OX4 1AW, UK
175 Fifth Avenue, New York, NY 10010, USA

Berg is the imprint of Oxford International Publishers Ltd.

Library of Congress Cataloging-in-Publication Data
Feminism in popular culture / edited by Joanne Hollows and Rachel
Moseley.
    p. c.m
    Includes bibliographical references and index.
    ISBN-13: 978-1-84520-223-1 (pbk.)
    ISBN-10: 1-84520-223-6 (pbk.)
    ISBN-13: 978-1-84520-222-4 (cloth)
    ISBN-10: 1-84520-222-8 (cloth)
  1. Feminism. 2. Popular culture. 3. Women in popular culture. I. Hollows,
Joanne. II. Moseley, Rachel.

HQ1111.F4644 2006
305.42--dc22
                                    2005028760

British Library Cataloguing-in-Publication Data
A catalogue record for this book is available from the British Library.

ISBN-13 978 184520 222 4 (Cloth)
  ISBN-10 1 84520 222 8 (Cloth)

    ISBN-13 978 184520 223 1 (Paper)
     ISBN-10 1 84520 223 6 (Paper)

Typeset by JS Typesetting Ltd, Porthcawl, Mid Glamorgan.
Printed in the United Kingdom by Biddles Ltd, King's Lynn.

www.bergpublishers.com

Contents

Notes on Contributors   vii

Acknowledgements   xi

1   Popularity Contests: The Meanings of Popular Feminism
     Joanne Hollows and Rachel Moseley   1

Part I: Inter-generational Relations of Feminism

2   Feminism in the News
     Susan Sheridan, Susan Magarey and Sandra Lilburn   25

3   The Feminist in the Kitchen: Martha, Martha and Nigella
     Charlotte Brunsdon   41

4   Feminism in the Classroom: Teaching Towards the Third Wave
     Kathleen Rowe Karlyn   57

Part II: Coming to Terms with Feminism

5   'Ally McBeal', 'Sex and the City' and the Tragic Success of
     Feminism
     Joke Hermes   79

6   Can I Go Home Yet? Feminism, Post-feminism and Domesticity
     Joanne Hollows   97

7   Sex Workers Incorporated
     Jane Arthurs   119

Part III: Negotiating and Resisting Feminisms

  8   Discipline and Pleasure: The Uneasy Relationship Between
      Feminism and the Beauty Industry
      Paula Black   143

  9   Learning from B-Girls
      Charla Ogaz   161

 10   Illegitimate, Monstrous and Out There: Female *Quake*
      Players and Inappropriate Pleasures
      Helen W. Kennedy   183

 Index   203

Notes on Contributors

Jane Arthurs is Head of the School of Cultural Studies at the University of the West of England, UK. Her teaching and research is in film, television and feminist cultural studies. She has co-edited *Women's Bodies: Discipline and Transgression* (Continuum, 1999), *Crash Cultures: Modernity, Mediation and the Material* (Intellect, 2002) and co-authored *The Crash Controversy: Censorship Campaigns and Film Reception* (Wallflower Press, 2001). Her most recent book is *Television and Sexuality: Regulation and the Politics of Taste* (Open University Press, 2004). She is also co-editor of the 'reviews and reports' section of *Feminist Media Studies*.

Paula Black is a lecturer in sociology at the University of Sussex, UK. She has previously taught at the University of Derby and the University of Manchester. Her research interests include sexuality, the body, the beauty industry and class in Higher Education. She is the author of *The Beauty Industry: Gender, Culture, Pleasure* (Routledge, 2004).

Charlotte Brunsdon teaches at the University of Warwick, UK. Her publications include *Everyday Television: 'Nationwide'* (BFI, 1978), *Films for Women* (BFI, 1986), *Screen Tastes* (Routledge, 1997), and *The Feminist, the Housewife and the Soap Opera* (Clarendon Press, 2000).

Joke Hermes teaches television studies at the University of Amsterdam. She is also a professor of public opinion formation at Inholland University, The Netherlands. Her latest book is *Re-reading Popular Culture* (Blackwell, 2005), which considers questions of popular culture, audiences, gender and cultural citizenship. With Ann Gray and Pertti Alasuutari, she is founding editor of the *European Journal of Cultural Studies*.

Joanne Hollows is Principal Lecturer in Media and Cultural Studies at Nottingham Trent University, UK. She is the author of *Feminism, Femininity* *and Popular Culture* (Manchester University Press, 2000), co-author of *Food and Cultural Studies* (Routledge, 2000) and co-editor of *Approaches to Popular Film* (Manchester University Press, 1995), *The Film Studies Reader* (Arnold, 2000) and *Ordinary Lifestyles* (Open University Press, 2005).

Kathleen Rowe Karlyn teaches film and media studies at the University of Oregon, USA. Her publications include the award-winning *The Unruly Woman: Gender and the Genres of Laughter* (University of Texas Press, 1995) and articles on feminism, film and cultural studies, including a widely anthologized essay on comedian Roseanne Barr. She is currently working on the family romance in contemporary film.

Helen W. Kennedy is Senior Lecturer, MA Award Leader and Chair of the Play Research Group in the School of Cultural Studies, University of the West of England. She has spoken at a number of both academic and industry conferences on the role of women in computer games and computer games culture, including the first UK international conference in computer games in 2001 entitled 'Game Cultures', which she co-organized, and two international symposia – 'Power Up: Computer Games, Play and Ideology' (2003) and 'Playful Subjects' (2005). She publishes widely on the subject of gaming, ideology and identity, and has a book, *Games Cultures*, with J. Dovey (Open University Press, 2005).

Sandra Lilburn was Senior Research Associate on the project, 'Faces of Feminism: representations of feminism in Australian print media, 1970 to 1995' from which her chapter here derives. She is currently the Deputy Director of the ACT Council of Social Service and works in the policy area of health and poverty

Susan Magarey is Adjunct Professor in the History Department of Adelaide University and was foundation editor of *Australian Feminist Studies*. Her most recent book is *Passions of the First Wave Feminists* (University of New South Wales Press, 2001).

Rachel Moseley is Lecturer in Film and Television Studies at the University of Warwick, UK. She has published on various aspects of popular film and television, is the author of *Growing Up with Audrey Hepburn: Text, Audience, Resonance* (Manchester University Press, 2002) and the editor of *Fashioning Film Stars: Dress, Culture, Identity* (BFI, 2005).

Charla Ogaz completed her doctorate in the History of Consciousness at the University of California, Santa Cruz. She is Assistant Professor of Liberal Arts at Savannah State University, USA.

Susan Sheridan is Professor and Head of Department of Womens' Studies at Flinders University in Adelaide, South Australia. Her most recent book is *Who Was that Woman? The Australian Woman's Weekly in the Postwar Years* (University of New South Wales Press, 2002).

Acknowledgements

This book has had a long gestation period, which was initially plagued by the curse of the lower leg. Thanks are due to so many people, who have each contributed in different ways. A big thank you to Tristan Palmer at Berg for being supportive, friendly and professional, and for taking on a book with feminism in the title, and also to Christine Cooper for her hard work on a wonderful chapter which, in the end, could not be included in this collection due to circumstances beyond our control.

Joanne would like to thank Dave and Roger for their parts in making it possible for her to not be programme leader while this book was completed and, more generally, the MCS team at NTU. Discussions with people at recent conferences and seminars really helped her to clarify ideas around the themes of this book, and she'd like to thank the participants. Thanks to David for suggesting we approach Tristan. As usual, she wants to thank Mark for lots but she'd like specifically to thank him for the ridiculous amount he did for her during the time of 'the leg illness' that marked the genesis of this book. Finally, thank you to Rachel for being so great to co-edit with!

Rachel would like to thank supportive friends for always being there to listen and in particular Helen and Helen. Of course, enormous thanks to Joanne and Jacinda for suggesting the project, for making it easy and especially for maintaining the momentum and doing so much of the work in the early stages when she was, quite literally, in pieces!!

Last, but absolutely not least, we both want to thank Jacinda, and to dedicate this volume to her.

CHAPTER I

Popularity Contests: The Meanings of Popular Feminism

Joanne Hollows and Rachel Moseley

Why feminism *in* popular culture? The decision to make this our focus, rather than the more usual formulation of feminism *and* popular culture, is fundamental to what we set out to do in putting this collection together. The idea of feminism *and* popular culture tends to presume that a 'real' and 'authentic' feminism exists outside of popular culture, and offers a position from which to judge and measure feminism's success or failure in making it into the mainstream. Such an approach also assumes that feminism, or the feminist, can tell us about popular culture, but does not examine what popular culture can tell us about feminism. In this chapter, we discuss in more detail the nature of these debates about feminism and popular culture, identifying how they developed and how they have been negotiated and challenged. In the process, we examine how debates about popular feminism, post-feminism and third-wave feminism have conceptualized the relationship between popular culture and feminism.

However, the idea of feminism *in* popular culture also gestures towards a generational politics of feminism and is shaped by our own experiences of growing up with feminism in the popular. Rather than first encountering feminism as a social movement in the 1960s, our initial ideas of what feminism was about were formed through the popular in the 1970s and 1980s. For example, Joanne's encounters with feminism came through reading popular feminist coming-of-age novels such as *Kinflicks* (Alther 1977) and *Memoirs of an Ex-Prom Queen* (Shulman 1973), 1970s independent woman movies and *Spare Rib* magazine. However, in her memories of this period, images of independent women, which she learned to equate with feminism at the time, also manifested themselves in disco songs like 'Native New Yorker' and magazines like *Cosmopolitan*. Therefore, her understandings of feminism were formed within the popular from sources that have been thought of as both feminist and anti-feminist.[1] In this way, it was feminism in popular culture that formed the basis for later feminist identifications and politics. For Rachel, an awareness of something called 'feminism' was not really given a name and a historical framework until university, but until that point had been part of a commonsense understanding about how the world might ideally work, rather than how it in fact functioned. Such 'commonsense' understandings of women's rights and potential came from popular cultural texts such as the 'Brat pack' films of the 1980s, television programmes like 'Charlie's Angels' (Spelling-Goldberg productions, 1976–81) and 'Wonder Woman' (Bruce Lansbury Productions/DC Comics/Douglas C. Cramer Co./WB, 1976–9), girls' magazines like *Jackie* and *Just Seventeen* and singers like Gloria Gaynor, Debbie Harry and later, in a more conscious way, Madonna. Her awareness was, thus, formed on the cusp of feminist and post-feminist discourse within popular cultural forms.

Our point is that, apart from women actively involved in the second-wave of feminism in the 1960s and 1970s, most people's initial knowledge and understanding of feminism has been formed within the popular and through representation. Rather than coming to consciousness through involvement in feminist movements, most people become conscious of feminism through the way it is represented in popular culture. Thus, for many women of our generation, formative understandings of, and identifications with, feminist ideas have been almost exclusively within popular culture (although clearly some women's formative identifications with feminist politics are still through work with political parties and unions, or around specific issues or campaigns). Because of this, we never had a clear sense of, or investment in, the idea of an 'inside' or 'outside' of feminism and, indeed, a post-structuralist turn within theory problematizes the very idea that there is an 'outside' of representation. Likewise, postmodern/post-structuralist feminist theory has also attempted to radically destabilize and deconstruct the binaries upon which representations, and indeed experiences, of gender have been understood and made (see Butler 1990 and 1993). Nonetheless, there remain powerful attachments in some feminisms to the idea that feminism can exist in an 'outside', and vanguard, position. It is partially this tendency, we suggest, which has underpinned the inter-generational disagreements over the relationships between second-wave and post- and third-wave feminisms.

Not surprisingly, what happens to feminism within the popular has been a major concern of feminist critics. However, as we go on to argue below, these accounts have frequently oversimplified the complex ways in which feminism and the feminist have been envisaged within the popular. As Hinds and Stacey argue, reviewing changing images of feminism in the UK press, it would be easy to construct a narrative which charts 'a shift from the *monstrous outsiders* of the 1960s and 1970s to the *incorporated* Ms of the 1990s. However, such a linear account of the move towards reconciliation leaves little room for the uneven and multiple significations of media imaging of feminism during this time' (2001: 155). It is these 'multiple and uneven' ways in which feminism is imagined that form one of the key concerns of this collection. While many of the chapters focus on the contemporary, Sheridan *et al.*'s chapter on representations of feminism in the Australian press clearly demonstrates how the meanings of second-wave feminism were frequently constructed within the media rather than 'outside' the popular.

Therefore, a major concern of this collection is to pay attention to how the meanings of feminism are processed within the popular. Rather than assuming that these processes are inherently conservative, we suggest that it may be more enabling to abandon such a priori assumptions. Nonetheless, the idea that we need to analyze how feminism is negotiated in popular culture underpins many of the chapters that follow. For example, Paula Black (Chapter 8), Charla Ogaz (Chapter 9) and Helen Kennedy (Chapter 10), in their essays on the beauty salon, B-girls and gaming respectively, address the ways in which the meanings of feminism have been articulated within these spaces. Furthermore, we would suggest that when feminism is refused within the popular, this does not necessarily imply a conservative agenda. As Hollows argues in Chapter 6 in her exploration of the 'problem' of home and the domestic for post-feminism, and the recent debate around middle-class women 'downshifting': 'we can't simply dismiss the appeals of going home as evidence of false consciousness but need to take seriously, and analyze, the cultural significance of wanting to go home'. Struggles in popular culture over the meaning of feminism – and about the feminist's authority to speak for all women – may offer a way of understanding the limitations of feminism.

SECOND-WAVE FEMINISM AND POPULAR CULTURE

Our argument that it is necessary to examine feminism *in* popular culture needs to be understood in the context of the relationship between feminism and popular culture in the second-wave feminism of the 1960s and 1970s. The women's movement – along with many other political movements of the time – was conceived of as a social movement that was 'outside' of, and frequently oppositional to, the dominant culture and therefore as offering an alternative set of ideologies that sought to challenge hegemonic ideas about gender. In this period, the women's movement was far more visible as a social movement engaged in struggles over a range of issues such as reproductive rights, equal pay for equal work, domestic and sexual violence, and the sexual division of labour. From such a perspective, the popular was seen as a site for the cultural reproduction of gender inequalities, although there was considerable discussion about how this was achieved and how feminists should offer a challenge. However, what tended to unite these diverse feminisms was an opposition between feminism and popular culture, and between the feminist who can see through the mystifications of the popular and the 'ordinary woman' who simply passively reproduces the dominant culture (Brunsdon 1997, 2000). In order to illustrate how second-wave feminism conceived of the relationship between feminism and popular culture, we want to briefly explore two examples.

The first is associated with what became known as the 'images of women' debate. The idea that women were socialized into 'false' images of femininity through popular culture was a key element of second-wave feminism. Influenced by Betty Friedan's (1963) foundational book for liberal feminism, *The Feminine Mystique*, in which she examined how the media played a role in socializing women into restrictive notions of femininity, feminist communications research in the 1970s claimed that media audiences were presented with stereotypical images of women that not only socialized girls into 'traditional sex roles', but also told them that they 'should direct their hearts towards hearth and home' (Tuchman 1978: 37). Furthermore, it was claimed that the media misrepresented what women were 'really' like. (For similar debates in film studies, see Rosen 1975 and Haskell 1975.) If the assumption that media messages had direct effects and were simply internalized by audiences was problematic, so was the idea that the media could simply offer 'a window on the world', that media images could, or should, simply reflect reality. From this perspective, popular culture demanded a feminist intervention in order to show 'real' images of women. Examples of such interventions took the form of feminist documentary film-making that offered an alternative to the 'false' images of women in Hollywood and would represent women, and feminism, with more 'accuracy' and 'honesty', frequently seeking to tell 'real women's' stories using an 'autobiographical discourse' (Kuhn 1982: 148).

Like the theoretical assumptions underpinning 'images of women' criticism, such an approach assumes that it is possible to identify what a 'real' woman looks like: as Charlotte Brunsdon has argued, 'Arguing for more realistic images is always an argument for the representation of "your" version of reality' (cited in van Zoonen 1994: 31). Frequently, 'real' images of women were equated with 'feminist' images of women, and this sets up a hierarchical relationship between the feminist who can identify 'real' images of women and her less aware audience who cannot. From such a position, there is the potential for feminism to enter the mainstream, but only as the result of a feminist 'makeover'. It is this form of intervention that has underpinned rare instances of overtly feminist television programming such as Channel 4's 'Watch the Woman' in the 1980s. Arguably, such liberal feminist themes are also more widespread in television, film and women's magazines as we go on to discuss below.

A second example is associated with feminist work that drew on semiotics, ideology and Lacanian psychoanalysis. Although theoretically diverse, these approaches worked from the assumption that 'representations were not expressive of some prior reality, but instead were actively constitutive of reality' (McRobbie 1997: 172). Although not inherent in the approach McRobbie describes, for many feminist critics working within these approaches in the 1970s (and later) the structures and processes underpinning the organization of meaning in popular texts inevitably reproduced patriarchal ideology and made culturally constructed gender differences appear as natural and inevitable (see, for example, Mulvey 1975 and Johnston 1973). From such a perspective, popular culture was seen as a patriarchal mass culture, which reproduced patriarchal ideology in its spectators. Only by using complex theoretical methods of reading texts could these texts be denaturalized, and the only way to challenge patriarchal meanings was to offer a radical challenge to the way in which meaning was organized. Feminist film-makers working in this tradition drew on avant-garde film-making techniques to create a 'non-narrative, difficult, even boring, oppositional cinema' that would subvert the pleasures of Hollywood cinema (Williamson 1993: 313). Examples include films such as Mulvey and Wollen's *Riddles of the Sphinx* (1977), Sally Potter's *Thriller* (1979) and *The Gold Diggers* (1983), which aimed to show how ideology was reproduced in classical Hollywood cinema by attempting to deconstruct the patriarchal text and demonstrate the 'invisible' language and structures that underpinned them (see also Chapter 3). Setting itself up in opposition to the popular, this form of feminist 'alternative' was doomed to remain marginal because it was addressed to an audience familiar with the codes of avant-garde artistic movements. In this way, such approaches were not only based on a refusal of popular culture, but also a refusal of the pleasures and meanings that 'ordinary women' brought to their lives.

Second-wave feminist work, therefore, not only presumed the authority of the feminist to designate what were correct images and ways of seeing for all women, but was also underpinned by a hostility towards the popular. This work often began from a position in which the feminist critic sought to measure how feminist a text was, usually finding these texts lacking. While many of these debates were developed in more theoretical terms in academic discussions, feminists working in academic disciplines were frequently active in the women's movement. Furthermore, similar relationships to the popular were adopted more widely within feminism. For example, a rejection of 'negative', 'demeaning' or 'restrictive' definitions of femininity underpinned protests against the 1968 Miss America Pageant in the US (Morgan 1970: 588), graffiti on advertising billboards, the production of feminist magazines to challenge mainstream women's magazines and the adoption of 'alternative' forms of dress (see, for example, Brownmiller 1984).

However, while as part of a political movement second-wave feminists sought to challenge mainstream political agendas, the opposition between feminism and the popular has also frequently disguised the extent to which some feminist ideas and themes were circulating within the popular in the 1960s and 1970s. For example, Betty Friedan was herself a journalist for the women's magazines that she criticized for painting a monolithic and uncontested portrait of the appeals of being 'a happy housewife heroine' (Meyrowitz 1994). More generally, elements of feminist discourse such as female independence and equal opportunities in employment were circulating in unlikely popular forms from disco music, to the independent woman's movie, to 'Charlie's Angels' (Brunsdon 1986; Levine 2005). This is not to argue that popular culture was made over in feminist ways in the 1960s and 1970s, but rather that feminine identities were already being negotiated during the period in ways that incorporated elements of feminism within the mainstream.

Furthermore, in the late 1970s and into the 1980s, feminist media and cultural studies began to take forms of feminine popular culture seriously. These approaches demonstrated that feminine texts such as soap operas, romantic fiction and women's magazines were worthy of analysis, arguing that their readers could not simply be dismissed as the passive 'dupes' of patriarchal culture and that popular forms and practices could offer possibilities for resistance (see, for example, Brunsdon 1981; Ang 1985; Radway 1987; Winship 1987; for an overview of these debates, see Hollows 2000). As Charlotte Brunsdon has argued, this work often involved an exploration of the pleasures that had been disavowed in the process of becoming a feminist academic, whereby 'the feminist academic investigates her abandoned or fictional other – the female consumer of popular culture' (2000: 5; see Chapter 3 for a return to these debates). This work formed the foundations for some of the debates about post-feminism we go on to discuss in the next section.

POST-FEMINISM AND POPULAR FEMINISM

In order to offer a way of understanding the significance of the debates in this collection, we want to chart some of the changing ways in which feminisms have expressed their relationship to the popular from the 1980s onwards, a period that is historically post-second-wave feminism. The inheritance from second-wave women's movements was a climate in which some feminist concerns had been 'incorporated' into mainstream political, cultural and legislative frameworks. For example, legal changes around equal pay, sexual discrimination in the workplace and domestic violence may have been divorced from some of the radical politics of feminist movements, but they nonetheless involved a mainstreaming of feminist politics, and secured some real advances in addressing gender inequalities. Our central concern in this book is the relationship between feminisms and cultural change at the level of representation and in everyday lived practices. However, cultural struggles are struggles over the legitimation of ideas necessary for structural change.

From the 1980s onwards, a range of different ways of conceptualizing the relationship between feminism and popular culture have emerged. This debate is complex, because key concepts such as popular feminism, post-feminism and third-wave feminism are used in a range of different ways in different historical and national contexts. For example, it is now clear that post-feminism has become a problematic term, because it is used in such a variety of ways. At stake in these debates are different modes of thinking about the relationship between feminism and popular culture. While we do not have the space here to provide an exhaustive survey, below we attempt to identify some of the key uses of these terms and how they are linked to different conceptions of the relationship between feminism and the popular.

Despite the substantial political changes achieved by feminism, the concept of post-feminism was used by critics such as Susan Faludi (1992) to identify a backlash against feminism that she argued had taken place in the US in the 1980s. Here, post-feminism is used to mark a negative and retrogressive move and refers to a cultural shift during the Reagan era in the US where an emphasis on 'family values' created a backlash against feminism. This backlash, which for Faludi had reached epidemic proportions across media forms, is identified as post-feminist because it claims that women have achieved equality, yet feminism has 'failed' women. Therefore, in Faludi's work post-feminism suggests an era based on the rejection of feminism, and she finds that representations of feminism within the popular are anti-feminist.

This idea of post-feminism as anti-feminism was appealing for some critics, because it helped to offer an explanation for why feminism as a social movement had seemingly lost its purchase. For example, Susan Danuta Walters (1995) saw young women who refused the identity 'feminist' as 'dupes' of the backlash. This fails to acknowledge the historical specificity of second-wave feminism and the generational politics at play between second-wave 'mothers' and their student 'daughters': refusing to accept the identity 'feminist' does not necessarily mean that someone is anti-feminist, but that they may be actively questioning the values of second-wave feminism, or that they find it impossible to reconcile the rhetoric and perceived 'rules' of second-wave feminism with their own experiences of growing up female and feminist in the 1980s and 1990s. Nonetheless, the equation of post-feminism with the idea that feminism is no longer relevant as women are now equal continues to have considerable purchase in communications research in the US (for example, Hall and Rodriguez 2003).

The association between post-feminism and backlash is frequently a highly inflexible and crude tool for reading the complex relations between feminism and popular culture from the 1980s onwards. Indeed, while Faludi speaks from a feminist location 'outside' the popular, like Friedan before her, she is a journalist whose work contributes to struggles over the meanings of feminism within the popular. In this way, Faludi operates within the zone of 'celebrity feminism', which describes how 'some form of feminist discourse' occurs across a range of popular forms (Wicke 1994: 765). By focusing on a backlash against feminism, this negative reading of post-feminism frequently neglects how the popular operates as a site of struggle over the meanings of feminism. Indeed, in the UK press, commentators often speak from a feminist identity in order to criticize other 'non-feminist' aspects of the popular. As Julia Hallam has argued, 'feminism as a (contradictory and unfixed) subject position is widely circulating as an interpretive strategy amongst ... journalists' (cited in Read 2000: 119). This position is backed up by studies of film reviews (Brunsdon 1997; Read 2000), the reception of television shows (Moseley and Read 2002) such as 'Ally McBeal' (Fox, 1996–2002) and debates about the re-emergence of the domestic goddess (Hollows 2003).

An alternative way of reading the relationships between feminism and the popular in the 1980s onwards emerged, largely but certainly not only, in the UK. This work rarely used the term post-feminism, frequently preferring the idea of popular feminism. Indeed, some of the critics we identify with this position would vehemently refuse the term 'post-feminism'. Nonetheless, there exists a body of work that is loosely underpinned by the idea that we need new ways of understanding the relationship between feminism and the popular, in a period that is historically post-second-wave feminism. In essence, such an approach need not imply that post-feminism is either a good or a bad thing but that it is 'used in a historically-specific sense to mark changes in popularly available understandings of femininity and a woman's place' (Brunsdon 1997: 101). Such approaches enabled a more fluid and complex portrait of historical changes in femininity that did not simply reduce them to being feminist or anti-feminist. As Angela McRobbie argued in relation to her work on young women's magazines, 'We have to look at what emerges between feminism and femininity and we have to attend to the inventiveness of women as they create new social categories' (1994: 8).

A broad range of work can be located under this umbrella. For example, McRobbie (1991, 1994, 1997) identifies how young women's magazines negotiate new modes of feminine subjectivity that do not identify themselves as feminist, but neither do they operate as the 'other' of feminism. Brunsdon's (1997) work on *Pretty Woman* (Garry Marshall 1990) and *Working Girl* (Mike Nichols 1988) demonstrates how these films are both informed by second-wave feminism, while at the same time disavowing elements of it. In their edited collection *The Female Gaze*, Lorraine Gamman and Margaret Marshment argue that because popular culture is a site of struggle, it is a space where the meanings of feminism can be contested 'with results that might not be free of contradictions, but which do signify shifts in regimes of representation. And thus perhaps commonsense notions about women' (1988: 4).

This focus on encounters between feminism and the popular also began to reveal how and why elements of feminism might be refused or disavowed. While feminists such as Walters bemoaned her students' refusal of the feminist identity, McRobbie acknowledged that the meanings of feminism must be left up for grabs for different generations of women, and argued that it was necessary to refuse 'the lure of believing that if we try hard enough we can reproduce our feminist selves and our feminist theory in our daughters and with our students' (1994: 9); these concerns are picked up by Kathleen Rowe Karlyn in Chapter 4. The refusal of the identity 'feminist' within the popular was also linked to the perception that feminism is a white, middle-class movement. For example, Tricia Rose (1994) identifies how black female rappers embraced many elements of feminism, but refused the identity 'feminist' because they were suspicious of claims of 'sisterhood' and the privileging of sexual politics over the politics of 'race'. Likewise, Kathleen Rowe Karlyn argues that 'Roseanne' (Casey Werner/Wind Dancer Productions, 1988–97) acknowledges elements of feminism, while critiquing its class politics and exposing 'her oppression as a working-class wife and mother, while at the same time finding dignity and fulfilment in these roles' (Rowe 1997: 47; see also Lee 1995). Therefore, while second-wave feminism offered a critique of popular culture, these studies, while remaining critical, began to identify how popular culture might have something to teach feminism.

However, while these debates about popular forms of feminism saw clear potential in the wider negotiation of feminist ideas, there was frequently a reluctance to give up the feminist's authority to decide what were 'good' and 'bad' forms of relationships between feminism and the popular. Many studies were underpinned by a desire to identify the extent to which popular manifestations of feminism measured up against 'the real thing'. A central theme in *The Female Gaze* is whether feminism is present in popular culture 'or whether, in order to enter the mainstream, feminism is co-opted by being harnessed to other discourses which neutralize its radical potential' (Gamman and Marshment 1988: 3), although the editors are careful to distance themselves from the limitations produced by a model of co-option. Nonetheless, this idea of co-option is a central one in many debates about the relationship between feminism and popular culture, where it is frequently claimed that those elements of feminism that can be 'sold' – for example, ideas of liberation, independence and freedom – are appropriated by consumer culture but, in the process, become detached from the feminist discourses that anchored their radical meaning. From such a position, popular feminism is feminism tamed and divested of its radical meaning, so that it can be articulated with more traditional notions of femininity.

At times, the uneasy relationship between feminism and popular culture appears to have been displaced onto an opposition between feminism and consumer culture. For example, work on women's magazines has criticized the ways in which feminist ideas are incorporated in order to enable women to be addressed as consumers (see Pleasance 1991 and, for a more nuanced account, McRobbie 1994). Debates about feminism in 'Sex and the City' (HBO, 1998–2004) raise similar themes, arguing that the freedom to enjoy the 'liberated lifestyles' promised by post-feminism depends on a class position from which these lifestyles can be bought (Henry 2004). For Susan Zeiger, the forms of public citizenship offered by 'Sex and the City' are organized around the construction of the feminine citizen as a shopping citizen: 'Through its narratives, the series represents women fashioning public identities through consumption; through spin off web and print hype and tourism, the series encourages actual women and men to refashion their own public identities by exercising consumer choice' (2004: 98).

However, as Gottlieb and Wald (1994) argue in their work on riot grrrl bands, an insistence that feminism needs to exist in opposition to consumer culture frequently precludes the possibility of feminism becoming mainstream. There has been little academic attention to the ways in which feminist femininities were themselves produced through specific forms of consumption – and 'anti-consumption' – practices (although see Forster 2003 for work that gestures in this direction, and Wilson 1985 on feminism and fashion). Furthermore, 'consumption' in these debates frequently becomes reduced to the act of purchase and the reproduction of consumer capitalism, ignoring the more extensive understandings of consumption that have been produced in other fields (see, for example, Miller 1995, 1998; Lury 1997; and Casey and Martens 2006 for work on consumption; and for work on television fandom and cultural consumption and production see Jenkins 1992; Lewis 1992; Radner 1995; Tulloch and Jenkins 1995).

Nonetheless, critiques of the commodification of feminism within the popular have noted how modes of popular feminism are frequently centred around white, middle-class femininities (for example, Lee 1988). As Bev Skeggs (1997) has argued, this works to cement the idea that feminism is a movement for the privileged who can 'have it all'. For example, Jane Arthurs argues that 'Sex and the City' had to be seen in a continuum with, but also in departure from, other 'postfeminist, woman-centred drama[s]...that in the wake of second-wave feminism selectively deploy feminist discourses as a response to cultural changes in the lives of their potential audience, an audience that is addressed as white, heterosexual, and relatively youthful and affluent' (2003: 84). In this way, she draws on a set of arguments about post-feminist television culture, which understands popular texts to represent feminist agendas in particular and selective ways which usually reinforce the omissions and blind spots of second-wave feminist agendas (namely, race, class and sexuality), or to nod to them in minimal ways.

Whether post-feminism is seen as anti-feminism or in terms of the contradictory ways in which feminism is manifested in the popular, many studies retain an implicit or explicit assumption that popular culture could still benefit from a 'proper' feminist makeover. Underpinning many discussions of popular feminism is the assumption that there is a better 'unpopular' form of feminism. Such assumptions lingered in Gamman and Marshment's argument that it is necessary for 'feminists to intervene in the mainstream to make our meanings part of "commonsense" – or rather to convert "commonsense" into "good sense"' (1988: 2). This reproduces the idea that the feminist has good sense and therefore the moral authority to legislate on gendered relations, and also reproduces hierarchical power relations between 'the feminist' situated outside the popular and 'the ordinary woman' located within it.

CURRENT DEBATES

Thus far, we have tried to map some key ways in which the relationship between feminism and popular culture has been imagined. However, our narrative has largely stopped short of mapping current key debates. Post-feminism remains a central term in these debates, although, as we go on to demonstrate, its usefulness as a concept is tempered by the differences in its use within and between geographical locations and different disciplines. Recent conferences and seminars in the field demonstrate this effectively. At the 'Interrogating Post-feminism: Gender and the Politics of Popular Culture' conference at the University of East Anglia, UK, in 2004, it quickly became clear that there was little consensus over *what* was being interrogated and key differences emerged in the ways in which UK and US critics were using the term. Nonetheless, most critics shared the idea that while post-feminism as a concept did conjure up some form of relationship between feminism and popular culture, and while post-feminist identities were being negotiated within the popular, there was no equivalent post-feminist identity that people were willing to identify with themselves. The act of distancing from feminism captured in phrases like 'I'm not a feminist but...' does not translate into the claim 'I'm a post-feminist'. The confusion over the term has recently inspired a number of critics to attempt to survey or pin down the different uses of the term 'post-feminism' (see, for example, Projansky 2001; Gillis and Munford 2006).

At an ESRC-funded seminar on 'New Femininities' at the University of Cardiff, Wales, in 2005, there emerged not only geographical differences, but also disciplinary ones: post-feminism had a currency in making sense of texts within film, media and cultural studies, but was outside the frame of reference of many scholars working in sociology and education. An emphasis on how feminism is represented in popular texts, combined with the rise of female-centred dramas in US prime-time TV, probably explains why debates about post-feminism have taken off in television studies in particular. In representing the 'liberated woman' in the 1980s and 1990s, American television has engaged consistently with shifting notions of feminist politics and the relationships between feminism and femininity, in programming which has frequently focused on the tensions between work and home, private and public space, and sexuality, motherhood and 'liberation'. For example, in the 1980s and 1990s, 'L.A. Law' (Fox, 1986–94), 'Murphy Brown' (Shukovsky English Entertainment/WB, 1988–98), 'thirtysomething' (Bedford Falls Productions/MGM, 1987–91) and 'Ally McBeal' focused increasingly on spaces in which work and home come into conflict (see, for example, the *Camera Obscura* special issue: 'Lifetime: A Cable Network for Women' 1994–5; Dow 1996; Lotz 2001; Moseley and

Read 2002). More recently, these themes have been considered in relation to 'Sex and the City': for example, the essays in Akass and McCabe (2004) situate the show in relation to debates about post- and third-wave feminisms and analyze the consequences of the show's desire to 'have it all' in relation to questions of identity, citizenship and consumption. These debates are picked up by Joke Hermes in Chapter 5, by Joanne Hollows in Chapter 6 in her consideration of domesticity, post-feminism and British television's recent interest in 'downshifting', while Jane Arthurs in Chapter 7 investigates other ways in which the relationship between feminism, sexuality and citizenship has been worked through on television.

While an emphasis on post-feminism has certainly proved useful in fields like television studies, the emphasis on feminism *in* popular culture in this collection is also a response to some of the limitations of the concept. Crucially, this book brings together people from different disciplines to demonstrate how elements of feminism are articulated within the popular in a range of cultural practices as well as in television and film texts. If the terms of debates about post-feminism have frequently resulted in judgements about progressive or regressive texts, thinking about feminism in popular culture can produce a more nuanced and complex engagement as well as enable new positions to emerge.

This emphasis on both texts and practices also emerges in debates about third-wave feminism. Like 'post-feminism', the idea of third-wave feminism is a fraught term used in multiple and uneven ways across geographical contexts: for example, it has more currency in the US and some parts of continental Europe than it appears to have in the UK.[2] Although there is considerable debate about who exactly is included in this third wave of feminism, it appears to emerge in the same period as debates about 'post-feminism', although, unlike post-feminism, it is far more frequently used to designate both an identity and a movement. Gillis *et al.* suggest that the idea of a third wave of feminism emerges from struggles about the ability of second-wave feminism to speak for an 'identity, unity and collectivity' called 'women' (2004: 1). If second-wave feminists frequently positioned themselves as 'outside' of popular culture, for Gillis *et al.*, many forms of third-wave feminism have been formed through the popular. As Rebecca Munford argues, 'third-wave feminisms have refocalized the traditionally fraught relationship between feminism and popular culture to re-examine the politics of subjectivity' including the opposition between feminism and femininity that structured second-wave thought (2004: 143–4). An embrace of some aspects of 'traditional' femininities can be seen in the centrality of 'girly' culture in third-wave feminism, followed by a more recent flirtation with aspects of domesticity in books like Debbie Stoller's (2004) *Stitch 'n Bitch: The Knitter's Handbook* (see Gillis 2005). Parallel interests can be charted in feminist media and cultural studies, often resulting in variations of the 'Ur-article' that Charlotte Brunsdon discusses in Chapter 3.

While we have generally experienced third-wave feminism as something happening 'elsewhere', there are clearly overlaps between the concerns of third-wave feminism and those of this collection (and a discussion of these issues appears in Ogaz's and Karlyn's chapters). Furthermore, the third wave has been criticized for embodying some of the problems also commonly associated with representations of post-feminism – with an emphasis on individualism and middle-class femininities (Heywood and Drake 2004). Moreover, despite the embrace of the popular, critics have been divided over how successful a strategy this is, in ways that are reminiscent of second-wave debates about the popular. For example, Garrison seems to want to maintain a notion of an 'outside' while realizing the impossibility of such a position when she draws on critics such as Jameson to argue that a feminism constituted within the 'mainstream' creates a situation in which 'the object of consumption – feminism – stands in for actual political relations' (2004: 27). However, Heywood and Drake take a more pragmatic and useful approach to feminism in popular culture, suggesting that '[t]hrough its celebratory and critical engagement with consumer culture, the third wave attempts to navigate the fact that there are few alternatives for the construction of subjectivity outside the production/consumption cycle of global commodification' (2004: 19).

If, by offering a model of feminism *in* popular culture, third-wave feminism clearly shares some sympathies with this collection, it is also caught up in the generational politics of feminism. If Brunsdon's chapter highlights a process of disidentifying with the second-wave feminist at play in some feminist media studies, then we also acknowledge how a specifically generational narrative structures this introduction (and has strongly influenced some of our other work, see Hollows 2000 and Chapter 6 in this volume). The very idea of successive 'waves' of feminism has been seen to produce – or reproduce – antagonistic relationships between generations of women structured along the lines of the bad mother–daughter relationship that prevents 'a constructive dialogue' (Gillis *et al.* 2004: 3) and stops an 'inheritance' being shared (Spencer 2004: 10). As Munford puts it, 'the domineering mother and the rebellious daughter are destructive caricatures' (2004: 150).

Nonetheless, the mother–daughter paradigm not only structures relations between those identified as second- and third-wave feminists, but also debates in feminist media and cultural studies about post-feminism. In some recent work, this marks a shift from an attempt to dissolve the boundaries between feminism and popular culture – and feminism and femininity – towards a position which attempts to reinstate an 'authentic' feminism outside of the popular from which popular 'post-feminist' texts can be judged as deficient. For example, in 'Post-feminism and Popular Culture', McRobbie seeks to revive, and theorize, the idea of post-feminism as 'backlash' because, she argues, while feminism is still present in the popular, it only exists to be 'repudiated' and portrayed as 'a spent force' (2004: 254). While some of this anxiety is, quite justifiably, located around a perceived dominance of discourses of individualism and choice in contemporary feminisms, which bypass any sense of collective action and political involvement, there is also a way in which McRobbie's argument expresses disappointment that the potential for breaking down existing binaries which, in earlier work, she had perceived, has not been realized in contemporary culture. Instead, she argues, 'the post-feminist generation' of 'young women recoil in horror at the very idea of the feminist. To count as a girl today appears to require this ritualistic denunciation' (2004: 258).

The problem here is that, if third-wave feminists have been rightly criticized for distancing themselves from second-wave feminism to such an extent that it precludes dialogue, then second-wave feminists have sometimes also distanced themselves from 'inauthentically' feminist generations. As Ednie Garrison argues, 'This longitudinally extensive "post-feminist generation" facilitates a cynical and apathetic view of youth at any point after the sixties', enabling the second-wave feminist to 'exist at a safe distance in a mythological past reviled, or romanticized, depending on one's investments in feminist ideology and politics' (2004: 31). The essays in this collection aim to show that what McRobbie calls 'the cultural space of post-feminism' cannot simply be equated with a denunciation of, and non-identity with, feminist politics (2004: 257). Indeed, the collection is constructed to create a space for inter-generational discussion about feminist identities rather than repudiation.

Underpinning this collection, then, is the idea that second-wave feminism was partly constituted through the popular, and that feminisms – in diverse and fragmented forms – remain part of the popular. Furthermore, academic and activist feminisms – however 'unpopular' they may be – are not 'outside' these popular manifestations of feminism, but are part of the same social and cultural struggles over the meaning of feminism. These struggles over the meaning of feminism are not new, and are a key means by which feminism can be strengthened through a process of self-critique. A refusal of the popular, and a refusal to engage with the lives of different generations of women whose experiences are cross-cut by other forms of difference, can only limit the ability of feminisms to adapt. The chapters in this collection demonstrate, in different ways, what we can learn from looking at feminism in the popular.

THE BOOK

The book is divided into three parts, which broadly address questions of generation, cultural texts and trends, and practices. The essays in Part I, 'Inter-generational Relations of Feminism', attempt to think across second-wave feminism's presence and impact as it has transformed across the past thirty-five years, in culture, scholarship and in the classroom. In 'Feminism in the News', Susan Sheridan, Susan Magarey and Sandra Lilburn consider the representation of feminism in the Australian print media from the early 1970s to the contemporary period, through a number of case studies including the publication of Germaine Greer's *The Female Eunuch* and the 1995 United Nations World Conference on Women in Beijing. Their research suggests that feminism should be understood primarily as a construction of the popular media. In 'The Feminist in the Kitchen: Martha, Martha and Nigella', Charlotte Brunsdon begins with the image of the feminist in the kitchen as a cipher through which the idea of feminism has been negotiated and transformed in culture. She considers the 'othering' of the feminist in popular culture and criticism, as she suggests the recipe for post-feminist criticism of popular culture which has emerged as the Ur text of feminist media studies. In the last essay in this section, Kathleen Rowe Karlyn also considers the phenomenon of the disavowal of feminism by young women. In 'Feminism in the Classroom: Teaching Towards the Third Wave', Karlyn offers an account of her own pedagogic practice around 'third-wave feminism' and girl-oriented popular cultural texts, through the particular example of the parodic teen horror film *Scream* (Wes Craven, 1996). The chapters that form the first part of this collection, then, demonstrate and reflect upon the ways in which feminism has been represented and transformed in popular culture, and consider the significance of those transformations for theory, criticism and teaching.

Part II, 'Coming to Terms with Feminism', brings together three essays which take television texts and cultural trends as their focus, in thinking about how culture has come to terms with and negotiated feminist discourse. Joke Hermes considers the 'tragic success of feminism' through her analysis of viewers' understandings of the internationally successful American post-feminist television comedies 'Ally McBeal' and 'Sex and the City'. Hermes considers both how feminism appears in these shows and uses viewer discussions from www. jumptheshark.com to investigate the resonance of these feminist discourses for their understandings of them. Hermes argues that it is important to consider these post-feminist shows as comedies, in order to understand the precise nature of the negotiations (and exclusions) around feminism and feminist identities, and their 'others', with which they are engaged. In 'Can I Go Home Yet?' Joanne Hollows considers the practice of 'downshifting' by middle-class career women and its articulation in recent popular literature and television, and looks at the difficulty which second-wave feminism and post-feminist theory and cultural criticism have had with domesticity and the home as sites of pleasure and cultural practice for women. 'While we might know quite a lot about what emerges between feminism and youthful femininities, and between feminism and the single girl', she argues, 'what emerges between the feminist and the housewife remains largely unexplored'. Jane Arthurs, in the final essay of the section, 'Sex Workers Incorporated', looks at this history of feminist debates around the subject of sex work, the articulation of feminist perspectives in television programmes about sex work, and the transformations which have taken place to enable the inclusion of feminist perspectives on this topic as the industry has developed and shifted. Arthurs argues that these discourses have been used both to critique and legitimate the commodification of sexuality within global capitalism, and have been increasingly incorporated into debate over the politics of immigration.

The essays that form the third and final part of the book, 'Negotiating and Resisting Feminisms', are concerned with understanding feminism within the popular cultural practices of the beauty salon, the breakdance arena and the cyberspace of gaming communities. In her essay, Paula Black considers 'the uneasy relationship between feminism and the beauty industry', and begins by tracing the debates within feminist cultural criticism around beauty culture and practice. She then juxtaposes this with an analysis of the ways in which users of beauty salons understand their own practices in relation to feminism. Black's chapter engages directly with the perceived contradictions within what is now widely understood as a 'post-feminist' position, in which feminism and femininity are no longer necessarily mutually exclusive terms. Similarly, Charla Ogaz's piece 'Learning from B-Girls' uses participant observation to think about the feminist politics exhibited in girls' breakdancing culture and practice. Moving across issues including b-girls' self-naming practices, exclusion from and occupation of public, masculinized cultural spaces and the complex identifications and conflicts around family, gendered and ethnic identities in b-girl culture, Ogaz argues that the b-girl testimonies she presents can be read as expressing a profoundly feminist, resistant position to patriarchal cultures. In the final essay of the book, 'Illegitimate, Monstrous and Out There: Female *Quake* Players and Inappropriate Pleasures', Helen Kennedy investigates the consumption and production practices of female computer gamers, and argues that the practices of women online game players can be read as feminist, and as profoundly subversive of what is a male-dominated cultural space.

However, there are omissions within this book that are beginning to be addressed elsewhere. This collection was put together during a period in which there has been a mainstreaming of lesbian and bisexual femininities in prime-time dramas, and this begins to challenge the heterosexuality of the subject of post-feminist texts. This mainstreaming of lesbian and bisexual characters, and of narratives that do not centre on heterosexuality (although they may work to reinforce a normative heterosexuality) in US shows such as 'Buffy the Vampire Slayer' (Fox/Mutant Enemy/Kuzui/Sandollar, 1997–2003), 'The O.C.' (WB/Wonderland/College Hill/Hypnotic, 2003–), 'ER' (Conrad/John Wells Productions/Amblin Entertainment/WB, 1994–) marks a departure from debates about 'the lesbian kiss' on 'L.A. Law' (Kennedy 1997) and 'Ellen' (Black-Marlens Company/Touchstone, 1994–8; McCarthy 2003). Although the way in which non-heterosexual sexualities have been dealt with in many of these shows is undoubtedly problematic, the intervention of people like writer/producer Jane Espenson and the introduction by Showtime of the 'lesbian' 'Sex and the City', 'The L Word' (Anonymous Content/Dufferin gate productions Inc./Showtime Networks inc./Viacom, 2004–) do signal some significant changes that need to be incorporated more clearly into debates about post-feminism.

NOTES

1. However, this narrative is problematized by a lack of historical awareness which also meant that pre-second-wave movies were thrown into this mix, such as Ingrid Bergman's *Joan of Arc* (Victor Fleming,1948), *Arch of Triumph* (Lewis Milestone,1948) and *The Inn of the Sixth Happiness* (Mark Robson,1958), which, in different ways, seemed to offer appealing notions of feminine independence.
2. Joanne is grateful to Suki Ali and Stacy Gillis for some of these observations.

BIBLIOGRAPHY

Akass, K. and McCabe, J. (eds) (2004), *Reading 'Sex and the City'*, London: I. B. Tauris.
Alther, L. (1977), *Kinflicks*, Harmondsworth: Penguin.
Ang, I. (1985), *Watching Dallas: Soap Opera and the Melodramatic Imagination*, London: Methuen.

Arthurs, J. (2003), '"Sex and the City" and Consumer Culture: Remediating Postfeminist Drama', *Feminist Media Studies*, 3,1: 83–98.

Brownmiller, S. (1984), *Femininity*, New York: Fawcett Columbine.

Brunsdon, C. (ed.) (1981), '"Crossroads" – Notes on Soap Opera', *Screen*, 22, 4: 32–7.

—— (ed.) (1986), *Films for Women*, London: British Film Institute.

—— (1997), *Screen Tastes: Soap Opera to Satellite Dishes*, London: Routledge.

—— (2000), *The Feminist, The Housewife and the Soap Opera*, Oxford: Oxford University Press.

Butler, J. (1990), *Gender Trouble: Feminism and the Subversion of Identity*, New York: Routledge.

—— (1993), *Bodies that Matter: On the Discursive Limits of 'Sex'*, New York: Routledge.

Camera Obscura (1994–5), (Special Issue) 'Lifetime: A Cable Network for Women', 33–4.

Casey, E. and Martens, L. (eds) (2006), *Gender and Domestic Consumption*, Aldershot: Ashgate.

Danuta Walters, S. (1995), *Material Girls: Making Sense of Feminist Cultural Theory*, Berkeley, CA: University of California Press.

Dow, B. J. (1996), *Prime-Time Feminism: Television, Media Culture and the Women's Movement Since 1970*, Philadelphia: University of Pennsylvania Press.

Faludi, S. (1992), *Backlash: The Undeclared War Against Women*, London: Vintage.

Forster, L. (2003), 'Liberating the Recipe', in J. Floyd and L. Forster (eds), *The Recipe Reader*, Aldershot: Ashgate.

Friedan, B. (1963), *The Feminine Mystique*, New York: Dell.

Gamman, L. and Marshment, M. (eds) (1988), *The Female Gaze: Women as Viewers of Popular Culture*, London: Women's Press.

Garrison, E. K. (2004), 'Contests for the Meaning of Third Wave Feminism: Feminism and Popular Consciousness', in S. Gillis, G. Howie and R. Munford (eds), *Third Wave Feminism: A Critical Exploration*, Basingstoke: Palgrave.

Gillis, S. (2005), 'Which Domestic Goddess are you? (Post)Feminism and the Fetishization of the Domestic', paper presented at the Society for Cinema and Media Studies Conference, University of London, March–April.

Gillis, S., Howie, G. and Munford, R. (eds) (2004), *Third Wave Feminism: A Critical Exploration*, Basingstoke: Palgrave.

Gillis, S. and Munford, R. (2006), *New Popular Feminisms*, London: I. B. Tauris.

Gottlieb, J. and Wald, G. (1994), 'Smells Like Teen Spirit: Riot Grrrls, Revolution and Women in Independent Rock', in A. Ross and T. Rose (eds), *Microphone Fiends: Youth Music and Youth Culture*, New York: Routledge.

Hall, E. J. and Rodriguez, M. S. (2003), 'The Myth of Postfeminism', *Gender and Society*, 17: 878–902.

Haskell, M. (1975), *From Reverence to Rape: The Treatment of Women in the Movies*, London: New English Library.

Henry, A. (2004), 'Orgasms and Empowerment: "Sex and the City" and the Third Wave Feminism', in K. Akass and J. McCabe (eds), *Reading 'Sex and the City'*, London: I. B. Tauris.

Heywood, L. and Drake, J. (2004), '"It's all about the Benjamins": Economic Determinants of Third Wave Feminism in the United States', in S. Gillis, G. Howie and R. Munford (eds), *Third Wave Feminism: A Critical Exploration*, Basingstoke: Palgrave.

Hinds, H. and Stacey, J. (2001), 'Imaging Feminism, Imaging Femininity: The Bra-Burner, Diana, and the Woman who Kills', *Feminist Media Studies*, 1, 2: 153–77.

Hollows, J. (2000), *Feminism, Femininity and Popular Culture*, Manchester: Manchester University Press.

—— (2003), 'Feeling Like a Domestic Goddess: Post-feminism and Cooking', *European Journal of Cultural Studies*, 6, 2: 179–202.

Jenkins, H. (1992), *Textual Poachers: Television Fans and Participatory Culture*, London: Routledge.

Johnston, C. (1973), 'Women's Cinema as Counter-Cinema', in *Notes on Women's Cinema*, London: BFI.

Kennedy, R. (1997), 'The Gorgeous Lesbian in L.A. Law: The Present Absence?', in C. Brunsdon, J. D'Acci and L. Spigel (eds), *Feminist Television Criticism: A Reader*, Oxford: Oxford University Press.

Kuhn, A. (1982), *Women's Pictures: Feminism and Cinema*, London: Routledge & Kegan Paul.

Lee, J. (1988), 'Care to Join Me in an Upwardly Mobile Tango? Postmodernism and the "New Woman"', in L. Gamman and L. Marshment (eds), *The Female Gaze*, London: Women's Press.

—— (1995), 'Subversive Sitcoms: "Roseanne" As Inspiration for Feminist Resistance', in G. Dines and J. M Humez (eds), *Gender, Race and Class in Media: A Text-Reader*, Thousand Oaks: Sage.

Levine, E. (2005), 'Feminism and Femininity in "Charlie's Angels", 1970s to Present', paper presented at the Society for Cinema and Media Studies Conference, University of London, March–April.

Lewis, L. (1992), *The Adoring Audience: Fan Culture and Popular Media*, London: Routledge.

Lotz, A. (2001), 'Postfeminist Television Criticism: Rehabilitating Critical Terms and Identifying Postfeminist Attributes', *Feminist Media Studies*, 1,1: 105–21.

Lury, C. (1997), *Consumer Culture*, Cambridge: Polity.

McCarthy, A. (2003), 'Must See Queer TV: History and Serial Form in "Ellen"', in M. Jancovich and J. Lyons (eds), *Quality Popular Television: Cult TV, The Industry and Fans*, London: BFI.

McRobbie, A. (1991), *Feminism and Youth Culture: From Jackie to Just Seventeen*, Basingstoke: Macmillan.

—— (1994), *Postmodernism and Popular Culture*, London: Routledge.

—— (1997), '*More!* New Sexualities in Girls' and Women's Magazines', in A. McRobbie (ed.), *Back to Reality? Social Experience and Cultural Studies*, Manchester, Manchester University Press.

—— (2004), 'Post-feminism and Popular Culture', *Feminist Media Studies*, 4, 3: 255–64.

Meyrowitz, J. (ed.) (1994), *Not June Cleaver: Women and Gender in Postwar America 1945–60*, Philadelphia: Temple University Press.

Miller, D. (ed.) (1995), *Acknowledging Consumption: A Review of New Studies*, London: Routledge.

—— (1998), *A Theory of Shopping*, Cambridge: Polity.

Morgan, R. (ed.) (1970), *Sisterhood is Powerful: An Anthology of Writings from the Women's Liberation Movement*, New York: Vintage.

Moseley, R. and Read, J. (2002), '"Having it Ally": Popular Television (Post-)Feminism', *Feminist Media Studies*, 2, 2: 231–49.

Mulvey, L. (1975), 'Visual Pleasure and Narrative Cinema', *Screen*, 16, 3: 6–18.

Munford, R. (2004), '"Wake Up and Smell the Lipgloss": Gender, Generation and the (A)politics of Girl Power', in S. Gillis, G. Howe and R. Munford (eds), *Third Wave Feminism: A Critical Exploration*, Basingstoke: Palgrave.

Pleasance, H. (1991), 'Open or Closed: Popular Magazines and Dominant Culture', in S. Franklin, C. Lury and J. Stacey (eds), *Off-centre: Feminism and Cultural Studies*, London: HarperCollins Academic.

Projansky, S. (2001), *Watching Rape: Film and Television in Postfeminist Culture*, New York: New York University Press.

Radner, H. (1995), *Shopping Around: Feminine Culture and the Pursuit of Pleasure*, London: Routledge.

—— (1987), *Reading the Romance: Women, Patriarchy and Popular Literature*, London: Verso.

Read, J. (2000), *The New Avengers: Feminism, Femininity and the Rape-Revenge Cycle*, Manchester: Manchester University Press.

Rose, T. (1994), *Black Noise: Rap Music and Black Culture in Contemporary America*, New England: Wesleyan University Press.

Rosen, M. (1975), *Popcorn Venus: Women, Movies and the American Dream*, London: Owen.

Rowe, K. (1997), 'Roseanne: Unruly Woman as Domestic Goddess', in C. Brunsdon, J. D'Acci and L. Spigel (eds), *Feminist Television Criticism: A Reader*, Oxford: Oxford University Press.

Shulman, A. K. (1973), *Memoirs of an Ex-Prom Queen*, Bantam: New York.

Skeggs, B. (1997), *Formations of Class and Gender: Becoming Respectable*, London: Sage.

Spencer, J. (2004), 'Introduction: Genealogies', in S. Gillis, G. Howie and R. Munford (eds), *Third Wave Feminism: A Critical Exploration*, Basingstoke: Palgrave.

Tuchman, G. (1978), 'The Symbolic Annihilation of Women by the Mass Media', in G. Tuchman, A. Kaplan Daniels and J. Benet (eds), *Hearth and Home: Images of Women in the Mass Media*, New York: Oxford University Press.

Tulloch, J. and Jenkins, H. (1995), *Science Fiction Audiences: Watching 'Dr Who' and 'Star Trek'*, London: Routledge.

van Zoonen, L. (1994), *Feminist Media Studies*, London: Sage.

Wicke, J. (1994), 'Celebrity Material: Materialist Feminism and the Culture of Celebrity', *The South Atlantic Quarterly*, 93, 4: 751–8.

Williamson, J. (1993), *Deadline at Dawn: Film Criticism, 1980–1990*, New York: Marion Boyars.

Wilson, E. (1985), *Adorned in Dreams: Fashion and Modernity*, London: Virago.

Winship, J. (1987), *Inside Women's Magazines*, London: Pandora.

Zeiger, S. (2004), 'Sex and the Citizen in "Sex and the City's" New York', in K. Akass and J. McCabe (eds), *Reading 'Sex and the City'*, London: I. B. Tauris.

Part I
Inter-generational Relations of Feminism

CHAPTER 2

Feminism in the News

Susan Sheridan, Susan Magarey and Sandra Lilburn

Feminism has always been newsworthy, but its appearance in the print media today is very different from the way it looked over thirty years ago when Women's Liberation first hit the headlines. Today media representations of feminism are plural and various, the varieties not necessarily compatible with one another. Feminism is sometimes seen as a political agenda or a political ideology, and this happens despite the premature announcements of its death that have dogged the women's movement over the decades. The political identity of feminism blurs with other more broadly cultural aspects of 'lifestyle', on the one hand, and with public concern over issues of sexual violence and abuse, on the other. Conservative opinion journalists may represent feminism as a dangerously powerful lobby group, as the principal cause of trouble between women and men, or as a manifestation of contemporary decadence. Pro-feminist writers may stress the unfinished revolution or affirm the social and cultural changes that can be attributed to feminism. Whether or not it is named by the 'f-word', feminism is today a familiar feature of the contemporary scene, and a force to be reckoned with.

By contrast, around 1970 the women's movement and its feminist ideas were 'in the news' for novelty value. Feminism attracted a good deal of intrigued, though rarely sympathetic, reportage. Commentary veered wildly between seeing 'women's liberation' as just the latest fashion in a dynamic and unstable political scene, and construing it – as it saw itself – as the longest, and last, social revolution.[1] But as the novelty wore off and the wild new ideas were domesticated or diverted, the news media had to devise ways of reporting feminist ideas and political campaigns. While feminist campaigns successfully demanded a place in the news, the faces that were drawn for the women's movement were often less than friendly. More recently still, in the reaction against so-called 'political correctness', feminism is seen as not only legitimate but also as part of the establishment, and is even sometimes blamed for causing women new problems.

THE 'FACES OF FEMINISM' RESEARCH PROJECT

The research on which this essay is based was a study of representations of feminism in Australian print media, 1970 to 1995. We researched a number of case studies – events and individuals – with the aim of determining how and what public faces were created in the Australian print media for the new women's movement of the early 1970s, and how these changed over the next two decades.[2] We began with two related premises. One was that feminism is in part a construction of the popular media. The other was that feminism also uses the media for its own purposes, to make its objectives and campaigns known to 'the public'. These premises signal a recognition that despite repeated complaints that the media, as a public and therefore patriarchal institution, misrepresents feminism, the movement and its ideas have always existed, in part at least, *in* the media. It is impossible to draw a firm line between feminism 'in actuality' and feminism in the media-sphere.

We also wanted to distinguish our research from commentary that assumes that 'the media' is some kind of unified monolith, speaking with a single voice. While we found plenty of examples of media hostility to feminism, it became evident that the reasons for this hostility might differ (for example, it might be part of a wider hostility to a political party seen to be sympathetic to a particular feminist campaign). We found instances of favourable reporting, too, that could be explained in a variety of ways, ranging from the political commitments of individual journalists to the international context in which an issue might be placed. We learned that media representations of particular events were often unpredictable, and unstable.

Such considerations prompted us to develop a methodology that has three main characteristics. First, because newspaper research is labour-intensive and low on return for effort, and yet we wanted to cover a sizeable period of time looking for changes, we decided to select a number of case studies in the print media. Second, as we began by recognizing the complexity of the relationship between feminism and the press, we carried out extensive contextual research on the campaigns and characters of our case studies. Third, we gave considerable attention to the placement and illustration of specific items in the newspaper as well as the genres and discourses employed in the story.

While the field of 'feminism in the media' is huge, including changing social attitudes to just about anything, and 'lifestyle' cultural issues of all kinds, we confined our study to feminism in the sense of a broad movement for social change, encompassing a range of different political positions. That is, we looked at representations in news reporting of feminism as politics, a relatively neglected topic for feminist media studies (van Zoonen 1994), rather than broader questions of feminist influence in the entertainment media. This focus, we proposed, would allow us to draw attention to the political differences that existed among feminist groups and spokeswomen, and thus to challenge the monolithic concept of 'second-wave feminism' that tends to recur in recent debates. We also chose to focus on news reporting on the assumption that it would be around famous names (like Germaine Greer) and newsworthy events (like election campaigns or new legislation) that media constructions of feminism would first lodge in people's minds, and that these 'faces of feminism' would become embedded in popular memory through repetition and familiarization. Within this definition of feminism, our 'case studies' are all of events and issues of national scope or interest, starting with Germaine Greer's 1972 Australian promotion tour for *The Female Eunuch* and ending with the 1995 United Nations World Conference on Women in Beijing.

RESEARCH ON FEMINISM AND NEWS MEDIA: OUR RESEARCH QUESTIONS

As Liesbet van Zoonen (1994: 152) has observed, in news and current affairs areas where the media take on the role of an 'agency of public knowledge', where journalists occupy the 'fourth estate', a major site of public politics, it is not unreasonable to expect responsible and accurate representations of feminism and other social-political movements. But this expectation has, since the beginnings of feminism's second wave, often been frustrated. Popular wisdom among feminist activists is that the media always tend towards hostile constructions of feminism, ranging from ridicule through trivialization to attacks on movement spokeswomen and female politicians. Most feminist analyses of news media confirm the predominance of such negative representations of the movement's aims and campaigns (for example, Huddy 1997; Bradley 1998). The results of such research in a number of different national contexts are very similar: persistent feminist concerns, not only with the relative absence of women and neglect of women's issues, but also with the way in which the press continue to demonize, trivialize and personalize feminists and their issues, and to polarize feminist struggles (Rhode 1995). Deborah Rhode lists, as well, repeated media announcements of the women's movement's demise; repeated stories about the tragedy of women remaining unmarried, or childless, because of feminism; repeated examples of the focus shifting from social transformation to self-transformation. Media analysts have offered explanations for these negative representations by identifying a number of framing devices used in news reporting which tend to delegitimate the political claims and demands of feminism (and other radical social movements). These include the distinction between soft and hard news, the '(only) two sides to every question' device and so on (Rhode 1995; Costain, Braunstein and Berggren 1997).

From cultural studies we developed the expectation that we would find a repeated structure of binary oppositions between feminists and ordinary women, between responsible feminists and the 'lunatic' radical fringe, or between feminism represented as a utopian call for universal sisterhood and as pragmatic piecemeal reformism. The news genre is seen to be especially resistant to the basic feminist attack on the distinction between the personal and the political, although there is recent recognition that traditional boundaries between news and entertainment are increasingly blurred, and the private is made public in new ways (Sreberny and van Zoonen 2000: 10–11). Yet it might be expected that, over time, the media's growing familiarity with new ideas might yield some noticeable improvements even in traditional news genres. Several major studies had suggested this. Rhode, citing Elayne Rapping, argued that feminist perspectives in the United States media have 'dramatically altered the ways in which the public understands gender relations' (Rhode 1995: 705). While the mainstream press in the early years were mostly 'uninterested or unsympathetic', and 'female journalists often lacked the critical mass and professional leverage to ensure systematic, evenhanded treatment of gender issues', this has 'changed dramatically in recent years, in part because of women's increasing involvement in the media and in part because of broader cultural changes in gender roles' – that is, 'the public' itself, with increasing concern for women's issues, has forced some change (Rhode 1995: 686).

Van Zoonen, too, conceded that by the 1990s in the British and European press there was a significant amount of serious reportage on feminist lobbying for social and legal changes of benefit to women. However, she argues that this represented only one side of feminism, its 'emancipatory interests', which can be accommodated into a liberal individualist equal rights framework. The news media, she objected, focus on individual rights at the expense of feminist cultural critique, with its radical challenges to norms of femininity and gender relations (van Zoonen 1994: 152). Patricia Bradley, a feminist media critic using a more Marxist approach to news reporting in the United States press, emphasizes the class and race issues that are invisible in this emancipatory liberal feminism, but her point is comparable to van Zoonen's that feminism's broad cultural critique is elided (Bradley 1998: 165).

Both of these observations seemed to confirm our own perception that liberal feminism had won the feminist media wars. Indeed, before we began this research, Susan Magarey had conducted a study of representations of feminism in the Adelaide daily newspaper, the *Advertiser*, during the 1970s, and had found persisting, if shifting, pairs of oppositions between reasonable and radical, between 'real' women and unrepresentative feminists (Magarey, 1999). In a later article, part of the project described here, she saw that binary opposition as having shifted considerably by the 1980s. Now, the opposition was between feminists, who were reasonable, and their opponents, the 'lunatic fringe' of anti-feminist 'Women Who Want to be Women', discussed below (Magarey 2004).

Our initial hypotheses were thus informed by both cultural studies analyses of news media texts and contexts, and by feminist content-analysis research within communication studies. We expected to find that structural features of news reporting would limit representations of feminism as a politics, but that the search for novelty would at the same time ensure continued exposure of feminist ideas. On the basis of others' findings we also hypothesized that over the twenty-five years covered by our study there would be an increasing acceptance of rights discourse without necessarily any acknowledgement of the broader feminist cultural critique of patriarchal power. Yet we were also wary of falling back into the assumption of an inevitable opposition between feminism and the press, and kept looking instead for evidence of a more complex relationship, focusing on the detail of our case studies.

THE CASE STUDIES

In the case studies of media constructions of a 'public face' for feminism, our starting point was Germaine Greer's visit to Australia at the beginning of 1972 to publicize the paperback edition of her best-selling book, *The Female Eunuch*. Celebrity, or the media individuation of key feminists, thus became the theme of the first study in the series: Greer's status as 'the saucy feminist that even men like', and the sheer volume of media space she could command for what were in 1972 a new set of issues requiring new kinds of media 'framing'. Greer presented a paradox in that, while she gave eloquent expression to classic feminist critiques of the media for ignoring or trivializing women and their concerns, she also presented herself not as a spokeswoman for the Women's Liberation Movement, but as a major news item in and of herself. She was as much a darling of the media as a critic of its sexist practices — and of the marginalization of women journalists. But it was as the media's darling that she effected her most dazzling disruptions of the respectable femininity that was dominant at the time. There was 'an element of recklessness in Greer's performance that women admired and men found sexy' (Nolan 1999). At least, the young rebellious women who were interested in women's liberation admired her; others, like her contemporary Beatrice Faust, one of the founders of the Women's Electoral Lobby (see below) were scornful of her antics, regarding them as deleterious to the serious cause of women's rights (Lilburn, Magarey and Sheridan 2000).

Another case study was the media career of Pat O'Shane, and her status as 'first Aboriginal woman' to achieve many kinds of public office. Trained as a lawyer, she has been head of the New South Wales Department of Aboriginal Affairs (the first woman to be appointed head of any government department), and the first Aboriginal woman to be appointed a magistrate (Mitchell 1984). While there is no contradiction between celebrity status and social marginality – there are several Aboriginal women activists in Australia today who could be described as media celebrities – O'Shane's usually controversial public statements are reported in terms which emphasize conflicts between her feminism and her Aboriginality, and also between these aspects of her identity and her public roles such as magistrate. In fact, these apparently conflicting aspects of her celebrity presence enable O'Shane to speak freely without being constructed as a representative of 'feminism' or 'the Aboriginal community'. It is a freedom that she exploits to powerful effect, just as Greer exploits her self-constructed outrageousness (Lilburn 2001). Both these celebrity feminist figures skilfully deploy media discourses and practices to highlight their views. This, in turn, can create media space for others to debate their claims and, in so doing, enact the diversity of feminist opinion that now exists.

However, feminist political groups using the media to publicize demands and campaigns bring out quite different aspects of the terrain of 'feminism in the news'. Two of our case studies involved significant political events in Australia in 1972–3: the formation of the Women's Electoral Lobby (WEL, comparable to NOW, the National Organization of Women, in the United States) and the appointment of the first Women's Advisor to the Prime Minister. Here we had expected to find confirmation of the popular view that the moderate, reformist wing of the women's movement represented by WEL, and by women politicians and bureaucrats, enjoyed pragmatic and effective relationships with the news media, while the more radical feminist groups, suspicious of media misrepresentations, were likely to attempt to subvert media power (see Barker-Plummer 1995). However, it soon became clear that, in the case of WEL's pre-election survey of candidates' attitudes to women's issues, an initially positive media representation was undermined when one of its concerns – support for women's reproductive rights – was hijacked for party-political purposes. The right to abortion, instead of being represented as an issue of women's rights, was reframed in traditional political style as a 'conscience vote', where members of the predominantly male parliament could vote as individuals, not as directed by party policy. Media reportage consequently shifted its focus from the feminist challenge to electoral candidates to relations between candidates and their party machines. Thus WEL's triumph of media management was overridden, and the pre-feminist distinction between legitimate public issues and issues traditionally held to be 'private', such as abortion, was reasserted (Lilburn 2000).

Then there was the Elizabeth Reid story. The first women's adviser to the Prime Minister, she was appointed, in April 1973, by the first Labor Prime Minister in almost thirty years of Australian politics. Reid's advocacy established the women's affairs section within the Federal bureaucracy to exert a feminist influence on public policy. Despite the lurch in WEL's pre-election campaign discussed above, it had been clearly established that some government response to the women's demands was called for (Curthoys 1992). The advertised position, and her appointment to it, raised intense public interest, with media reportage varying from the sensational ('Miz Liz', an 'outspoken women's libber') to the admiring (especially of her leading role in criticizing the formal proceedings of the 1975 United Nations International Women's Year Conference in Mexico City). Reid's resignation just two-and-a-half years later became a front-page drama in an unexpectedly public career. She herself publicly blamed the media for making her position untenable (cited in Moore 1985). However, in making this criticism she appeared not to recognize that her position in public debate would always be mediated, nor that the prime political target would be Prime Minister Whitlam's increasingly beleaguered government, of which she and her office were seen as offshoots (Magarey and Lilburn 2000).

What emerges strongly from our research is that, as in the examples we have outlined, feminist issues are overwritten or significantly reframed by traditional public-sphere concerns such as party-politics or nationalism. Two further case studies concerned events when feminist issues entered mainstream politics in a big way – the passing of the 1984 Sex Discrimination Act in the Federal Parliament of Australia, and the United Nations International Women's Conferences culminating in Beijing, 1995.

When the proposed Australian Sex Discrimination Bill was introduced into parliament, there was an outcry from conservatives, ranging from the wives of some opposition parliamentarians to a group that will go down in history for its name if nothing else – Women Who Want to be Women. This ultra-conservative lobby group had formed in 1979 in the lead up to the United Nations Mid-decade Conference on Women, and had invited United States anti-feminists Phyllis Schlafly and Michael Levin on speaking tours in Australia. Their objections to the bill were similar to, but not nearly so influential as, the objections of United States conservatives that had brought about the defeat of the Equal Rights Amendment just a few years before this. On the other hand, there was a great deal of support for the bill, especially, but not surprisingly, from women journalists. The bill, introduced into the parliament by Senator Susan Ryan (feminist Minister for Education and Minister Assisting the Prime Minister on the Status of Women in the Hawke Federal Labor government from 1983 to 1987), seemed to be the answer to many feminists' dreams. It outlawed discriminatory acts based on gender, marital status or pregnancy. This measure, legitimated by its status as a government bill in the Federal Parliament, was centrally positioned in media reports as part of a modern drive for equality to which reasonable citizens could not object.

However, after the bill was passed, there was a backlash from an unexpected quarter. Senator Ryan was shocked when, appearing on television with members of the Women's Electoral Lobby, she heard them attack the new law as tokenistic and toothless – largely because it lacked provisions for fining or otherwise punishing non-compliant employers (Ryan 1999: 243). Such objections had scarcely been heard in the press during the campaign, although radical and socialist feminist groups who, unlike WEL, placed themselves well on the margins of mainstream politics, made jokes about 'Equal Opportunism' legislation. There had been no significant reportage of their reservations about legislation that, they felt, would have limited benefits for the middle-class and none at all for poor and Aboriginal women. Such criticisms of the act as not radical enough, unlike the attacks of the ultra-right group Women Who Want to be Women, received little media attention and less comprehension. The opposition between more and less radical versions of feminism, as it emerges in this story of the 1984 Sex Discrimination Act, could not be construed as a media invention. It was WEL's use of a media appearance to voice its unexpected attack on the new act that suggested wide political differences between feminists in the mainstream, like Senator Ryan, and those more aligned with community activism (Magarey, 2004).

In other circumstances, disagreements among feminists may be seized upon as newsworthy; this view is especially evident in press reports on international women's campaigns and meetings. In the case of the UN Women's Conferences of 1975, 1985 and 1995, media constructions of feminism tended to emphasize the utopian nature of claims about women's shared experience and to reassert that national interests will 'always', in such global forums, take precedence and divide women from one another. In the reporting of the Beijing conference of 1995 there was little recognition of how recent the key successes of international feminism had been: the establishment of a high profile for women's issues within the United Nations, and the increasing capacity to use international agreements to pressure national governments to improve the situation of women.

One striking example in the Australian press was the way a videoed speech by Auung Suu Kyi, Nobel Peace Prize winner, was reported. The capacity of feminist ideas to cross national boundaries, and women's contribution to peace-making processes (a theme of the official conference) was the point of her speech highlighted by the Melbourne *Age* correspondent, who reported Suu Kyi's belief that 'Women have a most valuable contribution to make in situations of conflict by paving the way to solutions based on dialogue rather than viciousness and violence' (*Age*, 1 September 1995: 9). Yet the *Sydney Morning Herald*'s correspondent took a diametrically opposed point from the same speech when he quoted her as saying that 'The adversities that we have to face together have taught all of us involved in the struggle to build a truly democratic system in Burma that there are no gender barriers that can't be overcome' (*Sydney Morning Herald*, 1 September 1995: 9). Thus while one newspaper depicts Suu Kyi as saying that women contribute to international peace processes, the other represents her as concerned primarily with the struggles of one nation (Sheridan and Lilburn 2003).

Press stories in the lead-up to the Beijing conference, in Australia as in the United States, were marked by anti-Chinese sentiment, and criticisms of conference organization, especially security arrangements, outweighed discussion of substantive issues (Howell 1997; Akhavan-Majid and Ramaprasad 1998). During the conference, too, this anti-Chinese tendency shaped Australian media stories that showed Australian feminists engaged in fighting the good fight against an undemocratic and repressive regime, effectively representing feminism as a nationalist position. The reductive parameters of universal feminist consensus or inevitable nationalist conflicts predominated in media reports. Media focus on women's cultural and political differences, in this context, has the effect of undermining the legitimacy of feminism(s) as a (series of) political positions.

However, a remarkable feature of the Beijing conference – symbolizing the new political possibilities opened up by easy access to electronic media – was that new media technology made it possible for NGO delegates to check out CNN's coverage and send out their criticisms of media coverage, as well as their own accounts of events.

CONCLUSIONS AND FURTHER QUESTIONS

Our findings challenge certain widespread beliefs among feminists, and some orthodox positions taken by feminist researchers on the news media. We concluded that:

- Media constructions of 'feminism' and indeed of 'women' varied over time and in relation to different issues.
- In the Australian press at least, the location of feminist issues in mainstream political institutions like parliament or the United Nations produced much more serious and attentive reportage.
- By the same token, feminist claims in such institutional contexts could readily be overridden by mainstream party-political or national interests.
- Celebrity feminism was there from the beginning, and depends for its success on media-savvy individual subjects.

One limitation of this research project was that our choice of these particular public-political events meant that many of the most radical feminist challenges to the mainstream were underemphasized in our study – for example, the lesbian presence (including, at Beijing, within international feminism), and the radical feminist critique of new reproductive technologies. As a consequence, we no doubt missed a number of dramatic examples of the press demonizing feminism: for example, Susan Magarey found that the press reacted with horror at what they saw as irresponsible bad behaviour at the 'Women and Politics' conference held in Canberra in 1975, when some delegates took literally the invitation to dress in 'black tie' for the formal dinner, and also raided the male toilets (Magarey 1999; Genovese 2002). Furthermore, challenges to mainstream feminism from indigenous and immigrant women are hardly visible. It was our decision to concentrate on the print media's shaping of the most prominent 'faces of feminism' in popular memory that led us to focus on the mainstream.

In particular, our study does not touch upon what is arguably one of the major triumphs of feminist influence on public policy and on cultural awareness in general – the recognition of sexual violence against women as a major social issue. Growing public concern with sexual violence and abuse has both transformed and been constructed by press coverage of these issues, perhaps especially since the Australian Federal government campaigns against domestic violence in the 1980s and 1990s. But the downside of that new concern is a tendency to present violence against women and children in a protectionist way rather than turning the lens on norms of masculinity and male power. Another example is the current moral panic about paedophilia, which has been deliberately confused with homosexuality.

In the early years of the twenty-first century, really radical feminist positions rarely get an airing at all, and liberal reformist feminism occupies all the available pro-feminist media space. While gender issues continue to invite controversy, the 'lunatic fringe' to which 'reasonable' feminism is set in opposition is these days more likely to be patriarchs and their female apologists, rather than 'radical' feminists. Female anti-feminist opinion writers, like the Americans Christina Hoff Sommers, Katie Roiphe and crew, who emerged into the media limelight in the 1990s, have also sprung up like mushrooms in Australia, most notably the writers Janet Albrechtson and Angela Shanahan in the Murdoch press quality daily, the *Australian*. This anti-feminism, which takes up a lot of the debating space, construes liberal feminism as patronizingly victim-oriented or oppressively politically correct. It was the occasion of an Australian media storm in 1994 when well-known writer Helen Garner (a one-time anarchist feminist) published *The First Stone*, a work of investigative journalism which used fictional techniques to deplore the actions of a couple of younger feminists who successfully sought legal redress against the master of their university college for sexual harassment. For Ann Genovese and other younger Australian feminists, the *First Stone* controversy was a turning point. Genovese sees the whole raft of feminist rights discourse swamped, apparently forever (Genovese 2002). Yet things move on very fast in today's media, and within a year or so of her article's publication, we have seen the return of liberal equal-rights discourse from a previously unsuspected source: the Equal Rights Commissioner Prue Goward (formerly women's adviser to conservative Prime Minister Howard) passionately promoting the issue of paid maternity leave despite opposition both overt and covert from the government that appointed her.

THEORETICAL ISSUES

Van Zoonen, analyzing press accounts of the early days of Dutch feminism, looked closely at the media's available genres and structures and proposed that the 'prioritising of events over the analysis of ideas' means that the news genre could not accommodate the radical new feminist definition of politics as including the personal (van Zoonen 1992: 462). This perception is still relevant today, and in Australia our newspapers are more than ever divided between news (public) and lifestyle (personal) stories. For example, the Melbourne quality daily, the *Age*, quite literally divides them, having a separate section called 'The Culture'. It could be said that the tabloid press converts news into entertainment, a phenomenon discussed below. In Australia we lack, particularly, significant weekly or monthly news magazines to offer space for discussion of ideas. However, does this separation of events from ideas mean the print media cannot take on the feminist concept of 'the personal is political'? Is this still the case?

Australian media commentator and academic Catherine Lumby would say no – this separation no longer occurs, as the news media have been significantly 'feminized' in the process of becoming more tabloid. Just as the division between tabloid and quality news media is breaking down, she argues, so too is the division between serious public masculine 'politics' and 'personal' gender issues that have been politicized by feminism (Lumby 1999). Naomi Wolf has been known to make a similar case about TV talk shows raising issues that then president George Bush ignored at his peril (Whelehan 1995: 236–7). In fact, Lumby refuses the old distinctions between news and entertainment altogether, insisting that in the current media-sphere, news no longer holds pride of place, and a new diversity is made up of magazines, talk shows, talk-back radio and the Internet. Ordinary people get to have a say; they interact and make sense of what living is like now, and while 'this sense-making ... may be characterized at times by ignorance and prejudice' notes Lumby, 'it is certainly an active, volatile process' (Lumby 1999: xiii). In this new democratic arena, 'it's a rapidly changing montage of images and ideas in which attractive, lively and charismatic people are given far more space than measured and verbose experts. Does it follow, then, that we've become a less informed or less politically active community as a result?' Lumby asks rhetorically (Lumby 1999: 2).

There is, she claims, an eruption of 'new voices and groups identified by race, ethnicity, gender, sexuality, and allegiance to new political movements' – feminism, anti-racism, ecology, gay rights. She points out that this new media diversity also includes reactionaries like Pauline Hanson, founder in the 1990s of the racist One Nation Party, who appealed to an 'old Australian' identity politics that is white, anti-immigration, rural and socially conservative. The argument in favour of tabloid democracy is extended beyond this view of the diverse political identities to which it allows voice. Lumby also argues that the media is a democratic public space – indeed not a single space but many overlapping public spheres and discourses – which can in the process create new 'publics' (Lumby 1999: 245–7).

This and other recent discussions in media and cultural studies about 'publics' originate as responses to Habermas's concept of the public sphere. John Hartley, in his influential *Popular Reality: Journalism, Modernity, Popular Culture*, argues that there has been a definitive shift in media function from the dissemination of

information to the dissemination, construction and interrogation of identities
– and thus of communities. 'Publics', in this sense, are the creation of the media
(Hartley 1996). His recent work, *The Indigenous Public Sphere*, proposes that in
Australia today indigenous people experience greater cultural visibility and
possibilities of self-representation in the media than in parliaments (Hartley
and McKee 2000).

A different response to Habermas is offered by Nancy Fraser, whose critique
of the notion of the 'public sphere' begins from the proposition that there have
always been 'counterpublics', with their own discursive logic and rhetorical styles.
Her notion of strong and weak publics is not confined to the media-sphere,
and differentiates between the exercise of power through opinion formation
and through decision making (Fraser 1997). Sreberny and van Zoonen suggest
using this notion to link parliamentary activities on gender issues (a strong
public), grass-roots and institutional sites within women's movements (as
counterpublic), and, as the activities of a weak public, 'the day-to-day attempts
of women to gain control over their private and public surroundings' (Sreberny
and van Zoonen 2000: 7–9).

This notion of multiple publics with different kinds of power at play in
the media-sphere helps to illuminate our case studies. In the case of Elizabeth
Reid's relations with the media, the evidence suggests that her campaigns were
undermined more by growing opposition to the Labor government itself than
by specific opposition to her advocacy for women. Here the electoral 'public'
prevailed over the newly emerging feminist public. Or, you could say that party-
political discourse drowned out the new feminist discourse. All our research
has shown the public faces of feminism enmeshed in complex discursive forms,
neither completely marginalized nor ever entirely successful in getting their
agenda across in their own terms.

An important theoretical issue raised by this research is what difference
it makes whether we frame the problem as one of conflicting publics, or of
conflicting discourses. Do social movements make a difference by introducing
new discourses, new ways of framing new questions? Or is it the media creation
of new publics that makes the difference? On the evidence of our study, it
could be argued that throughout the 1970s and 1980s, new public voices like
feminism were still required to speak in the old languages, in order to be heard in
the news media. An example given by Ann Genovese is that Australian feminists
were forced to shift media representations of women away from the sexualized
'whore' image (which, she argues, the press deployed in relation to the radical
women's liberation movement), to the sanctified 'Madonna' image of woman
enduring brutalization at men's hands, in order to 'appeal to the *noblesse oblige*

of the masculinist public sphere to achieve change' (Genovese 2002: 161–2). If the 'new publics' (indigenous, feminist, gay) have had to frame their issues within the old discourses and their oppositional structures – two sides to every question, the reasonable and the radical – then how far can they really make a difference to public debate? Was it inevitable that liberal reformist feminism should come to stand in the place of all the diversity of feminist voices?

If Raymond Williams is right, with his Gramscian model of ideological hegemony, then the dominant discourse cannot completely frame or contain issues raised by dissident political interests. Ultimately, out of the conflict of dominant, emerging and residual discourses, the discursive frame must change (Williams 1977: 121–7). On the other hand, if John Hartley is right, then there has been such a significant historical shift in the postmodern media-sphere that Williams' model of conflicting discourses must give way to a model of conflicting publics. Does our research support Hartley's model of media power, or Raymond Williams'? Or neither? We found, rather, that it is Nancy Fraser's model, which takes into account discourse and rhetorical styles as well as differentiating between kinds of political power, that seems to offer more potential for nuanced readings than either a Gramscian-Marxist or a postmodern model of how the media-sphere works. Feminism in the news is most often a function of its various counterpublics (the variety of feminisms) interacting with its strong publics (to the extent that it has become institutionalized in electoral politics, law and education).

Despite their differences, all three analytical models share the view that 'the news' is an integral part of popular culture, no longer (if it ever did) belonging in some higher realm of rational discourse. News reportage on feminist issues and campaigns draws on the same social discourses that construct 'celebrity feminists' such as Germaine Greer, and feature stories about the good or evil social impact of feminist ideas. It proves to be impossible in practice to separate representations of feminism as a social and political movement from such popular images and polemics about 'feminism'. It is a mixture of all these different faces represented in the media-sphere that makes up the popular memory of feminism for the broad public of women and men.

NOTES

1. The title of Juliet Mitchell's early essay, 'Women: The Longest Revolution', (1966), echoed Raymond Williams' classic study of class, *The Long Revolution* (1961).
2. Research funded by the Australian Research Council.

BIBLIOGRAPHY

Akhavan-Majid, R. and Ramaprasad, J. (1998), 'Framing and Ideology: A Comparative Analysis of U.S. and Chinese Newspaper Coverage of the Fourth United Nations Conference on Women and the NGO Forum,' *Mass Communication & Society*, 1, 3 & 4: 131–52.

Barker-Plummer, B. (1995), 'News as a Political Resource: Media Strategies and Political Identity in the U.S. Women's Movement 1966–75', *Critical Studies in Mass Communication*, 12: 306–24.

Bradley, P. (1998), 'Mass Communication and the Shaping of US Feminism', in C. Carter, G. Branston and S. Allen (eds), *News, Gender and Power*, London: Routledge.

Costain, A. N., Braunstein, R. and Berggren, H. (1997), 'Framing the Women's Movement News', in P. Norris (ed.), *Women, Media and Politics*, Oxford: Oxford University Press.

Curthoys, A. (1992), 'Doing it for Themselves: The Women's Movement since 1970', in K. Saunders and R. Evans (eds), *Gender Relations in Australia*, Sydney: Harcourt Brace Jovanovich.

Fraser, N. (1997), 'Rethinking the Public Sphere', in *Justice Interruptus: Critical Reflections on the 'Postsocialist' Condition*, New York: Routledge.

Garner, H. (1995), *The First Stone: Questions about Sex and Power*, Chippendale, NSW: Picador.

Genovese, A. (2002), 'Madonna and/or Whore? Feminism(s) and Public Sphere(s)', in M. Thornton (ed.), *Romancing the Tomes: Popular Culture, Law and Feminism*, Sydney: Cavendish.

Greer, G. (1970), *The Female Eunuch*, London: McGibbon and Kee.

Hartley, J. (1996), *Popular Reality: Journalism, Modernity, Popular Culture*, London: Arnold.

Hartley, J. and McKee, A. (2000), *The Indigenous Public Sphere: The Reporting and Reception of Aboriginal Issues in the Australian Media*, Oxford: Oxford University Press.

Howell, J. (1997), 'Post-Beijing Reflections: Creating Ripples, But Not Waves in China', *Women's Studies International Forum*, 20, 2: 235–52.

Huddy, L. (1997), 'Feminists and Feminism in the News', in P. Norris (ed.), *Women, Media and Politics*, Oxford: Oxford University Press.

Lilburn, S. (2000), 'A WEL Made Public Debate? The Women's Electoral Lobby, the Media and the 1972 Federal Election', *Australian Political Science Association Annual Conference Proceedings 2000*, available online at http:/apsa2000.anu.edu.au/confpapers.

——— (2001), 'Being the First of a Kind: The Case of Pat O'Shane', unpublished paper.

Lilburn, S., Magarey, S. and Sheridan, S. (2000), 'Celebrity Feminism as Synthesis: Germaine Greer, *The Female Eunuch* and the Australian Print Media', *Continuum: Journal of Media and Cultural Studies*, 14, 3: 335–48.

Lumby, C. (1999), *Gotcha: Life in a Tabloid World*, St Leonards, NSW: Allen & Unwin.

Magarey, S. (1999), 'Reading Straight and Reading Queer: Liberty Bodiss in Queen Adelaide's Town', in J. Damousi and K. Ellinghaus (eds), *Citizenship, Women and Social Justice: International Historical Perspectives*, Melbourne: History Department, University of Melbourne.

——— (2004), 'The Sex Discrimination Act 1984', *Australian Feminist Law Journal*, 20: 127–34.

Magarey, S. and Lilburn, S. (2000), 'The Unexpectedly Public Career of Elizabeth Reid', unpublished paper.

Mitchell, J. (1966), 'Women: The Longest Revolution', *New Left Review*, 40: 11–32.

Mitchell, S. (1984), *Tall Poppies*, Ringwood, Victoria: Penguin.

Moore, K. (1985), 'Interview with Elizabeth Reid', *Labor Forum*, 7, 2: 10–15.

Nolan, S. (1999), 'Tabloid Women', *Meanjin*, 2: 165–77.

Rhode, D. L. (1995), 'Media Images, Feminist Issues', *Signs*, 20, 3: 685–710.

Ryan, S. (1999), *Catching the Waves: Life in and Out of Politics*, Sydney: HarperCollins.

Sheridan, S. and Lilburn, S. (2003), 'Fragments of an International Feminism', in W. Waring (ed.), *Casting New Shadows: Proceedings of the Australian Women's Studies Association Conference 2001*, Sydney: Institute for Women's Studies, Macquarie University.

Sreberny, A. and van Zoonen, L. (2000), 'Gender, Politics and Communication: An Introduction', in A. Sreberny and L. van Zoonen (eds), *Gender Politics and Communication*, Cresskill: Hampton Press.

van Zoonen, L. (1992), 'The Women's Movement and the Media: Constructing a Public Identity', *European Journal of Communication*, 7: 453–76.

——— (1994), *Feminist Media Studies*, London: Sage.

Whelehan, I. (1995), *Modern Feminist Thought*, Edinburgh: Edinburgh University Press.

Williams, R. (1961), *The Long Revolution*, London: Chatto and Windus.

——— (1977), *Marxism and Literature*, Oxford: Oxford University Press.

CHAPTER 3

The Feminist in the Kitchen: Martha, Martha and Nigella

Charlotte Brunsdon

Before Martha Stewart was indicted, and then imprisoned, for insider dealing, she was fascinating – and rich and famous – for her perfect domesticity. Cool, blonde, poised, efficient, organized, Martha, through her multimedia empire whose product was herself, inspired envy and emulation.[1] Making cachepots from pumpkins for Thanksgiving, sewing buttonholes into linen napkins, turning staircase balusters into candlesticks, growing and drying herbs, laying dinnerparty tables with individual place names drawn from the clip art Martha website, Martha offered a vision of a light, bright, spacious home where there was a place for everything and everything was in its place. Martha's lovely life, in which the home maker could concentrate on creative and imaginative domestic and garden tasks, whilst still being an efficient cleaner and cook and celebrating with friends and family, was brought to her many fans through two main platforms: her syndicated television show, 'Martha Stewart Living' and her magazine of the same name.[2]

Martha Stewart's greatest success came during the 1990s, a period which in Britain was marked by the rise of 'lifestyle' programming across all four main network channels. Suddenly, there was cooking and gardening on television nearly every evening, and if the USA had Martha Stewart, Britain had Delia Smith, the 'Two Fat Ladies' and Nigella Lawson as well as design and home makeover shows like 'Home Front' (BBC, 1994–) and 'Changing Rooms' (Bazal for BBC, 1997–2004). Many of these programmes were fronted by women, and I became intrigued by the relationship between this resurgence of the domestic on television and feminism. Where is feminism on television? What relation is there between being told what to do in your house and kitchen by these women and feminism? Is this post-feminism, when women on television are just so very much more authoritative about what they are always assumed to have known best?

To explore these questions I want to look at three women who have come to prominence on television as domestic authorities in the late twentieth century – since the second-wave feminism of the 1970s – Delia Smith, Martha Stewart and Nigella Lawson. I will start, however, with another Martha, the artist Martha Rosler, who, in 1975, in the middle of 1970s feminism, made a short videotape called *The Semiotics of the Kitchen*.[3] This was the period in which semiotics and structuralism were the height of intellectual fashion, and the science of signs was seen as a way of proving the veracity of radical readings of film and popular cultural texts. The systematic exploration of systems of meaning was seen as a radical gesture, as inspired by Roland Barthes' classic analyses of images such as the cover of *Paris Match* published in English as *Mythologies* (1972). *The Semiotics of the Kitchen* uses the format of a child's alphabet primer to explore the kitchen. Rosler, in medium shot, stands behind a table in front of her cooker and refrigerator: the classic television cookery set-up. 'A is for apron', she announces, as she struggles into one of those aprons that need to be buttoned up behind your head. B is Bowl, which she slams down on the table, blender and broiler. C is for cup (fairly innocuous), can-opener (still functional), cleaver (a little more threatening) and finally, chopper, which she wields with fury. As she proceeds through the alphabet, rendering egg-beaters, forks, hamburger presses and rolling pins as offensive weapons, it becomes clear, as she finishes on a Zorro gesture with raised knives, that the semiotics of the kitchen signify containment, fury, aggression, resentment and potential revenge. The semiotics of the kitchen has nothing to do with cooking.

This is a classic second-wave feminist text both in its anger and in Rosler's self-presentation, which is *'au naturel'*, unmade-up, with her long hair parted in the middle and hanging loose down her shoulders. It is also very funny, as each piece of equipment is rendered expressive and sometimes threatening. Unusually for a second-wave text the feminist is actually in the kitchen – however cross she might be.

While thinking about Martha and Martha, and what I was beginning to formulate as an essay about 'the feminist in the kitchen', I was also teaching a course on avant-garde and independent film. We looked at two rather difficult 1979 feminist films, *Light Reading* (Lis Rhodes, 1979) and *Thriller* (Sally Potter, 1979). These are significant films and Sally Potter has gone on to make a series of feature films, including *Orlando* (1992) and *The Man who Cried* (2000, with Johnny Depp). They come from the period of 'high theoretical' feminist film-making in the late 1970s and early 1980s, when there was a great deal of concern about the politics of showing a woman's body on the screen, and one of the most important debates was about whether a woman could be the subject of her own story, or whether she was always 'spoken' in stories told by others. As a result feminist films from this period are multilayered, dense and difficult. As I was explaining some of this background, including political contextual factors, like the 1975 Equal Pay Act in Britain, which marked the first time it became illegal to pay women less than men for the same work, I could see expressions of faint incredulity on some of the students' faces. In discussion, it emerged that they thought that these feminist film-makers had made things incredibly and unnecessarily difficult for themselves, and also that they felt pretty certain that things were not like that now.

This is the classic moment at which someone of my age says, 'well, of course, once you are out in the workplace and considering how to have a satisfying personal life which may include having children, things may look a little different. But I agree – things aren't like that now'. What those young women were saying to me, as they have said to other feminist teachers like Lynn Spigel (1995) or Angela McRobbie (2004), was that they weren't like that – it wasn't like that for them. And in doing that, they invoke a structure of othering which, I want to suggest, has been a key component of engagements with feminist thought for at least the last thirty-five years. Put at its simplest, this is the cry, 'But we're not like that'.

This was, of course, what the first of the second-wave feminists, in the late 1960s, said, in response to the images of women they found on television, film and in the media more generally. These are Martha Rosler's semiotics of the kitchen. What second-wave feminism said was 'we're not like that', and that kind of femininity is impossible. But if psychoanalysis and feminism have both taught us, in certain ways, about some of the impossibilities of femininity, what I want to suggest here is that there is a 'disidentity' at the heart of feminism. Disidentity – not being like that, not being like those other women, not being like those images of women – is constitutive of feminism, and constitutive of feminism in all its generations. For if second-wave feminists were not like the housewives and sex objects they saw in the media, they were in turn othered by the post-colonial critique of the 1980s. As second-wave feminism interrogated itself, the next generation of feminists felt compelled to declare their lack of identity with second-wave feminists. Second-wave feminism is remembered, and demonized, as personally censorious, hairy and politically correct, and has been the key other for younger women keen to celebrate the femininity and feminism of Buffy and Ally.

The debates about feminism and post-feminism, which I shall not reproduce here, circle around questions of generation, privilege, periodization and the validity and national specificity of notions of 'backlash' (see Chapter 1 of this

volume for a discussion of some of these debates). I am generally in favour
of the relatively neutral notion of periodization as a way of differentiating
second-wave feminism from what came subsequently, but here want to suggest
that the notion of genre might also be productive. My proposal is that there is
a discernible genre of feminist analysis of popular culture which is repeated in
scholarship across media, and which has a particular role in the construction
of a periodization for feminism and in constituting second-wave feminism as
horrible and, thankfully, over. Genre is relevant because it permits us to concep-
tualize a structural relation between articles, books and discussions across a
wide range of topics and media, and gives us a sense of certain repetitions
across continuing change and adaptation.

Thus I am suggesting that there is an Ur feminist article that feminist scholars
within textual studies have been writing for some time, which produces, within
its structure, a temporality and periodization for feminism, if often unwit-
tingly.[4] I've written it. I wrote it about 1970s Hollywood films like *An
Unmarried Woman* (Paul Mazursky, 1978) and *Alice Doesn't Live Here Anymore*
(Martin Scorsese, 1974) and then later on I wrote it again about *Working Girl*
(Mike Nichols, 1988) and *Pretty Woman* (Garry Marshall, 1990).[5] Studies of
Madonna may have been one of the first clusters of this type of work, but there
are several others and rather than go through a list of articles, at a point where
another cluster is in evidence, with many scholars having written it, or writing
it, about 'Buffy the Vampire Slayer' (Fox/Mutant Enemy/Kuzui/Sandollar,
1997–2003), 'Sex and the City' (HBO, 1998–2004) and 'Ally McBeal' (Fox,
1996–2002), I'd like to discuss it more abstractly.

What does this Ur article do? It takes a television programme or film that
has a central female character – or characters – and which is usually addressed
to a feminine audience, and explores it within the vocabulary and concerns
of feminism. The structure of the article usually involves setting up what is
proposed as an obvious feminist reading of the text in which the text – and
the heroine – fail the test. The heroine is not independent enough; she cares
too much about shoes; she is always confined to the domestic sphere; she's
always worrying about what she looks like; she just wants to find a man and
settle down. Then what the author does is to mobilize her own engagement
with the text, her own liking for the treatment of the dreams and dilemmas of
the heroine, to interrogate the harsh dismissal of this popular text on feminist
grounds, and to reveal the complex and contradictory ways in which the text
– and the heroine – negotiate the perilous path of living as a woman in a
patriarchal world. The text is redeemed, and precisely the features that made
it fail the feminist test render it more resonant, interesting, sympathetic and
realistic for women now.

The heroine of this genre is both the author and her textual surrogate, while her adversaries are both textual (vampires, fellow lawyers, magazine editors, ex-husbands) and extra-textual – those censorious feminists who will not let her like the story and its iconography, the accoutrements of femininity. There are some striking historical homologies here, most evidently the defence of feminine fictional pleasures against dismissal, which characterized the early feminist work on soap opera and romance in the late 1970s and 1980s. However, now, it is not a patriarchal academy that is invoked as the enemy, but second-wave feminism itself. So I am suggesting that the very project of much contemporary feminist film and television textual criticism involves an articulation of what I am calling this disidentity at the heart of feminism. Rather than sisterhood, it is not being like that other woman that is central. And of course, what this work does, as well as redeeming whatever text it is for the modern girl's consumption, is to remake the cultural memory of the censorious feminist.

This move is not limited to the academy. It is arguably the single trope through which feminism is most often invoked in popular culture and can take many forms, as I shall explore below.[6] It was expressed vividly in a 2004 British radio programme in a comment by Marian Keyes, author of a series of successful books such as *Lucy Sullivan is Getting Married* and *Rachel's Holiday*, which are marketed (very successfully) as 'chick lit'. Keyes' novels, which reach worldwide audiences, have focused on the drama of being a young woman in the late twentieth century, and, while published in the bright pastel purple, pink and mauve covers of chick lit, take this journey to include dysfunctional families and dark passages of drug and alcohol addiction. In this radio interview, Keyes was trying to place her work in relation to feminism, and was espousing the continuing relevance of feminist ideas for her readers. She did this, though, by describing herself as being part of 'a post-feminist generation', which grew up in fear of being 'told off' by feminists and 'having everything pink taken out of my house'.[7]

COUNSELS OF PERFECTION AND IMPERFECTION

What I want to do in the second part of this chapter is to look at three different domestic stars on television to trace this complicated structure of being and not being a feminist, exploring some of the different moves made in relation to feminism and the figure of the woman in the kitchen. In these programmes, we can see the different modes of 'feminism in popular culture' that Hollows and Moseley propose in the project of this collection. After second-wave feminism, I don't think it is possible to be a television celebrity of domesticity without some negotiation with both the feminist and the housewife, but these negotiations can be quite complex and subtle, leading to very different women in very different kitchens. My argument is that each, in some way, is constituted through not being that cross woman in the kitchen embodied by Martha Rosler. Each is compelled to make the 'I'm not like that' move.

My main interest here is in the contrasting ways in which Martha Stewart and Nigella Lawson can be seen to embody some of the contradictions of the relationships between feminism, post-feminism and domesticity on television. Stewart's highly publicized trial, conviction and subsequent imprisonment for insider trading in 2004 changed her location within the media topography. She moved from daytime television and lifestyle magazine racks to the rather less picturesque, if more prominent, news and financial pages – although even on these pages, reports have been nearly always illustrated with her photograph, and her choice of handbag alone generated semi-autonomous coverage.[8] The size of Stewart's commercial empire meant that she was in fact always to be found on the financial pages, but her downfall has concentrated attention on what subtended her domestic fragrance, rather than the good things themselves. My concern here, though, is not with this gloating and gleeful coverage, 'blondenfreude', as Stanley and Hays call it,[9] but the contradictions Stewart previously embodied. From the other side of her downfall, hindsight perhaps renders these more visible, but Stewart has always attracted deep ambivalence, both passionate fandom and the camp fascination exhibited in websites such as 'Is Martha Stewart Living?' or a 1998 academic call for papers which characterized her as 'über-wasp and Chief Executive Housewife, archetype of white femininity and immigrant dream.'[10]

Nigella Lawson is less well known outside Britain, and her semi-ironic inhabiting of the persona of a 'Domestic Goddess' (her second cookery book was called *How to Be A Domestic Goddess*) may not travel well, just as Stewart's domestic perfectionism seems both humourless and chilly in Britain. Lawson has had three successful television cookery series – and was invited, by the British government, to cook for President Bush when he visited Britain in 2003. To understand what she represents in British television, we need to remind ourselves of the dominant British television cook of the last twenty years, Delia Smith.

Delia Smith is so significant within British food culture that her first name has now become a noun, and appears as such in the latest edition of the *Oxford English Dictionary*. The noun comes from the usage in which people will say 'Oh I just did a Delia' when describing what they cooked for a particular meal.

'Doing a Delia' is something to which people refer so readily partly because of the reliability of her recipes: because they are extensively tested, even if you have never cooked that particular recipe before, it is likely to work if you follow the instructions. Delia is an assiduous instructor and facilitator, who has become increasingly concerned both to instil basic cooking skills in the wider population and to extend the range of the national palate.[11] She has a core repertoire of familiar British dishes, but is also indefatigable in tracing and adapting recipes from a wide range of international cuisines. She is concerned, above all, with showing the viewer how to do it, rather than constructing herself as a distinguished chef. This means that her self-presentation does not detract from what she is demonstrating. She is nearly always filmed in the same environment, which is built to appear as her conservatory kitchen at her home in Suffolk. She dresses simply, never wearing an apron, and there are always plants or flowers in the room, usually in shot. Her instructions are clear and precise, and she is reassuring about the way in which food, in preparation, often looks rather odd: 'Don't worry that it looks lumpy at this stage'; 'all this runny juice will become absorbed in the cooking' etc. It is possible for anyone to 'do a Delia' precisely because of the way in which she presents herself as an enabler and facilitator – she has a certain neutrality, which is of course very specific in class and ethnic terms in that she is a lower-middle-class white married woman (now very wealthy), part of the respectable core of English identity.[12]

Now in some ways there are affinities with Martha Stewart here. There is the same sense of total control: of operations that have been performed and repeated and which have then been broken down into component parts which 'anyone' who has been paying attention can perform. Their television homes share a certain uncanny tidiness, abundant with necessary ingredients conveniently to hand in attractive containers, but devoid of mess. There is the *mise-en-scène* of a woman of a certain age who is immaculately groomed – but Martha has the veneer of wealth in a way that Delia does not. Delia, on television, is just a cook. She has views on how things should be served, and what one might serve with what, on the meanings of festivals such as Christmas and the value of hospitality, but she does not have designs on your linen drawers, bedroom, garden, hobbies and crockery. Delia has made the fortunes of a couple of small manufacturers by recommending their pans or kitchen utensils, and the supermarkets like to be informed of ingredients she is likely to recommend, but her books and programmes retain a quite strong relation to the instructional and functional within the realm of cooking. She is trying to show you how to do something useful. That is not to say that her work is somehow outside or without ideology – a range of scholars have shown the complex imbrications of discourses of nationality, empire and class in cookery programming, and Delia's sense of what is appropriate in today's kitchen is a very particular formation of unthreatening but slightly adventurous English suburban.[13] We should also note here that while she does not make much play of this within her programmes, Delia is married, and marriage is present within the television programmes, as for example, when she confesses that her husband makes much better salad dressing than she does. At this moment, Delia confirms that whatever else she is, the woman in the kitchen is a wife. Martha is very substantially more ambitious, with designs on a whole life system, and a commercial empire to match, but she also has a different relation to utility, necessity and the functional.

It is not that she doesn't show you how to do things, because she does, up to a point, but it is more to do with the type of things these are. Activities in the Martha world, which require planning, application and an aesthetic sense, are generally governed by a pre-industrial calendar of the natural year and religious festivities in combination with a post-industrial absence of necessity. Thus in the monthly diary in the magazine *Martha Stewart Living* and the topics on the shows, life is a succession of special events such as Hallowe'en, Thanksgiving, Passover, Easter, anniversaries, antiquarian book fairs, birthdays, Martin Luther King day and gala dinners. This is a fantasy of a peculiarly multicultural life on the homestead, where seasons are significant and domestic and garden chores have a natural rhythm. Housework exists in an event form – 'unwrap and arrange garden furniture', 'polish silverware', 'wash and wax floors', 'harvest herbs for drying' or as the potentially dilettante activity of dusting. At the same time, the Martha world is removed from necessity. Food is generally being cooked for special occasions such as neighbourly brunches and little dinners, while specialist electrical equipment such as a drill is used for drilling gourds to make a dried gourd garland for Thanksgiving (*Martha Stewart Living* magazine, November, 2002). There is no want here, but there is, always, careful attention to what things cost and what quantities it is appropriate to buy. The Martha world, although full of personal touches like home-made paper chains and Easter baskets (April, 2001) and a constant attention to making things unique and special, is never an extravagant one.

The *mise-en-scène* of domesticity in the Martha world is individuated, tranquil and rewarding. Because time is predictable and cyclical, events and activities can be planned, even offering the promise of improvement next time round. With necessity banished, the homemaker viewer can concentrate on making things lovely. And this is clearly a key source of Stewart's appeal. Ann Mason and Marian Meyers, who interviewed ten women who self-identified as Martha Stewart fans, found that the variety of the domestic projects she fostered was particularly attractive. They quote one respondent who says: 'I'll pick up *Women's Day* and those kinds of things. I feel like I read the same things over and over again in those magazines. You know, women's issues – weight gain, your breasts, quick pick-me-up during the day, put banana mush on your face. It's just the same stuff – and her stuff's different' (Mason and Meyers 2001: 811).

This woman clearly recognizes Stewart as addressing women, but she also perceives this address as distinct from that of most women's magazines with their predictable agendas. Stewart is seen to extend the range of feminine concerns, or to represent them in a way that makes them interesting, challenging and stimulating. Mason and Meyers observe: 'Much of what Stewart presents in her media traditionally has been considered women's work, but Stewart offers a different type of domesticity from that of previous generations. For the women in this study, she represents a liberated, chosen domesticity. Indeed, Martha Stewart appears to be giving permission to be interested in the domestic arena' (2000: 818).

Martha Stewart is a housewife who is not a housewife. In her media – the media that she controlled – she exists within the domestic arena, but this domestic is devoid of the boredom, repetition and frustration characterized as the housewife's lot by 1970s feminism. The Martha world is a sublime reversal of the feminist domestic labour debate in the 1970s. There, the discussion was concentrated on the extent to which women created value through their labour in the home to reproduce both labourers and labour power. Frequently emphasized was the manner in which the sexual division of labour produced the home as a site of leisure for the male worker but labour for the housewife. In the Martha world, the activities performed are almost never those essential to the production and reproduction of labour power such as rearing and feeding a family.

However, there are myriad tasks to be undertaken which will contribute to the home, and which promise a sense of creative satisfaction if completed. But because they are not, in any strict sense, necessary tasks, their performance is a type of busy feminine leisure within the home. Here it is useful to remember Janice Winship's discussion of fantasy when writing about a sudden flourishing of practical women's magazines in 1980s Britain. Winship relates the attractiveness of these magazines to women not to their utility but to their promise. She observes, 'craft and practical homemaking cannot be the nub of a certain kind of fantasy until those practices are no longer part of the daily grind' (1992: 103–4). She continues, 'Meanwhile, in the absence of spare time, looking at pics, reading instructions, is sublime (pleasurable and unpleasurable) surrogacy for practices that might construct another self; another place for women?' (1992: 106).

This understanding of the role of practical instructional media as 'a certain kind of fantasy' and 'sublime surrogacy' can usefully be combined with some of the more recent discussions of the changing nature of leisure and labour. For example, Witold Rybczynski, writing, one imagines, mainly about men, points to 'an unexpected development in the history of leisure': 'For many, weekend free time has become not a chance to escape work but a chance to create work that is more meaningful – to work at recreation – in order to realize the personal satisfactions that the workplace no longer offers' (1991: 224).

While one might quibble about the categories of person to whom the workplace has historically offered satisfaction, there is here a useful notion of the satisfactions of 'working at recreation' which can be combined with Winship's notion of 'sublime surrogacy' when approaching the Martha world. Leisure has, for most classes of women, always been uncommon,[14] but in the Martha world we are offered a very particular version of it constituted through fantasy as both an image and a practice of homemaking. Viewing one of the daily programmes of 'Martha Stewart Living', full of ideas for house and garden, flicking through the magazine, with its glossy paper and spacious layout, for even more ideas, trying to make a pussy-willow Easter basket (April, 2003) or arranging your collection of vintage rolling pins are all forms of virtuous feminine leisure, the perfecting of a domestic *mise-en-scène*.

While the specificity of the Martha world is formed in the context of the late-twentieth-century USA, a context which is post-feminist in the sense that it was possible for a woman to both own and perform *Martha Stewart Living*, there are aspects of the Martha world which are illuminated by Thorstein Veblen's writing on the leisure class in the late nineteenth century, particularly his notion of the ceremonial character of much of life for the leisure class: 'But much of the services classed as household cares in modern everyday life, and many of the "utilities" required for a comfortable existence by civilized man, are of a ceremonial character. They are, therefore, properly to be classed as performance of leisure in the sense in which the term is here used' (Veblen 1970: 55). Veblen's notion of 'the performance of leisure' provides an elegant characterization of the activities of the Martha world, which can often involve quite arduous craft labour, while his notion of the 'ceremonial utilities required' reminds us that Stewart endorses a wide range of products, including a household range in the downmarket Kmart.

So Stewart has to be understood through a matrix of concerns including the changing role of the housewife and the increased number of women undertaking paid work outside the home; the historical gendering of leisure; the changing significance of craft practices and the increasing association of leisure with practices of consumption. If we think about her in terms of feminism, she is — or perhaps was — exquisitely both pre- and post-. In her self-presentation and demeanour, Stewart works to erase the unkempt anger here embodied by Martha Rosler in the kitchen. Stewart is blonde, highly groomed, controlled and pleasant. There is nothing nasty here, which is perhaps why press reports during her trial concentrated with such fascination on Stewart's off-air rudeness. In her lack of affect, despite the warm smile with which she insists that the little jewel-coloured jellies that have just been made on the show are 'a good thing', Martha is in some ways both post-industrial and postmodern in the slight sense of pastiche that is discernible in her productions from a certain angle. Just as Martha instructs us how to use beeswax to bring a warm, sweet-smelling shine to wooden floors in a nostalgic but unlikely procedure, so too there is something faintly uncanny about the perfection of her performance of ceremonial domesticity. And it is this, I speculate, which provokes that structure of furious disidentification again — we're not like that.

Nigella is a different matter. The first thing that must be said about her is that she is impossible without Delia. The neutral, ordinary, transparent authority of Delia is the screen onto which Nigella can be projected, just as Martha's perfection illuminates Nigella's humanity.

I want to conclude by discussing the way in which Nigella Lawson invokes the 'I'm not like that' move in her cookery series, 'Nigella Bites'. Lawson, beautiful, glamorous, university educated and upper-middle-class, for many years wrote a cookery column for *Vogue*.[15] Her father at one stage a senior member of Mrs Thatcher's government as Chancellor of the Exchequer, Nigella married to a journalist, was clearly a member of the chattering classes, but also one who had to earn her way. The publication of her cookery book, *How to Eat*, led to a Channel 4 cookery series, 'Nigella Bites' (Pabulam and Flashback for Channel 4, 2001), which was distinguished by her sensual enjoyment of her own cooking and her semi-ironic, sometimes wittily flirtatious mode of address. By the time of the television series, it was widely known that Nigella's husband, John Diamond, was dying of cancer, because he wrote a weekly column on this topic in a quality newspaper. The Nigella television persona developed in this period represents an inflection of the type of *überfrau* figure that we find with both Delia and Martha into something a little saucier and post-feminist in a slightly different way. Here we should note that Nigella is younger, she has more cultural capital, she has more formal education — and she uses more irony. She also inscribes a certain vulnerability into her performance, both through an explicitly autobiographical address and the repeated trope of stealing down to the fridge to eat cold food alone at night.

The *mise-en-scène* of 'Nigella Bites' is Nigella's domestic life with her two children and husband, and the series is partly filmed in their home. The sequence

I want to analyze is set on a weekday when Nigella is trying to have friends to supper after work as well as dealing with the everyday life of caring for her two children, feeding them, taking them to school, etc. Nigella is first shown filmed in her study where she gives a little introduction to the episode and, later, cooking while the children have breakfast and then taking them to school. She is, unusually, wearing glasses. This is serious Nigella. She is also wearing a denim jacket, which makes her outline much harder and sharper than normal, as she usually wears soft, tight-fitting brightly coloured knits.

For our purposes, there is a significant relationship between what she is saying and what she is doing. This is an early morning sequence, which starts with Nigella getting the children downstairs for breakfast. While the children are shown eating porridge and toast, the camera tilts up from the table to Nigella as she starts to prepare food for the evening. The menu (bitter orange ice cream, and pumpkin and coconut seafood curry) has already been announced, and Nigella commences by grating the peel off the oranges. As she does this, she reassures the viewer, 'Cooking something at breakfast time, mad though it seems, I promise you isn't about being any kind of deranged superwoman'. Once again we see the othering structure with which I have been concerned, but here it lies in the refusal to be the 1970s answer to feminism, the superwoman. A woman who has published a book, with its ironies and love of baking, called *How to be a Domestic Goddess* is very clear to specify that what she is doing is not about 'being any kind of deranged superwoman'. Just, perhaps a very busy woman, who works, runs a house, has children and a life, and thus has to become an expert at the gender-free activity of 'multitasking', which seems to have replaced the notion of the persona of the superwoman. Nigella's denial, though, is undercut by the *mise-en-scène*. Although the children reappear at the end of the episode to be taken to school, they are very noticeably absent from the key parts of explaining the recipe. Even the prop of the breakfast time mug of tea cannot quite disguise the fact that although Nigella might not be a deranged superwoman, this is still quite a thing to do at breakfast, and something that can certainly not be performed and filmed at breakfast. However, we must also note how different are the semiotics of this kitchen: familial, expressive and, above all, modern.

Nigella Lawson is privileged, educated and witty. In her disidentification with 'that deranged superwoman' thing, I suggest that she is making the same move that we see in what I have described as the feminist Ur article, and would suggest that this move is one of the primary ways in which feminism currently appears in popular culture. The Ur feminist article is structured in the denunciation of that which formed it, just as Nigella would not be able to be ironic in the kitchen if Martha Stewart and Delia Smith had not already been super-competent there,[16] Martha and Delia could not have become wealthy in the kitchen if Martha Rosler had not been cross there first. My argument is not for a return to being cross in the kitchen. As Marian Keyes observed, 'God knows, there's plenty wrong with feminism'. But there is a repetition in play, both in feminist scholarship and the broader culture, which reinscribes second-wave feminism as that one does not want to be associated with. As another student observed to me, 'Feminism – that's a bit of an old-fashioned word, isn't it?' This repetition enacts a paralysis in the field, for while it promises progress – we are moving on – the very move actually functions to fix all the positions, so that Martha is left, stuck in the kitchen forever, making her Zorro gesture with raised knives.

And young women, busy to insist that they are not like that, attend to the counsels of perfection which insist on the necessity of the self-respect of perfect grooming, the delights of clothes and shoe-shopping, the pleasures of cooking, hospitality and homemaking, the satisfaction and love in child-rearing – and a full-time job as well. The young women faintly puzzled by the ungainliness and anger of second-wave feminism are quite right – it's not like that for them. It is permitted to have pink things in your house, and it is not permitted to be cross or tired or fed up – because then you might look a bit like Martha with her raised knives.

ACKNOWLEDGEMENT

A shorter version of this chapter was originally published as 'Feminism, Postfeminism, Martha, Martha and Nigella' by Charlotte Brunsdon in the *Cinema Journal* (44, 2: 110–16), Copyright © 2005 the University of Texas Press. All rights reserved. Thanks to Sarah Thomas and J. C.-M. for research help with Martha and handbags.

NOTES

1. While Martha clearly inspired envy and emulation among her many fans (for an analysis of what fans say about liking Martha, see Mason and Meyers 2001), she also provoked much more ambivalent feelings and outright hostility (see, for example, Margaret Talbot 1996).
2. The magazine was first published in 1991 by Time Warner Inc. The TV show began in 1993, appearing first on the Lifetime network, and then moving in 1997 to CBS. These were preceded by a significant deal with Kmart. See Mason and Meyers (2001) and Christopher M. Byron (2002).

3. Much of Rosler's work has been concerned with the iconography of the American Dream, particularly, initially, in the context of the Vietnam war, and with the spaces in which we live and travel. See the catalogue for the 1998 retrospective of Rosler's work (de Zegher 1998). Rosler has engaged with food and the place of food in several other pieces, including *The Art of Cooking: A Mock Dialogue between Julia Child and Craig Claiborne* (1974) and in 1985, *Global Taste: A Meal in Three Courses.*

4. Production studies tend to have a different emphasis. See, for example, Julie D'Acci (1994) and Amanda Lotz (2006).

5. See the essays 'A Subject for the Seventies' and 'Post-feminism and Shopping Films' in Brunsdon (1997).

6. A germane discussion of the significance of violence in the representation of feminism can be found in Hilary Hinds and Jackie Stacey (2001).

7. Marian Keyes, 'Start the Week', BBC Radio 4, 7 June 2004.

8. Stewart's self-presentation was the subject of much commentary during her trial. On the topic of her handbag, see, for example, in British newspapers alone: Rowan Pelling, 'Is there anything sadder than the trophy handbag?', *Independent on Sunday*, 5 September 2004: 23; Hannah Betts, 'Claim of only one bag is open and shut case', *The Times*, 19 July 2004: 5; James Sherwood, 'Dress down, look innocent: what to wear in the dock', *Independent*, 6 March 2004: 28; Hadley Freeman, 'Is the verdict in the bag?', *Guardian*, 3 March 2004: 21; Marcus Warren, 'Martha goes for a Birkin in court battle of the bags', *The Daily Telegraph* 23 January 2004: 17. The savemartha.com website offered an imitation Birkin bag for $16.99 (US).

9. Alessandra Stanley and Constance L. Hays 'Martha Stewart's to-do list may include image polishing', *New York Times*, 23 June 2002: 1, quoted in Carole A. Stabile's 2004 discussion of news coverage of Stewart's indictment and trial in comparison with the coverage of the male executives accused in the Enron scandal.

10. Zoe Newman and Kyla Wazana, call for papers for the 1998 MLA Conference for a session on *Martha Stewart's Living*, http://www.english.upenn.edu/CFP/archive/19988–02, accessed January 2004.

11. Smith's cookery journey, culminating, as she herself suggests, in her 1999 BBC series 'Delia's How to Cook' (Spire Films for BBC Birmingham, 1999) which included instruction on how to make toast and boil eggs, commenced in 1971 with a book called *How to Cheat at Cooking*.

12. Smith's image was shaken in 2005 after she made an impassioned appeal to home fans at a football match between Norwich City (of which she is a

director) and Manchester City, which was captured on camera and broadcast to the nation. The footage replayed repeatedly on television news and also circulated on the Web to the soundtrack of Tracy Chapman's 'Fast Car'. Smith's commitment (emotional and financial) to Norwich City is well documented and there has been considerable attention to her involvement in the club's restaurants. On this occasion, newspaper and other media coverage repeatedly involved the speculation that 'there was too much sherry in the trifle' (Patrick Barkham, 'Guardian Profile: Delia Smith', *Guardian*, 4 March 2005: 16) or that 'Ms Smith is thought to have enjoyed corporate hospitality' (Matthew Beard, 'How to make a fool of yourself in public', *Independent*, 2 March 2005: 3).

13. Nick Clarke (2004: 170) quotes 'an unkind television producer': 'She has an unerring touch to render metropolitan chic down a couple of notches for the suburbs.' See Niki Strange (1998) and David Bell (2000) among others on ideologies of cookery programmes.

14. The wonderfully attractive essays on leisure that Rybczynski cites, such as Bertrand Russell's 'In Praise of Idleness' and G. K. Chesterton's 'On Leisure', in which he suggests that leisure comprises three different things: 'the first is being allowed to do something. The second is being allowed to do anything. And the third (and perhaps the most rare and precious) is being allowed to do nothing' (1991: 15), are, precisely, the work of male authors.

15. For a more substantial analysis of Nigella, see Joanne Hollows (2003).

16. Space forbids full acknowledgement of the long genealogy here, which includes, most notably, Julia Child, Fanny Craddock and Marguerite Patten.

BIBLIOGRAPHY

Barthes, R. (1972 [1957]), *Mythologies*, trans. Annette Lavers, London: Jonathan Cape.

Bell, D. (2000), 'Performing Taste: Celebrity Chefs and Culinary Cultural Capital', paper presented at Crossroads Cultural Studies Conference, University of Birmingham, June.

Brunsdon, C. (1997), *Screen Tastes: Soap Opera to Satellite Dishes*, London: Routledge.

Byron, C. (2002), *Martha Inc.*, New York: John Wiley & Sons Inc.

Clarke, N. (2004 [2003]), *The Shadow of a Nation: How Celebrity Destroyed Britain*, London: Phoenix.

D'Acci, J. (1994), *Defining Women: Television and the Case of Cagney and Lacey*, Chapel Hill: University of North Carolina Press.

Hinds, H. and Stacey, J. (2001), 'Imaging Feminism, Imaging Femininity: The Bra-burner, Diana and the Woman who Kills', *Feminist Media Studies*, 1, 2: 153–77.

Hollows, J. (2003), 'Feeling Like a Domestic Goddess: Post-feminism and Cooking', *European Journal of Cultural Studies*, 6, 2: 179–202.

Keyes, M. (1997), *Lucy Sullivan is Getting Married*, London: Arrow.

—— (1998), *Rachel's Holiday*, London: Penguin.

Lawson, N. (1999), *How to Eat: The Pleasures and Principles of Good Food*, London: Chatto and Windus.

—— (2000), *How to be a Domestic Goddess: Baking and the Art of Comfort Cooking*, London: Chatto and Windus.

Lotz, A. (2006), *Redefining Women: Television After the Network Era*, Champaign: University of Illinois Press.

McRobbie, A. (2004), 'Post-feminism and Popular Culture: Bridget Jones and the "New Gender Regime"', paper presented at the 'Interrogating Post-Feminism' conference, University of East Anglia, UK, April.

Mason, A. and Meyers, M. (2001), 'Living with Martha Stewart: Chosen Domesticity in the Experience of Fans', *Journal of Communication*, Dec: 801–23.

Rybczynski, W. (1991), *Waiting for the Weekend*, New York: Viking.

Smith, D. (1971), *How to Cheat at Cooking*, London: Coronet.

Spigel, L. (1995), 'From the Dark Ages to the Golden Age: Women's Memories and Television Reruns', *Screen* 36, 1: 16–33.

Stabile, C. A. (2004), 'Getting What She Deserved: The News Media, Martha Stewart, and Masculine Domination', *Feminist Media Studies*, 4, 3: 315–32.

Strange, N. (1998), 'Perform, Educate, Entertain: Ingredients of the Cookery Programme Genre', in C. Geraghty and D. Lusted (eds), *The Television Studies Book*, London: Arnold.

Talbot, M. (1996), 'Les très riches heures de Martha Stewart', *New Republic*, 214, 20: 30–33.

Veblen, T. (1970 [1899]), *The Theory of the Leisure Class*, London: Unwin Books.

Winship, J. (1992), 'The Impossibility of *Best*: Enterprise Meets Domesticity in the Practical Women's Magazines of the 1980s', in D. Strinati and S. Wagg (eds), *Come on Down? Popular Media Culture in Post-war Britain*, London: Routledge.

de Zegher, C. (ed.) (1998), *Martha Rosler: Positions in the Life World*, Birmingham. The Ikon Gallery; Vienna: Generali Foundation; and Cambridge, MA: MIT Press.

CHAPTER 4

Feminism in the Classroom: Teaching Towards the Third Wave

Kathleen Rowe Karlyn

Popular culture is the politics of the twenty-first century

Gale Weathers, *Scream 3* (Wes Craven, 2000)

Since the mid 1990s, teen girls have enjoyed an unprecedented visibility in mainstream culture.[1] With books such as Mary Pipher's *Reviving Ophelia* (1994) putting the troubled teen girl psyche on the US national agenda, an explosion of entertainment aimed at teen girl audiences has provided evidence that teen girls 'matter', at least as audiences and consumers of girl-oriented music, television shows, films and websites. 'Girl power', a term first associated with the underground riot grrrl movement in the late 1980s, has gone mainstream thanks to the brief but wildly popular reign of the Spice Girls.

At the same time, while girl power may be hot, feminism is not. Rarely has feminism been viewed in the culture with such ambivalence, indifference or downright disdain. Many women, especially young women, simply do not want to associate themselves with feminism, despite the belief of most self-identified feminists that women of all ages have benefited, and continue to benefit, from feminism as a political movement and a mode of cultural and political analysis. This repudiation has made it difficult for teachers to bring feminist perspectives into the classroom, or to name them as such, even when teaching the politics of gender, and even with students who may well be sympathetic to the basic principles of feminism.

There is no easy explanation for this apparent contradiction. Indeed, the feminist movement itself has experienced a 'relational crisis', in Carol Gilligan's words, with intense debate across generational, racial and national divides about how to characterize the various periods of feminism, as well as the evolving relationship between feminism and the popular. What language should be used to periodize the movement? Generations? Waves? In the US, for example, the term 'wave' was deliberately adopted by young feminists in order to avoid the overdetermination of mother–daughter relations.[2] And what makes a popular text feminist – or not? While there was some consensus in 1991 that *Thelma and Louise* (Ridley Scott) was a feminist text, what does it mean to say the same about the parodic slasher flick *Scream* (Wes Craven, 1996), a cult film for US teen girls, or the sweetly romantic *Bridget Jones's Diary* (Sharon Maguire, 2001), which holds 'near iconic status' as 'chick lit and 'chick flick', especially in the UK?[3]

In this essay, I will approach this tension between feminism and the popular not as a puzzle to be solved, but in terms of how it has influenced my teaching. I formed my feminist identity in the 1970s during what has come to be known in the US as feminism's second wave. For the past decade, much of my research has focused on girl culture and its relation to current feminism. In this essay, I will explain how that research has changed my teaching. I will argue that teaching girl-oriented popular culture provides teachers with opportunities (1) to reintroduce feminist histories and methodologies into the classroom; (2) to provide tools for students to develop their own positions on youth culture and gender politics; and (3) to develop their own strategies of feminist pedagogy. I will begin by laying out some of the arguments that have been made, especially in the US, for why current students resist feminism, and how those arguments manifest themselves in the classroom. Then I will map out a methodology I have developed for teaching feminism and popular culture, illustrating my ideas with a brief discussion of *Scream*, a highly teachable film that provides rich insights into girl culture and its relation to emerging feminisms.

WHO NEEDS FEMINISM?

One of the most puzzling elements in recent public discussions about feminism is the degree to which young women have disavowed the movement. Feminism has become an easy target for women who do not feel that they benefited from the highly touted booming economy of the late 1990s, and who in fact work harder than ever to get by, with less time to enjoy the rewards of family life and domesticity. At the same time, while young women of all races and social classes appear to be uncomfortable with the term 'feminism', most agree with many of the principles associated with it, such as reproductive rights and equal pay for equal work. Most young women also have little knowledge of the history of the women's movement, or of the restrictions on women's lives that existed a mere generation ago.

Explanations abound for this apparent turn against feminism. The most obvious targets the larger social formation in which feminism exists. In her 1991 book *Backlash: The Undeclared War Against American Women*, Susan Faludi argued that feminism became the target of a massive effort during the socially conservative 1980s and 1990s to reverse the gains achieved by the women's movement since the mid 1960s. From Faludi's perspective, if young women today believe in their unlimited freedom and opportunity as individuals, reject structural analyses of social power and avoid questioning the unequal effects of the period's economic boom, that is because of the political environment in which they grew up.

This environment also accounts for the wave of highly publicized books by women such as Naomi Wolf, Katie Roiphe and Rene Denfield who may identify themselves as feminists, but according to a new set of definitions built on an array of rhetorically savvy terms and misleading oppositions: 'victim feminism' vs. 'power feminism', 'gender' or 'difference' feminism vs. 'equity' feminism. Young, white, educated at elite institutions, these women conform to *Time* magazine's choice of Ally McBeal, a narcissistic, Ivy League educated lawyer, as the 'face' of popularized feminism. Other conservative voices with more established academic credentials have joined the chorus, including Elizabeth Fox-Genovese, Camille Paglia and Christina Hoff Sommers.[4] While claiming to refashion a 'new' feminism, however, these women have not learned the lessons about racial and class privilege so hard won by the old feminists.[5] And even though their ideas have been well refuted in more scholarly venues, the mainstream press has embraced these authors as the new voices of the women's movement, using their work as the basis for sensationalized discussions of the state of feminism today.

The 'backlash' argument is compelling, especially because it addresses the retreat not only from feminism but also from any kind of political engagement. It helps explain the faith of many young people in their freedom as individuals to achieve what they want. This faith is especially strong among the largely white middle-class students I teach in the Pacific Northwest, students who have had little reason yet to become politicized or to view their position in the world in structural terms. It is easy to blame a hostile political and social environment for the problems besetting feminism today; however, it is more productive to look within the movement itself for reasons why young women have resisted it. From this perspective, mainstream or 'hegemonic' feminism – still largely associated with the second wave – has lost its appeal because of (1) its failures

regarding class and race; (2) its censoriousness regarding sexuality, especially
heterosexuality; (3) its resistance to the pleasures of the popular; and (4) its
growing institutionalization and refusal to examine its own stakes in the power
structure. The second wave, of course, was hardly monolithic, despite efforts to
make it appear so and to reduce it to caricature. However, the new feminisms
have distinguished themselves from the second wave by staking out different
positions and priorities on these matters.

The most disturbing disaffection from feminism has historically been by
women of colour, in response to the overwhelming whiteness and middle-
classness of the second wave. Indeed, the failures of mainstream US feminism
to forge a racially inclusive liberation movement date from its earliest history
in the nineteenth century, when Susan B. Anthony refused to support the
enfranchisement of black men, despite the movement's roots in the abolitionist
movement. Second-wave feminism did engage with minority voices, but
in selective ways – the highly intellectual Gayatri Spivak or 'easily digested'
Maya Angelou. The resulting tensions came to a head at the 1981 National
Women's Studies Association Conference, when women of colour, angered by
the structure of the conference, launched a movement they identified as US
Third World feminism.[6]

The continued association of feminism with whiteness can be seen in the
most recent of *Time* magazine's covers about the movement (Bellafante 1998),
which depicted its historical phases with four white faces, the last being that
of the fictional TV character Ally McBeal – skinny, professional, neurotic
and white. This whiteness can also be seen in the recent texts and performers
that have attracted the attention of academic feminists interested in popular
culture: Madonna, Ani Di Franco, the Spice Girls in music; *Scream* and *Bridget
Jones* in film; 'Buffy the Vampire Slayer' (Fox/Mutant Enemy/Kuzui/Sandollar,
1997–2003), 'Alias' (Touchstone/Bad Robot, 2001–) and 'Sex and the City'
(HBO, 1998–2004) on TV.

Second, young women are particularly sensitive to elements of mainstream
feminism that they perceive as dogmatic, censorious and out-of-touch with the
everyday lives of women, especially in the area of sexuality. In *New Millennial
Sexstyles*, a bold and moving effort to chart the territory between the second and
third waves, Carol Siegel describes the alienating effects of the second wave's
'concessions to conventional morality and its role in the regulation of sexuality'
(2000: 2). Her critique of the second wave zeroes in on its failures to address
love and sexuality, especially heterosexuality, in ways to which many women
could relate. Not only did the second wave's orthodox analysis of sexuality
leave no place for 'non-complicitous heterosexuality', she suggests, but it also

reinforced larger structures of bourgeois capitalism in policing the anarchic power of Eros.

Finally, as the movement has become institutionalized, especially in academia, it has failed to recognize its own growing stakes in the establishment. As a result, according to Catherine Lumby in *Bad Girls: The Media, Sex and Feminism in the 90s* (1997), second-wave feminists have been blinded to crucial changes in the landscape of politics and public life, which today are being enacted in the realm of technology, mass communication and everyday culture. In particular, by failing to articulate 'a feminist vision of new technologies and its role in our lives', Lumby argues, second-wave feminists have inadvertently aligned themselves with conservative social forces. Catherine M. Orr takes a similar position in the conclusion of her thoughtful essay on third-wave feminism, pointing out the conservatism of many second-wave feminists regarding popular culture. She warns that academic feminists may find themselves 'positioned uncomfortably' against the populism implicit in feminism's newest wave, which is returning to the popular culture that in fact helped the second wave achieve its own political power (Orr 1997: 41).

NEW FEMINISMS AND THE THIRD WAVE

In response to these critiques, new forms of feminism have emerged with different names and valences. Post-feminism carries in its name many of the ambivalences felt by younger women towards the second wave. The term is commonly used in popular discourse to suggest that 'real' feminism is a thing of the past. It has been the subject of academic enquiry as well, especially in the UK.[7] US Third World feminism continues to develop as a theoretically sophisticated and inclusive movement that, like earlier feminism, focuses on identity as the basis for a politically engaged scholarship, but considers gender as only one of many identity categories. Despite its associations with a formidable array of scholars of race, decolonization, cyberfeminism and queer studies, including Chandra Mohanty, Cherrie Moraga, Trinh Min Ha, bell hooks, Lisa Lowe and others, this movement has remained peripheral to what Chela Sandoval, in *The Methodology of the Oppressed*, calls 'hegemonic feminism'. It has, however, been foundational to the third wave, a movement that has developed in the US out of a strong sense of both continuity with but distinction from the second wave.[8] Because the third wave conveys an explicit sense of itself *as* feminism and as arising from a younger generation, I have found it accessible to students.[9]

The third wave was first named by Rebecca Walker in a 1992 article published in *Ms.*, 'Becoming the Third Wave'. In this article, and in a later edited book *To*

Be Real: Telling the Truth and Changing the Face of Feminism, Walker expresses the third wave's need to define its issues and goals for itself, including its desire to engage with difference more effectively than the 'elders' of the second wave. Since then, young scholars, activists and artists have produced a body of work including *Third Wave Agenda* (Heywood and Drake 1997), *Manifesta* (Baumgartner and Richards 2000) and others, explicitly identified with the third wave. Typically combining critique with manifesto, and ranging from collections of personal testimonies to more academically oriented anthologies, this work is provocative, wide-ranging and difficult to characterize because its views and modes of address differ so widely.[10]

Despite these differences, several threads run through it. Unlike the feminisms popularized by Roiphe *et al.*, the third wave retains a political, activist dimension. It is built on racial and sexual inclusivity, and is global and ecological in perspective. Young campus feminists see environmental and international labour issues as deeply connected, and anti-sweatshop and workers' rights movements as central to feminist political action. Third-wave feminist theory also shows the influence of post-structuralism on its notions of identity and subjectivity. Embracing the popular and engaging with the pleasures of consumer culture, it takes a postmodernist, rather than modernist, orientation towards art and culture. It continues the second wave's critique of sexuality under patriarchy, but more openly explores sexuality and femininity as multidimensional.

In third-wave feminism, popular culture is a natural site of identity formation and empowerment, providing an abundant storehouse of images and narratives valuable less as a means of representing reality than as motifs available for contesting, rewriting and recoding. This perspective rests on a post-structuralist critique of the relation between language and the 'real'. If young women reject the label of 'feminist', that stance may result not only from backlash and a resistance to political affiliation but also from their scepticism about the capacity of language to represent the 'truth' of who they are. According to writings from the third wave, young feminists today resist the positivist epistemology of the second wave, and consider such categories as 'male' and 'female', 'black', 'white', 'lesbian' and 'heterosexual' as pragmatic bases for political action rather than transparent signifiers of 'the real'.[11] While uneasy about the political consequences of abandoning these categories, many third wavers also view them as markers of identity that can be borrowed, performed and pieced together ironically, playfully or with political intent, in a mode typical of postmodern culture.

According to familiar analyses of postmodernity, such as Fredric Jameson's, postmodern culture lacks the potential for political critique because its pastiche of signifiers and intertextuality no longer refers to a shared historical reality. However, for youth culture, the appropriation of diverse cultural labels, motifs or other signifiers may express an aesthetic and politics of hybridity consistent with its consciousness of multiculturalism and sexual diversity (see the introduction to Heywood and Drake 1997).[12] And so young women of all races and ethnicities borrow from hip hop, a powerful force in youth culture today, even though its roots are in urban, male African-American culture, in order to take up its politicized stance towards racial injustice (Neisel 1997). Similarly, young women freely engage in masculinity – within themselves as well as in male-oriented music and violent action films – in order to 'take up' the sense of power our culture still identifies with boys and men. The *Scream* trilogy of films, to which I will return, enables girls to reject codes of femininity familiar to them from the highly conventionalized genre of the teen slasher film in order to rewrite them in more empowering ways.

As Nina Maglin and Donna Perry argue in '*Bad Girls, Good Girls*', sexuality has become a 'lightning rod for this generation's hopes and discontents (and democratic visions)' in the same way that Civil Rights and Vietnam mobilized their mothers.[13] The regulation of female sexuality is deeply ingrained in our culture to hold the structures of patriarchy and heterosexuality in place, with mothers – even feminist mothers – who have internalized these lessons teaching their daughters from an early age about the need to 'police' their sexuality. Indeed, much adult concern about young women and popular culture arises from the treatments of teen girl sexuality in movies, MTV, magazines, advertisements, clothing and TV shows. As a result, many third wavers focus their attention on sexual politics as well as cultural production, viewing society's 'construction, containment, and exploitation of female sexuality in the 1990s … as a model for women's situation generally, particularly in terms of agency or victimization', two of the key topics of debate among the 'popular' feminists (Maglin and Perry 1996: xvi).

While the second wave generally tied (hetero)sexuality to oppression, the third wave is less conflicted about sexuality in any form. Through her own encounters with youth subcultures and provocative readings of alternative music, Carol Siegel finds an inclination in youth culture towards fluid categories of gender and wide-ranging sexualities, or 'sexstyles'. This development challenges power structures threatened by sexual practices such as S/M or fetishism that resist the ideological frameworks of both mainstream culture and the second wave. The insistence of young feminists on their right to define their political strategy as '[making] use of power and danger' (Heywood and Drake 1997: 3) or as guided by 'desire, pleasure and anger' may well unsettle older women concerned about girls' vulnerability to exploitation by men or experimentation outside the social norms of heterosexuality. However, feminism's 'elders', to quote Walker, need to understand more fully the intention that motivates this strategy, whether they agree with it or not. As Lisa Jones writes of the third wave, 'We are smartass girls with a sense of entitlement, who ... delight in our sexual bravura, and live womanism as pleasure, not academic mandate.'[14] Part of that pleasure involves reclaiming the right not only to the term 'girl' but also to 'girly pleasures' such as shopping and dressing up, trivialized by the culture at large and criticized by the second wave as complicitous in sexism. In a punchy and knowledgeable survey of girl culture, Ann Powers in *Spin* magazine describes how girls aggressively flaunt traits formerly viewed as demeaning by both feminists and misogynists: prettiness, brattishness and sexual flamboyance (1997: 77). And so, while retaining the critique of beauty culture and sexual abuse from the second wave, young women have complicated the older feminist critique of the male gaze as a weapon to put women in their place, and instead exploit the spotlight as a source of power and energy. Thus girls do not see a contradiction between female power and assertive sexuality. Girl-power icons can dress in provocative clothing while demonstrating fierce physical prowess (Buffy) or chant the virtues of female power and solidarity while wearing Wonderbras (Spice Girls). Powers' sharpest insight into the new girl culture describes its strategy as neither rational nor analytic, like the second wave, but 'mythic', manifesting itself in the symbols, rhythms and motifs of a media-infused age. Approaching this new culture on its own terms, seeking to understand its relation to a new feminism, is the challenge we face in the classroom.

FEMINIST PEDAGOGY: A CASE STUDY

In 1996, I created an undergraduate course on Teen Girls and Popular Culture, which I have since taught regularly. Considering the demographic homogeneity of the Pacific Northwest, the course usually draws a mixed group of students. Some are lesbians, most are heterosexuals. Some are rebels, others sorority girls. Some are women of colour, most are white. Several are international students. A few are older women, some mothers with daughters of their own, but most are in their early twenties. Most are women, although a small number of male students typically enrol as well. Most of these students have had little or no exposure to feminist theory or to critical studies of popular culture. My objective in this course has been to introduce students to a critical perspective on popular culture addressed to and popular with girls and young women. We consider examples of culture that girls engage with (music, films, TV, magazines) as well as how popular culture shapes girls' perception of issues that are important to them. We seek to discover what girls learn about issues that concern them (health, friendship, sex, family relations, braininess and so on) as these themes are represented in popular culture. I expose the class to various tools of critical media analysis with the goal of helping students to develop their own positions on gender and popular culture. The course does not emphasize feminism, but by focusing on girls and culture, it puts gender 'on the table'. By the end of the term, feminism emerges as a relevant consideration in the context of the work the class has already done.

In conceptualizing the course, I realized that I couldn't teach it in ways I had become accustomed to. Teaching experts routinely talk about student-centred classrooms and student-driven learning, especially as new technologies break down traditional classroom boundaries and hierarchies. We are often told that students have a good sense of what they need to know, and can teach themselves what they need to learn. However, in the courses I have taught on such topics as film history, genre studies, media aesthetics and women directors, I had become comfortable with a traditional teaching style, establishing course content with a carefully constructed syllabus, and controlling the classroom with a mixture of lecture and discussion. The kind of authority I exercised has been hard earned, especially for women in university settings, and I believe it is appropriate for professors to determine the content of their courses, subjects for discussion, parameters for papers, standards for exams and so on.

However, Teen Girls and Popular Culture required a different approach. Given the ephemeral and ever-changing texts of youth culture, I simply could not keep abreast of the raw material I wanted to incorporate into the course, and I didn't want to limit the texts we studied to ones I was familiar with. Nor did I wish to present myself as an authority on how my students have experienced gender politics, or to draw the theoretical component of the course primarily from the second wave. I decided that I would first bring these controversial subjects into the classroom by using a pedagogy that reflected my own understanding of feminist principles. On the first day, I explained that I had designed the course around principles from my own education in the second wave. That education encouraged an exposure to and questioning of relations of power in all institutions, including the classroom. I did not want to teach the course as an expert on the subject, but I also didn't want to surrender my authority or expertise where relevant. We would share responsibility for what we accomplished. Collaborative learning would be the primary means of achieving our goals. Students would produce knowledge through multiple strategies, make decisions through negotiation and consensus-building, and would work in groups as well as individually.

What resulted was a course that changes every time I teach it, but which retains a basic structure designed to shift major responsibilities from me to the students. The course challenges students to take a more active role in their own education, in both what they learn and how they learn it. Students decide a significant portion of what we study and teach it to the class. I teach the first third of the term and the final week, while students are researching the material they will teach the class later. This portion of the class establishes a common historical context and theoretical framework for students to use as they conduct research into the particulars of teen girl culture. I then turn the class over to student panels, which choose the specific examples of popular culture we will examine from a series of broad topics I provide. The last week I return to lead the class in a more explicit discussion of feminism. At this time, we also discuss ways to revise the class the next time I teach it.

During 'my' portion of the course, I use conventional teaching methods, making decisions about the readings and films we study, giving short lectures and nudging class discussions towards conclusions I wish students to consider. We discuss readings that approach girl culture from differing points of view on how teen girls interact with and are influenced by popular culture. Students read from academic and popular sources, including Joan Jacobs Brumberg's *The Body Project* (1997), a fascinating work of social history, to gain historical perspective on the issues that absorb many girls today and shape media aimed at them. Some assigned readings present protectionist arguments about sheltering young women from the violence and sexual content in popular culture.[15] This argument, often based on content analysis, is familiar to many students. I also assign readings that take more radical and complex approaches to media, advancing the idea that young people actively create meaning in the process of consuming culture. This approach is more challenging to students because it overturns conventional wisdom about female weakness and vulnerability. I encourage students to test these various approaches as they do their own research. As the class makes its way through this body of theory and criticism, we study several films that have been popular among girls or raise significant ideas about them: films written by John Hughes from the 1980s, such as *Pretty in Pink* (1986), which many of them loved as girls; videos by Sadie Benning; and the powerful *Thirteen* (Catherine Hardwicke, 2003), written by a thirteen–year-old girl. These texts provide rich material concerning representation of teen girls, how teen girls relate to popular culture, and teen girls as authors or artists.

Scream is a particularly effective film to teach in this part of the course, especially after studying a pre-third-wave film such as *Pretty in Pink*.[16] As a surprise cult film among girls, *Scream* played a key role in identifying the demographic power of this audience. The film's appeal is intrinsically generational, since most adults don't 'get' it or like it. Its broad and visible use of cinematic style helps students deepen their appreciation for the relation between cinematic form and content, and its themes address issues of vital concern to most young women: (1) How can they respond to the increasing pressures of sexuality, especially around virginity? (2) What kind of power and agency will be available to them as adult women? (3) How is their gendered identity shaped by popular culture? And (4) how do cultural constructions of an oedipalized 'family romance' shape girls' passages to adulthood, especially regarding their relationships with their mothers?[17] Before discussing how the film treats these issues, we study how its meanings are determined by important elements of form, including intertextuality, genre and tone. First, students see that by drawing so heavily on other films and televisual references, *Scream* is making a statement about popular culture and its relation to their lives. Second, because *Scream* is incomprehensible without an understanding of the ways it draws on the conventions of horror/slasher films, we examine how the film both parodies and revises these conventions, and why. The class compares the generic constraints of a romantic melodrama such as *Pretty in Pink* with those of *Scream*.

This exploration of form enables the class to consider critically the film's treatment of its thematic material. By revising the conventions of horror, *Scream* challenges multiple codes of gender. It rewards a girl for her seriousness, intelligence and righteous anger. By using a powerful metaphor (the 'boyfriend' turns out to be the killer), it dramatizes the ways heterosexuality as an institution 'kills' girls by seducing them into the inequities of adult femininity. Moreover, its decentring of male characters is not limited to building its plot around a teen girl protagonist. The narrative enigma that drives *Scream* and its two sequels originates with her mother, and the trilogy becomes a quest to uncover her story. With sympathetic depictions of mothers and mother–daughter relations so rare in mainstream films, *Scream* becomes an occasion to ask why.[18] Even though the film never mentions feminism, our discussion implicitly opens it up for feminist readings and prepares the class to return to the subject later in the term.

With this foundation in place, students take over teaching the class for the remainder of the term. During the first week, I place students in one of a group of panels on topics related to teen girl culture; students are expected to research their topic and teach it to the class. Assigning students at random means they are challenged to work on topics, and with classmates they might never have chosen themselves. The topics shift from term to term, depending on student feedback, but have included Popular Icons and Role Models; Music; Health and Well-Being; Family and Friends; Sex, Romance and Sexual Orientation; Money, Class and Consumer Culture; Smart Girls and New Technology; Girls and Social Justice and Girls Globally. I acknowledge that the second wave faltered in matters of difference, and that I expect each panel will include racial, sexual and other forms of difference in its approach to its subject. As a result, students begin to experience feminism as a movement that is not static and monolithic but one that has many shapes and histories, a topic I return to in the last week of the term. Students are accountable to each other and me for the work they do in the panel, and I give them a simple format to document their contributions to the panel. I also give detailed and open-ended suggestions for how panels might go about their research. The grade each student earns for the course is based on a combination of exams and work done in the panel and individually.

The panel-taught portion of the course is invariably dynamic and exciting. It reflects the students' most important work, beginning with their struggles over how to define, limit and then teach their assigned topics. The breadth of the topics requires each panel to reach a consensus about what would be most valuable to teach to the class. To demonstrate that the production of knowledge is contested and value-driven, panels incorporate their decision-making process in their presentation. Students are free to research their topics through any means they wish, and to use creative ways to engage the class with their findings. Their research can include teen magazines, websites, television and film; library research; fieldwork in local schools, hospitals, youth groups, Planned Parenthood offices, TV stations and shopping malls. They conduct interviews and run surveys outside the class and within it. To present their findings, some students have made short films or other creative projects; others have brought guests to class, staged debates or led discussion of media clips they have chosen or readings I have assigned in relation to their topic.

In the final week, I return to head the class in a discussion of 'girl advocacy', a topic that becomes almost inevitable in the climate that develops in the class. By this time, the class has covered a substantial array of topics that include not only the headway girls have made in some areas, such as athletics and technology, but also the acute conflicts girls continue to experience growing up in contemporary culture. They have evaluated the various models of femininity evident in films such as *Pretty in Pink*, *Scream* and *Thirteen*. They have analyzed how the torment expressed in the film *Thirteen*, for example, is compounded by girls facing other challenges related to class, race and sexual orientation. They have also come to see media not as the easy scapegoat it often is in conservative circles, but as a source of empowerment as well, for girls who find solidarity and community in their uses of media. At this point, I bring feminism more explicitly into the classroom and ask what role it might play in advancing the well-being of girls.

By this time, the students are prepared to re-evaluate their earlier ideas about feminism – the charges outlined earlier including racism and classism, dogmatism and conservatism, hostility to femininity and romance, and resistance to the popular. We debate what the term feminism means today, who defines it and why. By giving a brief outline of the history of the movement, I convey to them that feminism is not static but dynamic. By grappling with the limitations of the second wave, I attempt to counter the charges of dogmatism with a voice that is both more modest and more historically contextualized. As we discuss the emerging third wave, they see that just as the second wave is available for criticism, the third wave is there for their active participation in its construction. The course typically ends with little resolution or closure. Many students remain sceptical about the value of identifying with any movement, let alone third-wave feminism. But others begin to see the word feminist as available for reclaiming, redefining or at least reconsidering. I consider that a small but real success.

I believe that students can be encouraged to take this step towards a politic-ized view of gender and culture when their study of sexual politics begins with material they care deeply about and know well. Much of this material celebrates 'girliness', heterosexual romance, fashion and other pleasures students today assume are antithetical to feminism. However, by putting aside the effort to define feminism as a universal category, students are freed to develop informed positions of their own on the meaning and value of the popular culture they live in and its relations to the lives of girls and women. The anxiety of second-wave parents over their daughters' love of 'Buffy' or the 'guilty pleasures' of young feminists over their attachments to *Bridget Jones* can begin to give way in a more dispassionate climate of open-ended debate and analysis.

This method of teaching is not without its challenges for the teacher as well as the student. Material I would like to teach does not get covered. Points I would like to make get lost. I spend much more time with students outside the classroom than usual, meeting with groups. The course requires more detailed initial preparation for the class, more handouts outlining procedures and expectations, a more constant flow of papers to be graded throughout the term. However, I have found this method to be effective and rewarding. The student-driven portion of the course brings freshness, immediacy and engagement into the classroom, as well as allowing students to set their own agendas for learning. Time and again, students tell me that their most powerful learning occurred while researching their panel presentations. Collaboration in groups encourages them to work harder and learn more than they would have in a conventional classroom, and having to teach a topic to their peers inspires them to learn it with greater depth. Students also note the value of forming interpersonal relationships within the panels, often across divides they would not normally cross.

I now bring this approach into all my classes, even those in which gender is not a central component. While Teen Girls and Popular Culture lends itself to turning substantial portions of the course over to student panels, I have found all my courses – on film genres, theory or aesthetics – benefit from incorporating the principles of feminist pedagogy I have developed with Teen Girls and Popular Culture. By decentring my presence in the classroom, I clear a space for students to work more independently, to develop skills in collaboration and to take more responsibility for their own learning. Ideally, students will eventually engage with feminism as an academic subject and political movement in its own right, but this form of pedagogy brings feminism into the classroom 'through the back door'. It enables students to encounter its principles experientially and to begin to consider feminism not as a collection of old stereotypes but as a dynamic model for understanding and changing their world.

NOTES

1. With thanks to Julia Lesage and Chuck Kleinhans for their helpful comments. Portions of this article were published previously in Karlyn (2003).
2. The terminology of 'waves' has become familiar in describing historical stages of the feminist movement in the US. It was claimed in the early 1990s by women, then in their twenties and thirties, who led efforts to build a new feminist movement they called the third wave. The first wave refers to the movement to obtain the right to vote, which lasted nearly three-quarters of a century. The second wave refers to the women's movement of the 1960s and 1970s.
3. The term is from Cobb (2004). The book and film were the subject of much informal discussion at the 'Interrogating Post-feminism: Gender and the Politics of Popular Culture' conference, UEA, UK, April 2004, as well as in papers including those by Angela McRobbie (2004), Craddock (2004) and Garrett (2004).

4. See, for example, Fox-Genovese (1996), Hoff Sommers (1994, 2000).

5. For example, see Baker Beck (1998), Cole (1998) and Oakley and Mitchell (1997). See also the introductions to Heywood and Drake (1997) and Maglin and Perry (1996). Among the most powerful voices in this critique have been those of women of colour, such as bell hooks, Angela Davis and Rebecca Walker, daughter of novelist Alice Walker.

6. According to Chicana/o studies scholar Chela Sandoval, in her important essay 'Feminism and Racism: A Report on the 1981 NWSA Conference', 'As diverse as we were, we realized that we would have to hammer out (as part of our community building) issues as basic as finding the common ground for our "unity" – aside from the shared oppressions we experienced within the movement and society at large' (1990: 61).

7. See Projansky (2001).

8. As Chela Sandoval charges in *The Methodology of the Oppressed*, 'the academic erasure of US third world feminism is an ongoing disappearing trick' (2000: 186, note 9).

9. Maglin and Perry (1996) list the ages of each of their contributors, most of whom are in their early thirties, or as one (Layli Phillips) describes herself, 'too young to be a baby boomer, too old to be Generation X'.

10. Garrison (2000) provides an excellent overview of third-wave feminism and its relation to subcultural movements. Both Lotz (2001) and Projansky (2001) have analyzed post-feminism. Collections based partially or entirely on personal testimonies include Carlip (1995), Green and Taormino (1997), Walker (1995) and Baumgartner and Richards (2000). More theoretically oriented anthologies include Heywood and Drake (1997), Maglin and Perry (1996) and Dicker and Piepmeier (2003).

11. Today, studies of popular culture challenge and complicate the notions of identity, authority, authenticity that were foundational to the second wave. The early stages of literary feminism took as its project revising the canon to include works by 'great' women authors who were writing within what might be considered high culture but who had not been admitted to the canon because their work had been forgotten or never adequately valued by taste-makers. Their work, it was believed, refuted the 'false' representations of women that occurred in works by male writers and replaced them with 'true' representations. Later, the project shifted to challenge the very notion of a canon and the gendered assumptions on which that notion was based. That revision, supported by the increased influence of cultural studies, opened the way for the scholarly study of

       works from everyday life and popular culture that have been important to women but deemed unworthy of serious study.

12.   MTV, for example, despite its history of excluding black artists and promoting misogynistic videos, provided young people with enlightened depictions of homosexuality and interracial relations long before adult-oriented network and cable programme did. This play of contradictory messages is typical of popular culture.

13.   More 'bohemian' or 'outlaw' versions of feminism, which existed during the second wave, are also generally unknown by the third wave.

14.   Jones is describing one of her pieces of performance art, in Walker (1995: 255).

15.   Douglas (1994) is highly accessible to students. Jenkins (1997) has written more polemical works on radical pedagogy.

16.   The plot of the first *Scream* film, like many current teen movies, is set in an affluent, predominantly white, bucolic community being preyed on by a masked serial killer. It begins with the stalking and violent murder of a blonde teen girl, and then shifts its attention to another girl, Sidney, who becomes the killer's next target. Sidney, whose mother was raped and murdered the previous year, has been left alone by her father for the weekend. At the same time, because of unresolved grief for her mother, she resists her boyfriend's ongoing pressure for sex. Meanwhile, Gale Weathers, an ambitious TV newscaster, pursues the story of the new killings. Gale's appearance on the scene rekindles Sidney's anger at her coverage of the events around the mother's death. The sub-plots culminate at a party during which Sidney decides to have sex with Billy and the killer lays siege to the gathered teens. After a violent battle, a wounded and battered Sidney learns that the killer is Billy, who claims to have killed her mother as well because her affair with his father caused his own mother to abandon him. With the help of an equally battered Gale, Sidney kills him.

17.   For an extended reading of the three *Scream* films, see Karlyn (2003).

18.   See Karlyn (2004) for a discussion of the erasure of mothers in popular cinema.

BIBLIOGRAPHY

Baumgartner, J. and Richards, A. (eds) (2000), *Manifesta: Young Women, Feminism and the Future*, New York: Farrar, Straus and Giroux.

Beck, D. B. (1998), 'The "F" Word: How the Media Frame Feminism', *National Women's Studies Association Journal*, 10, 1: 139–49.

Bellafante, G. (1998), 'Feminism: It's All About ME!', *Time*, June 29: 54–62.

Brumberg, J. J. (1997), *The Body Project: An Intimate History of American Girls*, New York: Random House.

Carlip, H. (1995), *Girl Power: Young Women Speak Out: Personal Writings from Teenage Girls*, New York: Warner Books.

Cobb, S. (2004), 'Adapting Identity: Postfeminism and Intertextuality in *Bridget Jones's Diary*', paper presented at the 'Interrogating Post-Feminism: Gender and the Politics of Popular Culture' conference, University of East Anglia, April.

Cole, A. (1998), 'There are No Victims in This Class', *National Women's Studies Association Journal*, 10, 1: 72–85.

Craddock, L. (2004), '"We are Operating in an Ill-Defined Sea": Post-Feminism or Third Wave in Chick Lit', paper presented at the 'Interrogating Post-Feminism' conference, University of East Anglia, April.

Denfeld, R. (1995), *The New Victorians: A Young Woman's Challenge to the Old Feminist Order*, New York: Warner Books.

Dicker, R. and Piepmeier, A. (2003), *Catching a Wave: Reclaiming Feminism for the 21st Century*, Boston: Northeastern University Press.

Douglas, S. J. (1994), *Where the Girls Are: Growing Up Female With the Mass Media*, New York: Times Books.

—— (1997), 'Girls 'n' Spice: All Things Nice?', *The Nation*, 25 August/1 September.

Faludi, S. (1991), *Backlash: The Undeclared War Against American Women*, New York: Crown.

Fox-Genovese, E. (1996), *Feminism is Not the Story of My Life: How Today's Feminist Elite has Lost Touch With the Real Concerns of Women*, New York: Nan Talese.

Garrett, R. (2004), 'Postmodern Chick Flicks: The Reinvention of the Woman's Film in the 1990s', paper presented at the 'Interrogating Post-Feminism' conference, University of East Anglia, April.

Garrison, E. K. (2000), 'U.S. Feminism – Grrrl Style! Youth (Sub)Cultures and the Technologies of the Third Wave', *Feminist Studies*, 26,1: 141–70.

Gilligan, C. (1997), 'Getting Civilized', in A. Oakley and J. Mitchell (eds), *Who's Afraid of Feminism? Seeing Through the Backlash*, New York: New Press.

Green, K. and Taormino, T. (eds) (1997), *A Girls' Guide to Taking Over the World: Writing from the Girl Zine Revolution*, New York: St Martin's Griffin.

Heywood, L. and Drake, J. (eds) (1997), *Third Wave Agenda: Being Feminist, Doing Feminism*, Minneapolis: University of Minnesota Press.

Jameson, F. (1991), *Postmodernism, Or, The Cultural Logic of Late Capitalism*, Durham, NC: Duke University Press.

Jenkins, H. (1997), 'Empowering Children in the Digital Age', *Radical Teacher*, 50: 30–35.

Jones, L. (1995), 'She Came With the Rodeo (Excerpt)', in R. Walker (ed.), *To Be Real: Telling the Truth and Changing the Face of Feminism*, New York, Anchor.

Karlyn, K. R. (2003), '*Scream*, Popular Culture and Feminism's Third Wave', *Genders Online Journal*, 38.

—— (2004), '"I'm Not My Mother": *American Beauty* and the Incest Motif', *Cinema Journal*, 44,1: 69–93.

Lotz, A. D. (2001), 'Postfeminist Television Criticism: Rehabilitating Critical Terms and Identifying Postfeminist Attributes', *Feminist Media Studies*, 1,1: 105–21.

Lumby, C. (1997), *Bad Girls: The Media, Sex and Feminism in the 90s*, St Leonards, NWS: Allen & Unwin.

McRobbie, A. (2004), 'Post-feminism and Popular Culture', *Feminist Media Studies* 4, 3: 255–64.

Maglin, N. B. and Perry, D. (eds) (1996), '*Bad Girls, Good Girls*': *Women, Sex and Power in the Nineties*, New Brunswick: Rutgers University Press.

—— (2004), 'Post-Feminism and Popular Culture: Bridget Jones and the "New Gender Regime"', plenary paper presented at the 'Interrogating Post-Feminism' conference, University of East Anglia, April.

Neisel, J. (1997), 'Hip-Hop Matters: Rewriting the Sexual Politics of Rap Music', in L. Heywood and J. Drake (eds), *Third Wave Agenda*, Minneapolis: University of Minnesota Press.

Oakley, A. and Mitchell, J. (eds) (1997), *Who's Afraid of Feminism? Seeing Through the Backlash*, New York: New Press.

Orr, C. M. (1997), 'Charting the Currents of the Third Wave', *Hypatia*, 12, 3: 29–45.

Paglia, C. (1990), *Sexual Personae: Art and Decadence from Nefertiti to Emily Dickinson*, New Haven: Yale University Press.

Pipher, M. (1994), *Reviving Ophelia: Saving the Selves of Adolescent Girls*, New York: Putnam.

Powers, A. (1997), 'Everything and the Girl', *Spin*, November: 74–80.

Projansky, S. (2001), *Watching Rape: Film and Television in Postfeminist Culture*, New York: New York University Press.

Roiphe, K. (1993), *The Morning After: Sex, Fear and Feminism on Campus*, Boston, MA: Little, Brown.

Sandoval, C. (1990), 'Feminism and Racism: A Report on the 1981 National Women's Studies Conference,' in G. Anzaldua (ed.), *Making Face, Making Soul:*

Creative and Critical Perspectives by Women of Color, San Francisco: Aunt Lute Foundation.

—— (2000), *Methodology of the Oppressed*, Minneapolis: University of Minnesota Press.

Siegel, C. (2000), *New Millennial Sexstyles*, Bloomington: Indiana University Press.

Sommers, C. H. (1994), *Who Stole Feminism? How Women Have Betrayed Women*, New York: Simon and Schuster.

—— (2000), *The War Against Boys: How Misguided Feminism is Harming Our Young Men*, New York: Simon and Schuster.

Walker, R. (1992), 'Becoming the Third Wave', *Ms.*, January/February: 39–41.

—— (ed.) (1995), *To Be Real: Telling the Truth and Changing the Face of Feminism*, New York: Anchor.

Wolf, N. (1993), *Fire With Fire: The New Female Power and How It Will Change the 21st Century*, New York: Random House.

Part II
Coming to Terms with Feminism

'Ally McBeal', 'Sex and the City' and the Tragic Success of Feminism

Joke Hermes

'Ally McBeal' (Fox, 1996–2002) and 'Sex and the City' (HBO, 1998–2004)[1] are often mentioned in the same breath – quite amazing for two series that are so dissimilar. 'Ally McBeal' is a fifty-minute 'dramedy' with animated sequences that visualize the emotions of its heroine. 'Sex and the City' is a thirty-minute comedy with a reality twist around four New York women friends who talk about sex and relationships. My friends are divided into 'Ally McBeal' and 'Sex and the City' camps. If you like Ally, you are definitely less likely to be a 'Sex and the City' fan, and vice versa. But they too refer to the two shows together. This suggests that these shows' shared investment in and portrayal of independent women goes beyond what we have seen before.

Television comedy has a tradition of having 'feminist' characters and strong female friendships (Dow 1996; Henry 2004). 'Murphy Brown' (Shukovsky English Entertainment/WB, 1988–98), journalist and single mother springs to mind, as do 'Golden Girls' (Touchstone Television/Witt/Thomas/Harris Productions, 1985–92) and 'Roseanne' (Casey Werner/Wind Dancer Productions, 1988–97), with their strong bonding between women who could not care less about appropriate female behaviour and norms. 'Ally McBeal' and 'Sex and the City', however, are apparently different, signifiers of a moment of significant change in television. They were not only key agents in establishing the era of quality popular programming, or 'must see' television (Jancovich and Lyons 2003), but also they are popularly recognized as post-feminist television. What 'post-feminist' might be depends on the continent from which one writes (Moseley and Read 2002 vs. Lotz 2001) and whether 'post' means 'passé' or 'new phase of' (Arthurs 2003). Post-feminism may mean the loss of a political agenda, or the foundation for a new one, where it signposts the overcoming of unproductive old distinctions between feminist and feminine (Moseley and Read 2002).

Post-feminist television heroines can be recognized by their economic independence while employed in a respectable profession, by their provocative clothing styles and by the acceptance of their choices and lifestyle by their friends. The presentation of entire gangs of what by most standards would count as feminist women is perhaps their most outstanding feature. When the earlier comedies introduced independent women characters, they would usually also include storylines that criticized the independent character for how she lived her life. The case in favour of the two series denoting a more broadly significant moment of change is strengthened by the fact that not only American quality television presents this particular twist. So does Bridget Jones, who is English and not American, and who doesn't even have a good job, although she does have the friendship network and ambition to succeed in a career. These new popular texts suggest that feminist concerns, from being an unmentionable radicalism, now resonate with wider viewerships. Here we have a new type of heroine that attracts audiences and sparks debate, not just amongst those who consider themselves feminists, but also outside those hallowed circles as well.

'Ally McBeal', 'Sex and the City' and *Bridget Jones's Diary* (Sharon Maguire, 2001) are comedies that suggest a new status quo. If there is indeed a new status quo that allows for a new type of woman, there remain pesky questions. What is getting laughed at? Who is the joke on? Comedy, after all, will usually give with one hand and take with the other. Norms, traditions, distinctions and accepted knowledge are all regularly upset and held up for inspection in a comedy episode, while by the end of the episode things are more or less back to 'normal' (Marc 1997). Although there may be a residual effect of norms having been challenged, in the end hierarchy and authority have been re-established.

Kim Akass and Janet McCabe suggest that the humour in 'Sex and the City' works to redefine the tightly woven web of patriarchal notions of what being a woman means (Akass and MacCabe 2004). Female humour is presented as a counterculture that invests in breaking taboos and rewriting old truths about women's bodies and sexuality. Its power is mostly found in actual moments of women's exchange and solidarity over formerly individualized questions and problems. These, one can hope, offer glimpses of another sexual economy, however difficult it will be to realize such a change. In both series, the post-feminist heroines, like their more traditionally minded sisters, still dream of Mr Right. He has a much tougher job, though, now that he has to measure up to standards set not by one individual woman, willing, perhaps, to be lenient, but also by her friendship network as well. He is certainly no longer the sole guarantor of women's happiness and emotional health.

Although I recognize the pleasure of sharing in girl talk, I am not sure it will really change much. For one thing, such exchanges between women are hardly new; although they may feel that way for those raised in middle-class families. But mostly, I am wary of expecting too much of these series, because they are comedies. Comedies are a key cultural form under hegemonic cultural conditions. Humour has always been a way of making temporary space for alternative formations and discourses, condoned by the powers that be, which never acquire any real status because jokes, like boomerangs, return to where they came from. Because 'Ally McBeal' and 'Sex and the City' are branded as comedies, and received enough Emmy Awards to prove that that was a clever choice, they are granted space for breaking taboos. For the same reason, they are also taken less seriously for doing so than any other cultural or political form.

We need to ask ourselves therefore, how do the friendship networks and professional identities anchoring our new heroines in the world stand up to the undermining power of comedy? We need to know what status quo is challenged in post-feminist television? Our well-heeled heroines can hardly be counted as being outside patriarchy or outside capitalism. They are white; they are straight; they work (well) with men. The only way that the 'Sex and the City' heroines upset the order of things, to come back eventually into its fold, is, it seems, by talking dirty. At face value, in any case, the only taboo really broken, despite the show's reputation for continually doing so, is that nice girls do not talk like lower-class sluts. 'Ally McBeal' shares 'Sex and the City''s outspoken interest in sex, and in women talking about men and sex freely, although as a network show, it can hardly have the explicit content that HBO as a subscription cable network can afford. Importantly, there is a class-sensitive link too. The success of the lawyers in the firm Ally works for has little to do with knowing the law but everything to do with putting up a good show. Earning money is not based on (intellectual) merit or hard work, but on being able to pull the wool over other people's eyes. Those earning high salaries might be sluts, and chances are they are clever frauds.

Has feminism fallen victim to repressive tolerance? Is it invoked in popular culture to be subtly ridiculed? Akass and McCabe feel that the opposite is the case and that discourses of appropriate behaviour for women and men are in the process of being rewritten in 'Sex and the City'. What do other viewers, whether professionals or engaged lay viewers, think? The next section will take a closer look at the series, in order to establish, briefly, common ground for this discussion. I will then move on to look at how viewers evaluate both series in terms of feminism.

THE SERIES

'Ally McBeal', a drama series around a Boston lawyer surrounded by a large ensemble cast, had very funny animated sequences, which in a self-reflexive manner observed the rules of male-to-female sexism and turned the tables on it. Ally's tongue is shown rolling out like a lizard's, ready to lick up Greg, love interest of the moment. Fighting her biological clock while kicking (mostly imaginary) babies around, also made Ally very funny. Some of the best sequences in the show have the two central male characters interacting; they are Richard Fish and John Cage, owners and managing directors of the law firm that also employs Ally. The relationship between the two men is intimate and full of jokes and criticism of traditional masculinity. When Cage lets Fish know he loves him ('A kick in the head', aired 2002), Fish jumps back and asks Cage whether he is gay, in which case he would be happy to allow him the freedom of this choice. Cage interrupts and reassures him that of course he is not gay – but meanwhile he has (very nearly) kissed the other man in a loving gesture. This is unexplored territory in drama, and comedy usually turns it into a big routine in which the abhorrence over the possibility of gay male intimacy is enough to fire up entire storylines. 'Ally McBeal' goes much, much further. Comedy is a guise, here, to explore the issue of straight masculinity and the ban on male intimacy that is not punished (as in the action film, for instance, see Willis 1998, or in sports, Poynton and Hartley 1990). The show is in fact much more than a comedy: it is a piece of satire of basic assumptions regarding the construction of femininity and masculinity.

Of course 'Ally McBeal' never really crosses sensitive bridges. There is a short flirtation with lesbianism (Ally and Ling, another female partner in the law firm, kiss, 'Buried pleasures', aired 1999), which does not include sex. Male homosexuality is mostly ignored, except for a set of episodes that deal with a gorgeous transsexual woman who still has a penis – much to Richard Fish's regret and abhorrence. It is also a very white show, with only a small number of African-American characters: Ally's room-mate Rene, her ex-lover Greg, who is a doctor, and one Chinese colleague. All non-white characters are racially stereotyped. However, 'Ally McBeal' did put issues of the construction of gender on the agenda. It engages with the tension between professionalism and femininity, which women are usually punished for (while men who are involved, caring professionals are revered for such behaviour). It is vanguard television in terms of style and the mixture of animation with realist drama and comedy routines.

'Sex and the City' is a comedy, though without the living room couch. Unlike almost all other comedies, its four heroines – among whom is the central character Carrie Bradshaw – do not present themselves as a (semi-) family group to be looked at, while seated together. Rather we see four women friends around a table in a public space, usually a café, discussing sex and relationships. Often, one of them has to run off to meet the demands of a busy work life (public relations manager, lawyer, gallery owner), while Carrie, a sexual anthropologist and journalist, muses over human mating habits, often in voice-over. All episodes have her posing a question, which is the tag line for her weekly column, as she pursues the meaning of sexual behaviour, often via participant observation. Carrie Bradshaw and friends co-own Manhattan; they feel free to move through it and explore it. The feminist slogan 'taking back the night' was never given meaning so directly or fully. Remarkable, too, in the wide range of relationships portrayed in the series, is the room given not only to gay male relationships, but also to lesbian relationships (Merck 2004).

'Ally McBeal' and 'Sex and the City' are post-feminist, then, in that they feature no-longer-young women who easily earn their own living and enjoy autonomous love lives. The Carrie Bradshaws and Ally McBeals are not much interested in traditional forms of caring – that is to say, not as part of the ongoing series. 'Ally McBeal' ended with McBeal choosing motherhood over her career and partnership in the law firm where she worked. Miranda, one of Bradshaw's friends and initially a single parent, in 'Sex and the City''s last season decides to move to Brooklyn with her partner and child. Charlotte, another of the four friends, adopts a baby. Woman's traditional destination has become the object of deferred gratification, the assurance of a partner, offspring and the regulation of one's sex life postponed to the very last episodes or after. Motherhood, Akass and McCabe note, may well be the last taboo (2004: 193).

THE PROFESSIONAL VIEW

Viewers and fans of the two series include many a professional writer. Their views suggest that the popularization of feminism in post-feminist television is by no means a cut and dried affair. Moseley and Read concluded after looking at the debate 'Ally McBeal' engendered in the British press that the combination of feminine and feminist discourse was considered to be particularly unpalatable: a grotesque creation of male fantasy masquerading as feminist role model for the 1990s (2002: 232). The press, it can be concluded, lag seriously behind current feminist work on popular culture that no longer starts from the assumption that feminist and feminine are mutually exclusive (Moseley and Read 2002:

234 and see also Braidotti 1991). The fact that the post-feminist position (female pleasure on female terms, as Moseley and Read put it 2002: 241) is always open to patriarchal recuperation is a risk viewers will gladly take.

Print journalism, in Britain as much as in the Netherlands where this essay is written, meanwhile prefers to remain mired in its 1970s definition of feminism, which dictates that feminists are against men, and that lesbianism is its strongest political expression. On www.salon.com this state of affairs, apparently also characteristic of the United States printed press, leads Carina Chocano (2002) to remark that it is 'unsettling to see how few, if any, farewell-to-Ally pieces have been written by women that do not emphatically put a disgusted distance between themselves and the skinny, nervous ditz in micro-minis.' Ally, pioneer of what Chocano calls 'the girl-in-the-city' genre, is bearing the brunt of a widespread feeling that these representations of women are all material for *Backlash II*, follow-up to Susan Faludi's shocking feminist deconstruction of the myths about women (single women, older women) propagated by American media (Faludi 1992). Chocano points out that a series such as 'Ally McBeal' also gave us a number of highly neurotic (though lovable) male characters, including sexist Richard Fish ('bygones').

Media critic Stine Jensen opened her remarks about 'Ally McBeal', *Bridget Jones's Diary* and 'Sex and the City' in a Dutch quality newspaper by stating that 'feminists are furious about the hunt for men in TV series "Ally McBeal"' or the movie *Bridget Jones's Diary*. But Ally and Bridget are 'heroines for our time' (2001). Jensen, apparently not a feminist herself, goes on to argue the qualities of these programmes. She suggests that these lie in how Ally and Bridget's tendency to self-diminishment also indicates their willingness to accept their own insecurities and 'loving yourself as you are'. The cartoon-like self-descriptions in *Bridget Jones*, the animated sequences in 'Ally McBeal' that tend to focus on her uncouth feelings of lust (Ally's tongue rolling out like the proverbial red carpet when she first meets doctor Greg) or anger (growing huge boxing mitts to punch someone out) are both comical and critical of how we envision ideal femininity. Jensen concludes that this new trend in popular culture is emblematic of 'lipstick feminism': feminism dressed up nicely and out to seduce men, a mere form of entertainment that does not include her as viewer or as journalist in any other capacity than a professional one.

According to journalistic critical response to this new wave of 'liberated women's fiction', there is no question that heterosexuality remains central to ideologies of femininity (it is the old sexual order turned upside down: now women lust after men). Professionalism seems to have become less entwined with masculinity, while male sexual codes (of looking at and hunting a desired object) have not led to happiness but to increasing cynicism as the man hunt goes on (see Shalit 1999; van Erp 2002). The only respect in which post-feminist entertainment is recognized as really feminist is in its empty celebration of being single as a new variety of the feminist wish for women's autonomy. The happy single is a myth, is the conclusion of Dutch journalist van Erp (2002), a theme echoed in much web journalism as well (Shalit 1999). The strong suit of women's friendship and bonding is hardly recognized at all. Rather than acknowledge how feminism has become rooted in popular imagination, journalists prefer to hold onto outdated notions of feminism. Their work offers little means for more open exploration of the attractions and possible ideological pitfalls in the narrative and representational practice of these new series. How about (critical) viewers?

'JUMP-THE-SHARK'

> I like that while Kim Cattral is older she is portrayed as the sexy one, which is so true. Older women can be sexy and guess what ... we are all going to get old!
>
> Appreciative viewer commenting on 'Sex and the City',
> posted on www.jumptheshark.com

'Jump-the-Shark' is an intriguing website that chronicles critical viewers' comments on, by now, an enormous range of television shows. It provides a rich source of comments on post-feminist television – by others than those of us who are professional critics. I will use it here to find out how viewer appreciation and criticism of 'Ally McBeal' and 'Sex and the City' is structured, and to see whether these comments shed light on what I sense might be the tragic dimension – the drama, if you will – in post-feminist comedy.[2]

'Jump-the-Shark' is a portal to lists of anonymous comments on hundreds of television shows, some of which have been discontinued, most of which still run. These comments have only one purpose: to decide whether or not a show has lost 'it'. Are its writers and producers still doing a good job, or are they committing crimes against the show's audience by losing a particular character, or not writing good storylines for a show's lead? The aim of the lists is to find out when exactly a show stopped being rewarding and what caused it to flunk. As such they provide a (fully typed) gold mine of material for an audience researcher. Via the title of a particular show, the moments can be accessed at which a particular show 'jumped the shark', followed by comments.[3]

Most of the comments are short, no longer than a few lines, and anonymous. Reading comments on 'Jump-the-shark', it is clear that viewers who contribute are convinced that the television industry regularly checks what they are writing. In fact, the tone of the entries suggests that viewers consider the television shows and their central characters as their property.

Throughout what turned out to be 'Ally McBeal's last season (2001–2), I followed new entries on 'Jump-the-Shark' for 'Ally McBeal' and 'Sex and the City' (which was also rumoured to be coming to the end of its run), and reread the heated debate of the years before, which has been 'archived' online. The representation of gender roles in post-feminist television elicits much comment (positive and negative) from viewers, in a markedly different vein from journalistic commentary. Three related qualities are appreciated in the two series, across the lists and comments. They are (1) the notion of the happy single woman as not a mother (Miranda's pregnancy and Ally becoming a mother are not felt to be amusing); (2) the never-ending romance rather than marriage (critique of the death of Billy as a focus for Ally's romantic longings; Carrie accepting a marriage proposal); as well as (3) heterosexuality (Samantha's lesbian affair is voted down, as well as – though much less so – the episode in which Ally engages in kissing with Ling).

The fun in being a woman, judging by comments on 'Jump-the-Shark', is a matter of extending the best stage of a woman's life: after achieving a career (and income) and before motherhood, with heterosexuality a comfortable given providing for women's needs much like a good department store. Within these parameters, viewers are more than happy to think about gender roles and what makes women (and men) attractive. Looks and bodies are discussed with gusto. Much time is spent denouncing what is perceived as Ally McBeal's anorexia. For example: 'Finally, can anybody give Calista Flockhart some food, the anorexic look is out babe' (Calista Flockhart plays Ally). Or: 'She looks like death on a stick', and: 'I am tired of hearing about how Calista Flockhart is healthy, even though she is very obviously underweight. Making women and girls everywhere thinking you not only can't be fat, but you have to be underweight to be pretty and acceptable.' Some are not only dismissive or upset, but also use swearing to denounce Flockhart, and call her names (e.g., 'bag of bones').

The role model theme is strong here. Ally is a 'stereotype'; 'she makes women look neurotic'; she is a 'stupid anorectic who dresses like a prostitute'; 'Ally is all that is dysfunctional about American women'. The 'Sex and the City' characters are 'whores'. Like the journalists, viewers understand the series as providing examples to evaluate gender ideals. Unlike the journalists, 'Jump-the-Shark' viewers commented a great deal on the representation of the men as well. Billy (erstwhile lover of Ally McBeal, later colleague and married to someone else, but continuing love interest until his death at the end of the third season) is much discussed for two remarkable moves on the character's part: he dyes his brown hair white, and later takes up a pimp-like attitude and has himself chaperoned by a bunch of black-latex clad women (the Robert Palmer girls). He also propagates male machismo as an ideology of male self-respect that needs to be revived. The hair and the girls net him a lot of comments (though not as many as his death), which make it clear that although weird, this is seen as an interesting experiment in redefining masculinity in the context of a show that is clearly in favour of women having careers. His lapse into a conservative ideology of masculinity is not seen as despicable, but as an interesting taunt.

The 'Sex and the City' posts, too, tend to be unforgiving to men showing sensitivity or weakness. Men should act out the male prerogative. Carrie's ongoing feelings for Big, who treats her like dirt, is discussed in terms of her behaviour, but not his. When she introduces her then fiancé Aidan to Big, Aidan's friendliness counts against him: 'If I were Aidan, I would have more than a few choice words for "Princess Carrie"...' and 'She f*cks Big behind Aidan's back, tells Aidan and gets dumped, begs her way back to Aidan then invites the man she cheated on him with to HIS cabin! I know SATC isn't realistic on a lot of levels, but that episode was just ridiculous. It made Aidan look like a milquetoast...': And about Big: 'When Big showed up looking all broken and pathetic at Aidan's country house to cry over that movie star lady, that was pretty much it for me. I've always looked at Big like Mr Macho, cool as a cucumber, and that episode made him look about as cool as a wet noodle.'

Two strands of argumentation cross in these comments. On the one hand, there is genuine conservative criticism of the representation of gender in the two series. Women characters should not behave like whores; men should be strong. More interestingly, notions of strong masculinity are also part of a different, romantically oriented discourse that is built on the notion that a good romance/sexual encounter needs feisty females and real men. Any threat to ongoing romance or romantic possibility is not appreciated. When in 'Sex and the City' Miranda decides not to have an abortion and instead have a baby, and the other women are in, or contemplating, monogamous relationships, this, for many 'Jump-the-Shark' viewers, spells the end of the singles' dream of a fun-, sex- and friendship-filled life: 'Season finale. Miranda is having a baby. Charlotte's already married. Then Carrie said yes to Aidan's marriage proposal. There won't be much Sex in the City if the women are tied down to husbands and babies. We've already been there and done that with Thirtysomething.' Or: 'But now this formerly sharp, funny show about fabulous single chicks has weighed down its cast with domestic baggage.' And: 'Why ruin a fun, hip show? Parenthood is not sexy. Save it for the bland network sit-coms.' And it goes on: 'Why can't we just watch interesting women go out to eat and wear cool clothes and talk about sex with new people? Those of us who *are* married and *have* kids want to live vicariously.' More complaints: 'This was an awesome show; for once women were not represented as complicit broodmares. They dated men; they had sex; they had fun! Now what is it with !@£$% babies? I have no interest in babies, yet networks seem obsessed with them.' A last one: 'Babies? Cancer? Country houses? For God's sake – this show used to be about fun and frivolous things. Hot clothes, hot dates, hot sex and hot restaurants.' Of course, apart from the baby, the disaster is averted; Carrie breaks it off with Aidan, Charlotte's marriage is over. And as for the baby, a lone soul suggests that maybe Steve (the father of the baby, with whom Miranda does not want to live) could take care of the baby? The resolution to all of this in the 2003/4 season, may quite possibly not have been to the delight of these viewers.

DISCUSSING REPRESENTATIONS OF GENDER

In discussions of post-feminist comedy on 'Jump-the-Shark', feminist notions and ideology are emphatically present. The posters hardly ever refer to the representation of women as successful professionals, or as 'invented family', which arguably is accepted practice, 'even' in what the 'Jump-the-Shark' posters call 'bland network comedy'. The more interesting presence of feminist ideology is in the strong sentiments against any form of right- or left-wing conservatism: both political correctness (the left-wing variety) and outdated ideas that women should not talk about sex are slighted.

> I have one question for some of the posters above: why do you feel that nudity on the part of SJP [actress Sarah Jessica Parker] or KD [Kristin Davies] would be good for the show, while having full frontal nudity on a man sign that this show has 'jumped the shark'? I hate to break it to all you disillusioned males, but women do like to see naked men, women do enjoy having sex and women LOVE to talk to their girlfriends about it.

Or a post on 'Ally McBeal':

> For once we have a thinking, feeling lead female, but she is not the 'ideal' looking kind of female or the 'normal' kind of pretty, and what do we all do? We bash her (jealous?) and any more talk of the show is gone. 'Ally eat a burger', and we end it

right there. Men can be neurotic and insecure, too, but god help you if you are a pretty, skinny girl, because THEN if you have any doubts, any longings, any visions of another life but you are not exactly sure of how to get there, admit you're not perfect (like I'm sure 90% of America feels) it means, well you can just chalk it up to the 'female' stereotype of being whiny and wishy-washy. Men could act the same way and we would probably call them sensitive or thoughtful or funny. The stereotypes are just killing me.

Clearly the posters, a group of television-literate viewers, who have a strong sense of how fiction television is produced, have easy recourse to feminist argumentation. The role model discussion, the delight in television that is different, the references to other shows (bland network comedy, and generic references to other shows in which lead characters have had babies such as 'Murphy Brown' and 'Mad About You' [In Front/Nuance/Tristar, 1992–9]) and the suggestions to the writers, all point to more than familiarity and knowledge. There is a sense of proprietorship, even if a viewer's hold on a series is, by definition, tenuous. These viewers know they are instrumental to a show's success. Their assertiveness, moreover, extends to accepting the premise of the possibility of a feminine feminism. Post-feminism might – at times – be challenged for its hedonist consumerism, but not for lack of a sense that women have rights, including the right to the pleasures of their choice, as much as men.

What, then, is characteristic of this new popular cultural feminism? Discussion of 'sexiness' is a good example. It is a strong underlying concern throughout all comments. The codes of sexiness appear not to be related to an older Platonic ideal of the coming together of the beautiful, the good and the truthful, but to a Foucauldian disciplinary system that is structured around a central norm: the posts make it clear that women should be thin, but not too thin. Shows should break the mould but not too much. Emancipated women can talk about sex, but not too much.

The pleasure in criticizing the shows is partly one of denunciation: whatever is on the show is excessive and food for criticism. This, in a sense, mirrors the cultural form of the comedy, which likes to challenge social norms, in order to then come back to the status quo. But feminism has also added a dimension, which is that even those in positions of relatively little power (such as the television viewer) may legitimately claim a position to comment on, or symbolically have a stake in, the cultural production of meaning. Feminism, after all, has more than laid claim to discussions of gender, it has also problematized questions of power and enunciation (Riley 1988), and how the gendering of roles or activities may have far-reaching consequences (Probyn 1993; Hermes 1997).

'Jump-the-Shark' is an invitation to take up strong viewer positions. In comments on post-feminist television, these viewer positions are connected with strong normative systems. Their bottom line is a discourse of self-distinction, both for the posters themselves as discerning viewers, and in what they expect of the characters. In answer to the original question of this chapter then, it can be concluded that interpreting these shows as poking fun at the (accepted) notion that women know what they want and their ability to realize those goals must be discarded.

Viewers are both irritated by and defensive of their heroines, but they certainly do not interpret them as dupes. Ally is admired and berated for her neurotic behaviour, but it is recognized as a highly specific and original style. As with Bridget Jones, there is admiration for a woman doing things her own way, buffoon or idiot she may sometimes show herself to be. Likewise the four 'Sex and the City' friends are judged and admired for 'doing their own thing', whether in bed or out of it, and in relation to their sense and style of dress. The anorexia comments usually understand the actresses to bow to an outdated norm of feminine beauty, and implicitly this is replaced by a norm of 'strength' (of character) for both the women and the men. Sensitivity is only OK if presented in a self-assertive manner (Ally), while it is never hip or sexy in a man (this is Aidan's predicament). Any reliance on received notions of what a woman, a man or a feminist should be like is disapproved of. A wish for strength of character and freedom to do as one chooses is the ideological uptake of feminism, according to viewers, in popular culture.

BY WAY OF CONCLUSION: THE TRAGEDY IN COMEDY

While as a viewer and in agreement with the viewers quoted above I appreciate the pleasure in tough-but-reflexive characters, this is not the entire story to be told about post-feminist comedy. Viewer comments, like television criticism, also lay bare a preference for a particular type of heterosexuality. Marriage, motherhood, lesbianism, and lack of strength in male characters have the 'Jump-the-Shark' viewers up in arms. All fall outside of their romantic ideal, which is for older women to enjoy themselves as if they were young and unencumbered. Age has become more and more elastic, and to settle down is to fall victim to the trap of traditional femininity. It is not sexy or exciting, and it offers no good reasons for living your life vicariously.

Young-heterosexuality-for-older-women goes well with a particular type of hero: strong, straight males remain the norm. This does not bode well for those neither strong nor straight. Although the introduction of (male) gay men and couples, and of transsexuals in both series has been lauded (*The Advocate*, 14 September 1999), alternative sexualities are used ultimately not to progressive ends (as in a role model and visible political rhetoric), but to make fun of, and then resort to, the straight norm. David Greven (2004) offers this very argument when he points out that men in 'Sex and the City' are used for a freak show. One after the other, he argues, male sexual partners are only used as exemplars of not-being-the-right-one and are discarded at the end of the episode often for reasons that turn them from 'men' into beasts and perverts. Is the joke on men then?

Apart from David Greven, neither critics, nor journalists, nor viewers seem to take the fact that 'Ally McBeal' and 'Sex and the City' are *comedies* very seriously. They have been popularly appropriated as post-feminist *television*. Women's independence and right to a free sexuality are, and remain, key elements. The viewer posts on the website suggest that the joke is not on feminism or on women generally. Neither women, nor women's independence are set up to be undermined, even if notions of professionalism are, to say the least, presented in an unconventional manner in 'Ally McBeal'. Since Ally and her similarly if not more unconventionally working male colleagues are successful at what they do, this is not where comedy plays out its insidious undermining and re-establishing of the status quo. Representation of male characters, though, is a different story.

Our expectations of the portrayal of men in relation to strong women characters in television drama have been shaped by comedy, by network comedy to be more precise. Comedy, generally, is one of the few genres that have strong and large female casts, as has been noted in the introduction to this chapter. Comedy, more than other genres, also allows men to show their emotional side, more, I suspect, even than soap opera. Good, Porter and Dillon (2002) counted for eleven of the then most popular comedies (unfortunately selecting their sample the year before 'Sex and the City' and 'Ally McBeal' started) how men are portrayed in self-disclosure. They find that in sitcom, contrary to stereotype, ('Frasier', 'Friends', 'Spin City', 'Will and Grace', 'Home Improvement' and six other shows[4]), it is acceptable for men to talk about themselves to other men. 'It thus appears', they conclude, 'that the contemporary sitcom genre cultivates the message that "guy talk" includes self-disclosure, and that men will not typically experience ridicule or shaming responses from others to their disclosures' (2002: 5). This is quite a different story from the abuse (wet noodle, milquetoast) aimed at Big and especially Aidan in 'Sex and the City', or the approval Billy in 'Ally McBeal' nets for returning to Neanderthal standards for masculinity.

The brunt of the joke, in the end, in post-feminist television comedy (key example of the new 'quality television'), is on men not measuring up to very traditional standards, in which a real guy is not gay, always sports a stiff upper lip and so on. With only a few exceptions, men are paraded in a freak show, whether as discarded sexual partners deemed unsuitable, or as gay men. In the network show 'Ally McBeal', gay masculinity is only hinted at; in 'Sex and the City' to be gay, or even bisexual, as a man means that not much pleasure awaits you. 'The series may be steeped in gay sensibility, but (Carrie's gay friend) Stanford's erotic prospects must be wrung out and left out to dry' (Greven 2004: 41). If I am right, post-feminist television, however pleasurable to watch in some respects, represents a tragic success, with its unintended but all the more painful exclusion of gay happiness, and its resurrection of highly traditional notions of masculinity, despite its 'progressive' reputation. While I admit that having a laugh at the expense of men makes a welcome change, the representational politics, laid bare here, are less amusing.

There is, I suppose, one reason not to despair. The branding of 'Ally McBeal' and 'Sex and the City' by the network and cable stations might be a mere marketing ploy. These series may not be comedies by any old standards, but romantic comedy or even romance in a new guise. This is to take up Jane Arthurs' (2003) suggestion that new television shows are remediated amalgams of existing media formats, aided by the synergy created in the multimedia corporations that rule not only audio-visual but print media as well. Arthurs' interest is in the link of the glossy women's magazine to 'Sex and the City'. I am, as will have become clear, much more an 'Ally McBeal' fan, and recognize in her the enormous change wrought in the former Mills and Boon romantic heroine. Tough and sensitive, a professional and a klutz, blessed with a strong fantasy life and a sharp tongue, these are all qualities that romantic heroines have long had (see Modleski 1984). Such heroines need strong guys to match their own inner strength. Such storylines require recognizable difference rather than sameness or partnership/comradeship. Such an interpretation explains the horror at motherhood and same-sex sexuality effectively. It makes clear why, for someone adhering to this interpretation (such as me), the difference between 'Sex and the City' and 'Ally McBeal' is so obvious. Some readers like the family saga, others the short romance.

Last but not least, such an interpretation also comfortingly reassures me that television, old-fashioned and slow-to-change medium that it is, is not suddenly ahead of the times. On the contrary, it has yet to find out the sexiness and fun in gay romance, long discovered in novels and thrillers, and the attractions of the mothering male, long ago recognized by romance readers and much experimented with since in romance novels themselves (Radway 1984). Believe me, feminist romance, whether marketed as comedy or not, has a long way to go. The joke may well, with some interpretative sleight of hand, ultimately be on television itself. Popular culture, meanwhile, continues to be a domain that has long shown itself to be open to exciting new definitions and identities, also of feminist origin. The trouble for us critics is that it does not replace old representations, but adds new ones. There is a lot of feminism in popular television, but there is also a lot of old rot, that, it needs to be said, apparently continues to offer a great many viewers much pleasure.

NOTES

1. Both are in syndicated reruns in the United States and programmed over most of the globe.
2. I have also used 'Jump-the-Shark' comments on 'Ally McBeal' and 'Sex and the City' in *Re-reading Popular Culture* (2005), where I use (analysis of) the material as part of an ongoing argument about cultural citizenship.
3. The name 'Jump-the-Shark' refers to the last season of the TV show 'Happy Days' in which the main character, Fonzie, literally jumps a shark while waterskiing. This was so patently ridiculous that even die-hard fans of the series were disgusted and felt that the writers had run out of ideas. Hence 'jumping the shark' points to a series losing what made it attractive.
4. Respectively: Grub Street Productions/Paramount, 1993–2004; WB/Bright/Kauffman/Crane Productions, 1994–2004; DreamWorks/Lottery Hill Entertainment/Ubu Productions, 1996–2002; KoMut/Three Sisters/NBC/Everything Entertainment/New Dominion Pictures, 1998–; Touchstone Television/Wind Dancer, 1991–9.

BIBLIOGRAPHY

Akass, K. and McCabe, J. (2004), 'Ms. Parker and the Vicious Circle: Female Narrative and Humour in "Sex and the City"', in K. Akass and J. McCabe (eds), *Reading 'Sex and the City'*, London: I. B. Tauris.

Arthurs, J. (2003), '"Sex and the City" and Consumer Culture: Remediating Postfeminist Drama', in *Feminist Media Studies*, 3,1: 83–98.

Braidotti, R. (1991), *Patterns of Dissonance: A Study of Women and Contemporary Philosophy*, Cambridge: Polity.

Chocano, C. (2002), 'Bye-bye, Dancing Baby', available online at www.salon. com, Arts and Entertainment, (accessed 11 June 2002).

Dow, B. (1996), *Prime-Time Feminism: Television, Media Culture, and the Women's Movement Since 1970*, Philadelphia: University of Pennsylvania Press.

Faludi, S. (1992), *Backlash: The Undeclared War Against Women*, London: Vintage.

Good, G. E., Porter, M. J. and Dillon, M. J. (2002), 'When Men Divulge: Portrayals of Men's Self-disclosure in Prime Time Situation Comedies', in *Sex Roles: A Journal of Research*, 46: 419–27.

Greven, D. (2004), 'The Museum of Unnatural History: Male Freaks and Sex and the City', in K. Akass and J. McCabe (eds), *Reading 'Sex and the City'*, London: I. B. Tauris.

Henry, A. (2004), 'Orgasms and Empowerment: "Sex and the City" and Third-Wave Feminism', in K. Akass and J. McCabe (eds), *Reading 'Sex and the City'*, London: I. B. Tauris.

Hermes, J. (1997), 'Gender and Media Studies: No Woman, no Cry', in J. Corner, P. Schlesinger and R. Silverstone (eds), *International Media Research: A Critical Survey*, London: Routledge.

—— (2005), *Re-reading Popular Culture*, Oxford, Blackwell.

Jancovich, M. and Lyons, J. (2003), 'Introduction', in M. Jancovich and J. Lyons (eds), *Quality Popular Television*, London: BFI.

Jensen, S. (2001), 'Lippenstift feminisme. De neuroses van *Bridget Jones* en 'Ally McBeal', in *NRC Handelsblad*, 26 Januari, available online at www.nrc.nl/ cultuur/ (November 2001).

Lotz, A. (2001), 'Postfeminist Television Criticism: Rehabilitating Critical Terms and Identifying Postfeminist Attitudes', *Feminist Media Studies*, 1,1: 105–21.

Marc, D. (1997), *Comic Visions*, second edition, Oxford: Blackwell.

Merck, M. (2004), 'Sexuality in the city', in K. Akass and J. McCabe (eds), *Reading 'Sex and the City'*, London: I. B. Tauris.

Modleski, T. (1984 [1982]), *Loving with a Vengeance: Mass-produced Fantasies for Women*, New York: Methuen.

Moseley, R. and Read, J. (2002), '"Having it Ally": Popular Television (Post)Feminism', *Feminist Media Studies*, 2, 2: 231–49.

Poynton, B. and Hartley, J. (1990), 'Male viewing', in M. E. Brown (ed.), *Television and Women's Culture: The Politics of the Popular*, London: Sage.

Probyn, E. (1993), *Sexing the Self: Gendered Positions in Cultural Studies*, London: Routledge.

Radway, J. (1984), *Reading the Romance: Women, Patriarchy and Popular Literature*, Chapel Hill: University of North Carolina Press.

Riley, D. (1988), '"*Am I That Name?" Feminism and the Category of "Women*"' in History, Basingstoke: Macmillan.

Shalit, W. (1999), 'Sex, Sadness and the City', *Urbanities*, 4, 4 (Autumn), available online at www.city-journal.org (accessed 27 November 2001).

van Erp, B. (2002), 'Dertiger, hip, vrouw en ongelukkig', *Vrij Nederland*, 30 maart.

Willis, S. (1998), *High Contrast: Race and Gender in Contemporary Hollywood Film*, Durham, NC: Duke University Press.

CHAPTER 6

Can I Go Home Yet? Feminism, Post-feminism and Domesticity

Joanne Hollows

This chapter examines the problematic place of 'home' and domesticity in debates about post-feminism. In the process, I explore how the impact of second-wave feminism on debates about post-feminism produces significant problems in talking about what domesticity means to women today. The chapter attempts to find a way out of this impasse by analyzing some of the ways in which the meanings of domesticity, and domestic femininities, have been transformed in a historical period that is post-second-wave feminism. Therefore, my chapter aims to trace some of the characteristics of post-feminist domesticity.[1]

The neglect of domesticity in debates about post-feminism in media and cultural studies takes place in a wider context in which some academics have turned homewards. Although debates about globalization have frequently worked to privilege the public sphere and reproduce the idea that public identities are the site of 'important' politics, critics such as Massey (1994) and Morley (2000) have reminded us that thinking globally remains an abstraction and becomes limiting if it is divorced from the lived experience and more 'mundane' politics of the local and the domestic where globalization is 'experienced'. Likewise, studies of consumption have shifted away from an emphasis on spectacular modes of semiotic creativity in public space to the more routine or unspectacular modes of consumption that create and sustain our classed, gendered and 'raced' experience of everyday life (see, for example, Jackson and Moores 1995; Clarke 1998; Miller 1998; Bell and Hollows 2005; and Casey and Martens forthcoming). Similarly, feminist cultural history has questioned the neglected place of the domestic and the gendering of everyday life in theories of modernity, arguing that exploring things from the point of view of a gendered experience of the domestic problematizes many of the narratives through which we have conceptualized both past and contemporary experience (Felski 2000 and Giles 2004).[2]

My interest in the relationships between feminism, post-feminism and domesticity is partly fuelled by the strange trajectory of my own research, where I have been simultaneously working on cooking and food on the one hand, and on the relationships between feminism, femininity and popular culture on the other. As I became increasingly interested in cooking as a form of domestic culture, I also became increasingly aware that debates about post-feminism and 'new' femininities that I was exploring elsewhere had very little to say on the domestic.

However, this chapter is also fuelled by those more 'everyday' experiences that also shape research questions. Early on in the academic phase of my working life, I remember being surprised by the lack of fit between people's houses and their professed politics. I saw Frankfurt School influenced critics of consumption swan around their custom-made designer kitchens and watched feminist critics who were scathing about domestic enslavement serve up elaborate multi-course feasts. At this stage I (perhaps naively) expected people's domestic consumption to match their academic political positions, and would ask my partner in an exasperated manner, 'How can they be into Adorno and have THAT kitchen?' Feminists clearly do cook, decorate and clean yet, as Margaret Horsfield has argued 'cleaning house has become an activity for which no politically correct woman in her right mind would dare show much enthusiasm' despite the fact that 'there are a lot of clean – or at least clean-ish – homes out there, and a great deal of time and effort goes into keeping them that way' (1997: 5–6; see also Martens and Scott 2005). It would seem that academic feminist identities have frequently been constructed through a kind of 'life laundry' in which the clutter and investments of everyday life are conveniently parcelled off elsewhere. In what follows, I want to question whether the (hidden) investment that many feminists have in domestic life means that they also have an investment in maintaining some aspects of the sexual division of labour, or whether these investments might suggest that there is more to domesticity than the maintenance of the sexual division of labour.

However, perhaps most crucially for what follows, this chapter is shaped by an awareness of an increasing fascination with the domestic as a forbidden pleasure among my contemporaries. I appear to know a fair number of feminist-influenced women in academia in their thirties and early forties who have a secret fantasy of giving up their careers in order to bake cakes, tend the garden, knit or do home improvements. Judging by conversations I had as a result of presenting the original version of this chapter at a conference on post-feminism, my friends, if not typical, are certainly not simply aberrational wannabe Stepford Wives (and our comments on domesticity and third-wave feminism in the opening chapter of this book also reaffirm this point). I should also make it clear that I include myself among these women (most of my fantasies seem to centre around rhubarb). What interests me is why highly educated women who have secured good middle-class jobs and were well-versed in feminism (who might not identify themselves as feminists but who nonetheless identify with many aspects of feminism) have fantasies about giving up their jobs to make jam. What I find equally interesting is why, in their academic writing, these fantasies remain secret when the same people have 'come out' about their investments in 'Buffy the Vampire Slayer', designer clothing and *Pretty Woman*.

It would seem that, despite its absence in writing on post-feminism, domesticity is part of the lived experience of a post-feminist period. In the following section, I seek to understand why debates about post-feminism have a problem with the domestic, and explore how these debates reproduce second-wave feminism's rejection of domesticity. In the remainder of the chapter, I go on to examine some examples of contemporary popular forms and practices in the UK where there is evidence of an attempt to think through what might emerge between feminism and femininity in a domestic context. In the process, I examine how what might be classified as post-feminist domestic femininities need to be understood in relation to the lifestyle choices through which fractured middle-class identities are formed.[3]

My aim here is not to create some form of manifesto for going home and embracing a life of domesticity. Nor am I trying to deny that the sexual division of labour continues to be central to the creation and maintenance of gender inequalities. However, domestic tasks – which may or may not be experienced as domestic labour – continue to be done, even by feminists. Demonstrating how domesticity contributes to gender inequalities is crucial but it does not exhaust the cultural significance of domesticity. Furthermore, these issues intersect with current policy debates about women and work, and about work-life balance. Catherine Hakim's (2002) 'preference theory', which aims to show how women's employment is best understood in terms of work-centred or home-centred attitudes among women, has recently caught the attention of policy-makers in the UK and elsewhere. She argues that far fewer women than men have 'work-centred' attitudes, and that many more are adaptive or home-centred. This, she believes, is the key influence on women's labour market participation. So, for example, she argues, education levels have little impact on attitudes to work. From this she concludes that 'Women who enter higher education are not "investing" in a future employment career... but in the marriage market' (2002: 445). While both the claims to the scientific power of her preference theory and quantitative methodology make Hakim's work problematic for feminist cultural studies, as do her emphasis on choice and her similarities to theorists of a reflexive modernity such as Giddens (1991), there is also clearly something going on here. We can't simply dismiss the appeals of going home as evidence of false consciousness, but need to take seriously, and analyze, the cultural significance of wanting to go home. It seems that feminist cultural studies is caught in some kind of refusal to take on these issues (and for an extended discussion of these issues in relationship to Hakim, see Johnson and Lloyd 2004).

LEAVING HOME: SECOND-WAVE FEMINISM AND DOMESTICITY

Judy Giles has observed that, in many feminist narratives, '"leaving home" … is a necessary condition of liberation' (2004: 141–2). For Giles, rather than challenging the opposition between public and private that has structured theories of modernity, feminists have frequently reproduced this opposition, preferring to become 'culturally "one of the boys"' (Thornton 1995: 104) by identifying with the adventure of urban, public space rather than re-evaluating the contribution to modern life of practices in private suburban space. In this way, feminist theory often shares with other theories of modernity a vocabulary that is 'anti-home' and which 'celebrates mobility, movement, exile, boundary crossing. It speaks enthusiastically about movement out into the world, but is silent about the return home' (Felski 2000: 86). 'Home', like the women who remain there, becomes associated with 'familiarity, dullness, stasis' (Felski 2000: 86). Therefore, in second-wave feminism, domesticity was frequently represented as 'something that must be left behind if women were to become "modern", emancipated subjects' (Giles 2004: 142). As Elspeth Probyn has noted, within much social and cultural theory, an investment in the domestic has come to signify 'narrowmindedness' (Probyn 2005).

Both Felski and Giles provide spatial dimensions to Charlotte Brunsdon's arguments about feminism's ambivalence towards domesticity. Brunsdon has charted how 'the opposition feminist/housewife was polemically and historically formative for second-wave feminism' (2000: 216). Just as the identity 'feminist' was predicated on an escape from 'home', so it was predicated on a distance from the woman who lived there, 'the housewife'. Brunsdon's argument is neatly demonstrated in second-wave feminist writing on housework. For example, in her research into housework, Ann Oakley claims that 'An affirmation of contentment with the housewife role is actually a form of antifeminism, whatever the gender of the person who displays it. Declared contentment with a subordinate role – which the housewife role undoubtedly is – is a rationalization of inferior status' (1974a: 233). Yet, despite this, Oakley also acknowledges elsewhere that 'Most of the women interviewed for this study have the idea that feminists are not interested in housewives – that they "look down" on them, and consider the occupation inferior to a job or career outside the home' (1974b: 194). While popular representations of feminists in the 1970s frequently constructed them as 'anti-housewife' (Brunsdon 1997: 186), such conclusions are not difficult to draw from feminist scholarship.

The opposition between these two different femininities – the feminist and the housewife – identified by Brunsdon made it very difficult for second-wave feminism to deal with domesticity. Domesticity and a suburban 'home' were things associated with the feminist's 'other', and therefore needed to be kept at a distance. This is neatly illustrated by Janet Rée's recollections about her 'inappropriate' behaviour at an early women's group meeting:

> One woman stormed out because she said I was always trying to make people feel at ease… She said she was fed up with people just sitting around, middle-class women not getting out and actually doing things. I was always smiling at people. It was awful. I was a hostess – can you imagine, I always made cakes. And tea and coffee. I've always loved making a kind of home. All the peripheral things like cooking and sewing, having a nice warm room, all that. It was really important. But I was mortified and recognised the justness of that description of myself. I might as well have been hosting the Women's Institute. That was the subtext. (cited in Brunsdon 2000: 23)

While the politics of housework and suburban privatized domesticity could be objects for feminist analysis, they needed to be kept well away from the feminist subject.

Nonetheless, such characterizations of feminism are not only problematized by the differences between feminisms generally, but also more specifically by differences between the modes of feminism that emerged in different national contexts. In a UK context where socialist/Marxist-feminism was frequently theoretically dominant, the emphasis on 'home' in relation to domestic labour and the reproduction of the family is not surprising (see Giles 2004: 143). However, the US provides a more complex picture. On the one hand, the liberal feminism associated with Betty Friedan portrays the housewife as a passive, conforming, dehumanized 'anonymous biological robot' (1963: 296) and she argues that this condition is brought about by 'a feminine mystique' that promoted a domestic femininity. Friedan's solution to this 'problem with no name' was for women to give up their search for domestic fulfilment, get a life and commit to the masculine world of work. In Friedan's work in the 1960s, an investment in domesticity is clearly pathological and the opposition between feminist and housewife, public and private, is clearly policed. (See Bowlby 1992; Meyerowitz 1994; Hollows 2000; Giles 2004.)

However, on the other hand, radical feminists in the US were far more sceptical of this embrace of masculine values: although they tended to see the housewife as being duped by patriarchal values, their rejection of 'home' was less clear-cut. In its cultural feminist variations, radical feminism rejected both the artifice of femininity as a product of patriarchal male values and searched for a 'female essence… in an effort to revalidate undervalued female attributes' (Alcott 1988: 408). Therefore, while patriarchal notions of domesticity and its practitioner, the housewife, were rejected, the domestic space of the home could operate as a site for 'the nurturance of a female counter-culture' (Echols 1989: 51) where domestic skills and crafts might be revalued as a challenge to a male-dominated value system. As I go on to explore in the next section, these 'quilt-ridden' forms of 'folk feminism' resurface in debates about post-feminism.

'I CAN NEVER GO HOME ANYMORE': POST-FEMINISM AND DOMESTICITY

The problematic place of domesticity in second-wave feminism has influenced debates about post-feminism and its ability to deal with the domestic. In order to explore these problems, I have adopted a rather more schematic approach to post-feminism than those associated with critics such as Sarah Projansky (2001). Instead, I want to concentrate on two key strands of post-feminism: a largely pessimistic position that equates post-feminism with 'backlash', and a sometimes optimistic position which concentrates on what has developed in a post-feminist context in which new femininities have emerged 'between feminism and femininity'.

In the pessimistic 'backlash' versions of post-feminism, the opposition between the feminist and the housewife is invoked to demonstrate how post-feminism represents an attempt to turn the clock back to pre-feminist times. Such approaches tended to emerge at the close of Reaganite America, arguing that the emphasis on family values under Reagan had produced a backlash against feminism. In these debates, domesticity was seen as part of a 'new traditionalism' associated with television shows such as 'thirtysomething'. In the more complex and productive analyses of this new traditionalism, critics such as Probyn (1990) treated television's return home historically, demonstrating that post-feminism's take on the home was not straightforwardly an attempt to turn back the clock but instead articulated the home as 'a choice'. However, in more simplistic accounts associated with the backlash thesis's 'celebrity' proponent Susan Faludi (1992), the backlash treats femininity in far more ahistorical terms: the association between women and home becomes renaturalized as if feminism had never happened.

If critics like Faludi tended to associate domesticity with an anti-feminism that characterized the backlash, a more productive line of argument is offered by Judith Stacey in her analysis of the 'new traditionalism' she found lurking in the work of allegedly 'feminist' critics. Preferring the term 'conservative pro-family feminism' to 'post-feminism', Stacey argues that '"old" conservative themes present in the domestic feminism of the nineteenth century' were circulating in the work of critics such as Germaine Greer, Betty Friedan and Jean Bethke Elshtain in the 1980s (Stacey 1986: 244). These critics, she argued, had abandoned an examination of sexual politics in favour of 'a "pro-family" stance' that 'celebrates traditionally feminine qualities, particularly those associated with mothering' (1986: 222). These themes, as I noted above, were also circulating in cultural feminism in the 1970s where feminine virtues could be found in womanly domestic traditions which were the part of an 'authentic' women's culture that presumably 'existed isolated like some deep-frozen essence in the freezer of male culture' (Parker and Pollock cited in Bennett 1986: xii).

However, rather than simply seeing 'conservative pro-family feminism' as an attempt to turn the clock back to pre-feminist times, Stacey instead proposes a structural and historical explanation of why such manifestations of post-feminism had come about. The explanation lies in 'the collective biographical roots of a particular generation of feminists' who had found the experience of combining being a feminist with building relationships and doing mothering painful and/or unfeasible (Stacey 1986: 238). Therefore, while Stacey has little sympathy with what she identifies as conservative feminism, she nonetheless argues that 'unreconstructed' feminists must find a way of dealing with the problems that reconstructed conservative feminists have identified.

Two interesting issues emerge from Stacey's argument. First, she seems to acknowledge that the identity 'feminist' sat uncomfortably with some women's lived experience in the clutter of everyday life (while, at the same time, continuing to reproduce the opposition between feminism and the domestic). Second,

Stacey's argument returns us to historical questions about shifting relationships to feminism in a way that the backlash thesis cannot handle. Her argument also acts as a reminder of the autobiographical impetus behind much feminist theory with its roots in consciousness-raising. If Ann Oakley's *Housewife* begins by acknowledging that 'it is obligatory for me to thank my own family for the experience of my oppression as a housewife' (1974a: x), then this seems to be different to the experience that fuelled the reflections of Stacey's conservative feminists. And, more crucially for my argument in what follows, it is also a different experience to that of middle-class professional women today who have grown up in conditions that are both shaped by second-wave feminism, and which are also the product of a time that is historically post-second-wave-feminism. How can women now leave home when they've never been there?

However, before addressing this question, I want to return to the second type of approach to post-feminism. While it would be misleading to describe this as a more optimistic characterization of post-feminism, it is an approach that has nonetheless been prepared to look more positively at 'what emerges between feminism and femininity' in popular culture from the 1980s onwards. This approach examines how elements of feminist discourses have been articulated within the popular to produce new feminine subjectivities that are partly informed by feminism but refuse the identity 'feminist' (Brunsdon 1997). The focus here tends to be on fashion and youth cultures (for example, McRobbie 1991, 1994 and 1996), girly movies such as *Working Girl* and *Pretty Woman* (for example, Brunsdon 1997) and recent TV shows such as 'Sex and the City', 'Buffy the Vampire Slayer' and 'Ally McBeal' (for example, Moseley and Read 2002). However, what is distinct about much of this work is that the emphasis is on youthful or non-domestic femininities (although exceptions exist such as Rowe 1997). In debates about what emerges between feminism and femininity, while the relationships between public and private are explored (as Ally juggles professional life and personal relationships and Buffy juggles saving the world with her 'family' responsibilities), what distinguishes these femininities is that they are primarily defined by their roles in the public sphere (Ally as lawyer and Buffy as vampire slayer). Therefore, while backlash critics condemn post-feminism through its association with domesticity, these critics use a more positive conception of post-feminism by avoiding domesticity. While we might know quite a lot about what emerges between feminism and youthful femininities, and between feminism and the single girl, what emerges between the feminist and the housewife remains largely unexplored.

'THE GREEN GREEN GRASS OF HOME': BETWEEN THE FEMINIST AND THE HOUSEWIFE

A recent example of 'chick lit' for the 'older' Bridget Jones, Alison Pearson's novel *I Don't Know How She Does it* opens with her heroine's account of 'roughing-up' a packet of mince pies from Sainsbury's supermarket in order to give them a 'home-made' quality. The heroine observes 'Women used to have time to make mince pies and had to fake orgasms. Now we can manage the orgasms but we have to fake mince pies. And they call this progress' (Pearson 2003: 5). Pearson's novel has a modern-day fairy tale ending in which the girl gets to downshift from inner-city London to a northern rural idyll, 'a place on the edge of a market town with a view and a paddock' (2003: 349). She gives up the corporate ladder to become a good mother, rescue her marriage and, by chance, become a socially responsible entrepreneur rescuing the female employees in a floundering doll's-house factory. While in the 1980s, *Baby Boom* (Charles Shyer, 1987) – with its narrative centred around a high-flying urban professional who retreats to the country after inheriting a baby only to find a fulfilling relationship and found a baby-food empire – was frequently seen as one of the quintessential backlash texts, by now it is beginning to look like it captures an emergent structure of feeling.

If cultural studies has largely ignored what emerges between the feminist and the housewife, then the rest of this chapter examines some recent examples of domestic post-feminist identities and narratives within the popular to explore how new domestic femininities have emerged between these figures. In what follows, rather than seeing post-feminism as inherently conservative or progressive, I want to employ Brunsdon's less value-laden and more historical approach that suggests that post-feminism is best 'used in a historically-specific sense to mark changes in popularly available understandings of femininity and a woman's place' (1997: 101). In this context, what interests me is how the figures of the feminist and the housewife are imagined within the popular in a 'post-feminist' period.

As my earlier work on Nigella Lawson demonstrates, the British press frequently draw on feminist discourses to present the housewife as a prob-lematic figure (Hollows 2003). Indeed, if, as Angela McRobbie (2004) has suggested, the feminist is frequently represented as an anachronistic figure who has gone to live in a 'retirement home' in a 'seaside resort', then the housewife is frequently presented as fit for the asylum or located in a retro-dystopia. Therefore, while Lawson's *How to be a Domestic Goddess* was a collection of baking recipes, it provided some columnists in the British press with an opportunity to rehearse the difference between their feminist-identified selves and the housewife. The book provoked a huge debate in the press about the relationship between feminism, femininity and baking, with Lawson being variously positioned as the pre-feminist housewife, as an anti-feminist Stepford Wife, as the saviour of downshifting middle-class career women, and as both the negative and positive product of post-feminism. For some critics baking was associated with false consciousness, as they suggested there was but a short step from baking to domestic enslavement (Tyrer 2000) and a pre-feminist world of backstreet abortions (Moore 2000). Nigella Lawson was demonized in the name of 'famous feminists': Gillian Glover asked, 'didn't Marilyn French, Erica Jong and Germaine Greer free us from our need to please the genie of the Fairy Liquid bottle?' (2000: 9). Such comments frequently assumed a straightforward choice between feminism and domestic femininity in which feminism could be the only 'rational' response: 'Could it be that the real reason women hate baking is because cake-baking epitomizes our status as domestic slaves? Most men secretly love the idea of a Stepford Wife, programmed to eager servitude, be it sex or baking' (Tyrer 2000: 47). Burnside sneered that 'For women who have given up career jobs to make packed lunches and sew Tweenie costumes', *Domestic Goddess* was 'affirming stuff' (2000: 16). The coverage devoted to the book would seem to support Julia Hallam's argument that 'feminism as a (contradictory and unfixed) subject position is widely circulating as an interpretive strategy amongst... journalists' (cited in Read 2000: 119).

However, Lawson's *Domestic Goddess* also negotiated the opposition between the feminist and the housewife: rather than prescribing a return home, Lawson offers the opportunity to experience at the level of fantasy what being a domestic goddess would *feel* like. Her address is frequently to the harried, working middle-class woman and she suggests that sometimes 'we don't want to feel like a post-modern, post-feminist, overstretched woman but, rather, a domestic goddess trailing nutmeggy fumes of baking pie in our languorous wake' (Lawson 2000: vii). In this way, Nigella acknowledges the temporal constraints that produce, for many women, the experience of contemporary femininity. *Domestic Goddess* does not suggest women can 'have it all' (indeed, as Charlotte Brunsdon suggests in her chapter in this volume, she rejects the figure of the 'superwoman'), but offers us the experience at the level of fantasy of what other 'retro-femininities' might feel like. It is precisely the time-consuming nature of baking that offers a temporary escape from the pressures of managing time, which, for many women, constitute the contemporary feminine experience of modernity. Alison Light has argued that fantasy allows us to explore 'desires which may be in excess of the socially possible or acceptable' (1984: 7). As the press coverage of Nigella demonstrates, being 'just a housewife' is frequently presented as neither possible nor desirable. In such a scenario, the desire to experience 'a bit of the (forbidden) other' can be a source of pleasure.

Although the publication of Lawson's *Domestic Goddess* was a high-profile example of popular debate about the housewife, the publication of Cheryl Mendelson's (2003) *Home Comforts: The Art and Science of Keeping House* and Danielle Crittenden's (2004) *amandawright@home* has also generated large amounts of public debate about the relationship between feminism and the housewife. Indeed, press coverage frequently reinforces the impasse between the two: 'Read Betty Friedan's *The Feminine Mystique*, published in 1963', suggested Kate Carr in the *Times*, or 'failing that, if you find yourself being berated by one of these Marie Antoinette types to get in touch with your inner housewife, chop off her head' (2003: 27). However, these (frequently PR-generated) clusters of debate exist alongside a wider interrogation of the meaning of domesticity today. These debates are wide-ranging and diverse, and are given additional complexity as many simultaneously interrogate the roles of housewife, feminist, career woman and mother. Whereas feminist cultural studies has tended to keep the housewife at a distance from the feminist, these popular debates are frequently far more messy, articulating and disarticulating different feminine identities with and from feminism in a variety of ways.

If Nigella plays with feminist discourses to offer her readers the opportunity to experience home, then other narratives have surfaced that seemingly legitimate going home in feminist terms. In the late 1990s and into the 2000s, the British media have shown an apparently endless fascination with downshifting narratives, amid wider debates about 'work–life balance'. While downshifting is not straightforwardly a female pursuit, although Ghazi and Jones (2004) suggest that more downshifters are women than men, it would be very easy to read the key downshifting narrative as a classic backlash tale. Indeed, downshifting has certainly been read as a 'failure of nerve', and as a refusal by women to fight to 'have it all'. Downshifting businesswomen add 'weight to the argument that women no longer want to – or can't – have it all. Yet there are thousands of professional working mothers who relish running a home and a hectic career' claimed Diana Appleyard (2003: 26) in the *Daily Mail*. Likewise, *Observer* columnist Christina Odone claimed that women who thought that 'having it all ... was no longer feasible' were 'being defeatest' (2004: 25). However, for its advocates, downshifting was an opportunity to interrogate the very notion of 'having it all': 'The point is that the old feminist battles have become obsolete. The argument now is no longer about *whether* women should pursue career or motherhood or both. It is about *how* they can best combine whichever roles suit them' (Ghazi and Jones 2004: 131). Debates about downshifting then offered the opportunity to revisit debates about the meanings of contemporary femininity that were constructed through lifestyle choices.

However, I want to suggest, there is more at stake than this in the fascination with downshifting. The term downshifting encompasses a range of practices, but usually involves a reduction in the number of hours worked and/or a voluntary drop in income. Estimates of the extent of downshifting vary wildly: when broad definitions are taken, Clive Hamilton has suggested that as many as '25 per cent of British adults aged 30–59 have downshifted over the last ten years… The proportion rises to 30 per cent if those stopping work to look after a baby or set up their own businesses are included' (Hamilton 2003: vii). Hamilton claims that the majority of downshifters are in fact suburban, and contrasts this 'reality' with the 'widespread myth' that 'downshifting means selling up in the city and shifting to the countryside to live a life closer to nature' (2003: vii). However, this 'myth' is one replayed across the British media and there are many television shows that employ this narrative. For example, property shows 'Relocation, Relocation' (IWC Media for Channel 4, 2003–) and 'Escape to the Country' (Talkback for BBC, 2002–) frequently centre around people searching to reorient their lives by swapping the urban for the rural, while 'No Going Back' (Ricochet for Channel 4, 2002–4), and 'Get a New Life' (Brighter/Endemol for the BBC, 2003–4) frequently give a spin on the downshifting narrative in the pursuit of a 'rural idyll' outside the UK.[4] Alternative versions of this narrative were dramatized in TV cook Hugh Fearnley-Whittingstall's series focusing on his smallholding experiment based at River Cottage in Dorset, and in the accompanying cookbooks.[5] Furthermore, as Robert Fish (2005) has suggested, *Country Life* magazine frequently coheres around *Baby Boom*-esque narratives of downshifting urban businesswomen whose pursuit of the good life in the country results in the establishment of an innovative and successful rural business (a scenario reproduced in Pearson's novel).

These downshifting myths are popular then, but what do they tell us about the relationship between feminism and home? Many of these narratives are not gender-specific; indeed, they are largely constructed around heterosexual couples and, most frequently, 'conventional' families. I would suggest that one significant feature of downshifting stories is their ability to seemingly resolve the problems of modern femininity through geographical relocation. The pressure to 'have it all' and the problems of achieving a 'work–life balance' are magically resolved through the process of relocation as urban femininities are abandoned in favour of rural femininities, which seem imbued with the balm of the 'rural idyll'.

Although research into the lived reality of rural heterosexual femininity suggests that it is well-policed along conventional lines (Little 2003), the downshifting narrative enables elements of feminism to be articulated within the transition from urban to rural femininities. The downshifting narrative promises that one can give up careers (or at least minimize paid work) in order to spend more time at home without simply becoming 'a housewife'. By transforming giving up careers into 'leaving the rat race', the downshifting narrative enables voluntary domesticity to become a critique of the masculine values of corporate culture. Furthermore, by associating the need to work 24/7 with the need to consume an infinitely expanding range of consumer goods, the rejection of corporate culture is coupled with a rejection of consumer culture – 'the "work-spend-consume" straightjacket' (Ghazi and Jones 2004: 44) – in order to opt for 'voluntary simplicity'.

In the process, the meanings of going home are seemingly transformed. The suburban Mrs Consumer, Friedan's 'Happy Housewife Heroine' who has swallowed 'the feminine mystique' is transformed into a *No Logo*-reading anti- or ethical consumer whose lack of microwave and dishwasher signifies her moral/ political/spiritual superiority. Indeed, there are some strong similarities between post-second-wave ecofeminists and these downshifted rural femininities. For example, in *Ecofeminism*, Mies and Shiva argue that there is a need to 'transcend… the consumerist model' through 'a voluntary reduction in the living standards and a change in consumer patterns by the rich countries and classes' calling for new conceptions of 'the good life' (1993: 253). Ghazi and Jones claim that:

> Greater spending power has brought Westerners previously undreamed-of lifestyles and travel opportunities… But many people are beginning to sense that indefinitely expanding the boundaries of our lifestyles is likely to take a heavy toll on ourselves, our society and the environment in which we live… In response, a growing minority of people are tuning out mall culture and switching gear to simpler, more self-sufficient and affordable lifestyles. (2004: 12)

In this way, going home to make jam can be legitimated through its implicit association with an ecofeminist consciousness which prefers the 'moral economy' of 'ecological sustainability' and 'self-reliance' to the world of corporate capitalism and an expanding consumer culture (Mies and Shiva 1993: 256–7).

If the downshifting narrative promises alternative versions of 'the good life' in which a new hybrid form of domestic femininity might emerge between the feminist and the housewife, it is obviously not without its problems. Most crucially, the downshifting narrative is a classed narrative, as I go on to discuss in the next section. Furthermore, the rejection of dishwashers, washing machines and microwaves cannot simply be equated with a rejection of consumption: buying and using a rustic antique mangle might signify a critique of the compulsory obsolescence and the unnecessary overproduction of consumer goods, but it also helps to construct a lifestyle through consumption that is 'distinguished' from the time-poor, the economically poor and the 'cultural poverty' of those who wish to flaunt their economic capital. Indeed, in many downshifting narratives, voluntary simplicity does not necessarily equate with the loss of the washing machine because going home becomes a lot less appealing without one. The downshifting narrative in its ecofeminist-inspired manifestations can too easily reproduce some familiar and long-standing ideas about femininity which articulate the performance of 'care' with 'respectability' (Skeggs 1997): indeed, they can work to essentialize notions of women's 'nurturing' natures.

Finally, there also remain problems around the putative power of relocation to transform gendered identities. The downshifting narrative rests on relocation to a 'rural idyll' that, despite the anti-consumerist ethic implied in downshifting narratives, is itself thoroughly commodified and frequently conservative (Bell 2005). The rural idyll is also a product of modernity, 'idyllization ... is a symptom of urbanization' (Bell 2005: page numbers not available). In this way, rather than opening up 'home', the pursuit of the rural can be seen to fit into existing structuring oppositions between modernity and domesticity discussed above: the distinction between urban and rural is easily mapped onto existing dichotomies between public/modernity/masculinity and private/tradition/femininity.

However, this is not necessarily straightforward. Domesticity has traditionally been associated with immobility and stasis, and against the adventurous spirit of modernity. Feminist discourses have frequently reproduced these associations and have, in the process, distanced the feminist from images of spatially fixed classed and gendered figures epitomized by the (affluent working and middle-class) suburban housewife. From such a position, 'going home' is associated with other, and othered, femininities. The downshifting narrative recasts many of the assumptions of theories of modernity, including many forms of feminism, by investing 'going home' with mobility and with a spirit of adventure: people seeking out home-based lifestyles (that both reject, and depend on, late modernity) in rural locations become the new frontierswomen.

CONCLUSIONS

My interest here has been less in the 'reality' of downshifting and more in the current preoccupation with the downshifting narrative in the UK. It would be very easy to read this narrative as evidence of a backlash against feminism (and I briefly toyed with my own downshifting fantasy in which I would 'do a Faludi', write *Downshifting: The New War Against Women* to huge commercial success, give up my job and downshift to a cottage by the sea). However, unfortunately for my bank balance and dreams of days filled with making crabcakes, I think that downshifting appears to be a rather more contradictory phenomenon. The downshifting narrative tries to imagine something between feminism and 'traditional' femininity, it tries to imagine a solution to the problems of inhabiting contemporary femininities. Although, as I discuss below, it is caught up in a rhetoric of choice, and while it may ultimately reproduce certain dichotomies, it is nonetheless a compelling fantasy which offers the possibility to also think through the relationships between public and personal, work and leisure, feminism and femininity, paid work and domesticity. As Elspeth Probyn has argued, we need to be aware of the affectivity of such images, the way in which 'representations of choice can translate into feelings of possibility', the possibility of rearranging the 'feel of the material' (1993: 283).

However, the downshifting narrative is a profoundly classed narrative. One of the key features of the examples I have discussed above is the way they centre around choices for those who inhabit specific middle-class femininities. This is hardly surprising as these 'post-feminist' femininities are produced in relation to second-wave feminist femininities which themselves were profoundly middle-class (and many debates about post-feminism generally frequently focus upon middle-class experience). Indeed, the emphasis on choice and lifestyle, which many attribute to post-feminism, was frequently a feature of second-wave feminism itself. Just because fantasies and narratives of domesticity are classed does not, in itself, undermine their significance as long as the specificity of the experiences discussed are acknowledged and analyzed. Conceptions of the feminist subject have been rightly criticized for their tendency to universalize middle-class experience but this does not mean that middle-class femininities should not be analyzed in their particularity and regarding how they are positioned in relation to 'other' femininities.

As Elspeth Probyn has argued, middle-class femininities are a product of choices between identities 'in which feminism itself is bound up with a discourse of choice' (1993: 284). Choices are offered between feminism and domesticity, between workplace and family, between paid work and domestic labour, between what Bell (2002) has called 'work-work' and 'leisure-work'. Both paid labour (and the economic capital that is generated by paid labour) and the 'work' of consumption and leisure are crucial to maintaining distinctive contemporary middle-class lifestyles. As Gregson and Lowe (1995: 95) argue, many forms of domestic labour are time-consuming and hard work, yet contribute little to classed lifestyles and notions of 'quality time'. Therefore, middle-class professional women may opt to pay someone else to carry out the 'less pleasant' aspects of domestic labour so they can invest in 'the more pleasurable domestic tasks of childcare activities and cooking' (1995: 95). Indeed, many of those elements of domesticity which have received renewed attention are those which are consistent with new middle-class lifestyles, elements that can be appropriated as pleasurable forms of labour/leisure which help maintain middle-class identities (such as baking cakes with Nigella). Less pleasurable and creative aspects of the 'housewife role' are then carried out by working class domestic labour whose relationship to the domestic is less about choice and identity and who remain economically, culturally and socially fixed by their relationship to the domestic. The ability of some women to choose lifestyles must always be contexualized by considering those who are positioned outside of this discourse of choice (see Skeggs 2004).

Yet paid work is also central to contemporary middle-class femininities and definitions of success. Not only is economic capital necessary to produce middle-class lifestyles, but career success in liberal feminist terms is also crucial to the social capital upon which these lifestyles also depend. For example, the middle-class thirtysomethings in Joanna Brewis's study of the aspirations of female urban professionals 'talk resentfully of what they see as a London tendency to define others using their jobs' (2004: 1831). To not work is seen as a threat to class status and this is backed up by studies that suggest that 'middle-class women are becoming increasingly "polarized"' as women who chose to become full-time mothers lose their social capital (Elliott and Iredale 2003: 6). In the same news story in the *Times*, it was claimed that this lack of social status was linked to increased isolation experienced by urban housewives, citing economic historian Jane Humphries who claimed, 'In a rosy pre-war village you would have much more contact with your neighbours and wider kin, society was much less mobile and housing patterns led to the development of closer ties' (2003: 6). Within this article, the pattern of the downshifting narrative begins to take shape: the urban is associated with the middle-class working woman, and the 'rural idyll' with middle-class lifestyles that are not centred around 'careers'.

It would appear that elements of liberal feminism are central to the identities of many 'post-feminist' middle-class urban professional women (Brewis 2004). Indeed, in many ways an investment in elements of liberal feminism forms part of the social and cultural capital upon which these femininities frequently depend. Put another way, for many women, elements of feminism are closely tied in with narratives of class mobility through education and/or paid work. Women who are 'securely' middle-class, who possess the security of reserves of economic capital and the security of their middle-class habitus, risk less in choosing domesticity over careers: if they give up work, they are still middle-class women with reserves of capital that legitimate their choices. Giving up paid work not only requires significant reserves of economic capital, it also requires a confidence in the security of your class position outside of professional assets. For women who have achieved class mobility through education and employment, the choices may be different to those whose middle-classness is inherited rather than achieved. For professional, socially mobile women, a middle-class femininity, informed by feminism, has often been achieved by distinguishing themselves from those middle-class and working-class figures who are bound by the domestic.

These specific historical configurations of class and gender, informed by feminism, may begin to explain why highly educated women, who had secured good middle-class jobs and were well-versed in feminism, fantasize about giving up their jobs to make jam. If Judith Stacey's article, which I discussed earlier, from a different historical and national context was called 'Are Feminists Afraid to Leave Home?', it would seem that it would be more appropriate to ask now 'Are we allowed to go home?' For women who used higher education to gain good jobs in the 1980s and 1990s, one of the profound differences to feminists of earlier generations is that being 'just a housewife' was never really an option (although being a mother was). Therefore, it is perhaps hardly surprising that there should be a return of the repressed and that women should fantasize about domesticity (and there is nothing inherently heterosexual about these fantasies). For some sections of the middle-class, full-time domesticity may be a desirable and realizable option. For others, domesticity operates as a site of fantasy and a means of exploring feminine identities that may not be realizable, or indeed desirable, outside of fantasy.

To reiterate, I'm not suggesting that we all give up our jobs and don aprons instead. However, I do want to suggest that if we want to understand contemporary relationships between feminism and its othered femininities, we can't just ignore how relationships between feminism and femininity are being negotiated in relation to the domestic. Likewise, the domestic can't be simply celebrated as a site of feminine virtue or as a site of pre-feminist subordination. Instead, the meanings of the domestic, and domestic femininities, are contextual and historical and what operates as a site of subordination for some women may operate as the object of fantasy for others.

NOTES

1. I have given versions of this chapter as a paper a number of times. I would like to thank the range of people who have offered useful advice and criticism.
2. Since writing this chapter, I have come across another key recent text in this debate. In *Sentenced to Everyday Life*, Johnson and Lloyd (2004) offer an extensive and valuable discussion of the problematic place of both domesticity and the figure of the housewife in feminist thought. While their account is far more detailed than I can offer here, there is some overlap between the arguments they advance and my own arguments in this chapter.
3. Within contemporary debates about domesticity, there is obviously considerable overlap between practices/identities associated with motherhood on the one hand, and domesticity/homemaking on the other. My emphasis here is on domesticity because it has troubled feminist frameworks rather more than motherhood does. While to be a feminist and a mother has not, on the whole, been seen as incompatible, to be a feminist and homemaker is far more problematic. Nonetheless, motherhood is crucial to many downshifting narratives – indeed, for many women, it may be a motivating force – and this issue clearly needs to be developed in future work. Likewise, it is worth noting a couple of further caveats. My focus here is on middle-class femininities but I certainly do not mean to suggest that the fantasies of domesticity I discuss here are only middle-class fantasies. Furthermore, I have largely bracketed questions about 'race' because, in the texts I refer to, class appears as a far more forceful organizing category than 'race' (although there is clearly further work to be done here given that the countryside is frequently associated with 'whiteness'). Finally, as I make clear later in this chapter, there is little evidence to suggest that there is anything inherently heterosexual in many elements of the fantasies about domesticity I discuss.

4. Although there are exceptions to these conventions, the dominant one appears to be in relocations to Australia where many participants seem attracted by their ability to better pursue a suburban dream in Australia, and in a better climate.

5. The TV series include 'Escape to River Cottage' (Keo Films for Channel 4, 1999), 'Return to River Cottage' (Keo Films for Channel 4, 2000) and 'River Cottage Forever' (Ricochet/Keo Films for Channel 4, 2002), 'Tales from River Cottage' (Keo Films for Channel 4, 2003) and 'Beyond River Cottage' (Keo Films for Channel 4, 2004). These spawned *The River Cottage Cook Book* (Fearnley-Whittingstall 2001), *The River Cottage Year* (Fearnley-Whittingstall 2003) and *The River Cottage Meat Book* (Fearnley-Whittingstall 2004).

BIBLIOGRAPHY

Alcott, L. (1988), 'Cultural Feminism Versus Post-structuralism: The Identity Crisis in Feminist Theory', *Signs*, 13, 3: 405–36.

Appleyard, D. (2003), 'Yes, You Can Have It All!', *Daily Mail*, 7 January: 26–7.

Bell, D. (2002), 'From Writing at the Kitchen Table to TV Dinners: Food Media, Lifestylization and European Eating', paper presented at 'Eat, Drink and Be Merry? Cultural Meanings of Food in the 21st Century', Amsterdam, June.

Bell, D. (2005), 'Variations on the Rural Idyll', in P. Cloke *et al.* (eds), *Handbook of Rural Studies*, London: Sage, page numbers not yet known.

Bell, D. and Hollows, J. (eds) (2005), *Ordinary Lifestyles: Popular Media, Consumption and Taste*, Milton Keynes: Open University Press.

Bennett, T. (1986), 'Introduction: Popular Culture and "the Turn to Gramsci"', in T. Bennett, C. Mercer and J. Woollacott (eds), *Popular Culture and Social Relations*, Milton Keynes: Open University Press.

Bowlby, R. (1992), *Still Crazy after all These Years: Women, Writing and Psychoanalysis*, London: Routledge.

Brewis, J. (2004), 'Sex and Not the City? The Aspirations of the Thirty-Something Working Woman', *Urban Studies*, 41, 9: 1821–38.

Brunsdon, C. (1997), *Screen Tastes: Soap Opera to Satellite Dishes*, London: Routledge.

—— (2000), *The Feminist, the Housewife and the Soap Opera*, Oxford: Oxford University Press.

Burnside, A. (2000), 'Lessons from a Goddess', *Sunday Herald*, 3 September: 16.

Carr, K. (2003), 'Let Them Bake Cakes', the *Times*, Weekend Review, 4 October: 27.

Casey, E. and Martens, L. (eds) (forthcoming), *Gender and Domestic Consumption: Material Culture and the Commercialization of Everyday Life*, Aldershot: Ashgate.

Clarke, A. J. (1998), 'Window Shopping at Home: Classifieds, Catalogues and New Consumer Skills', in D. Miller (ed.), *Material Cultures: Why Some Things Matter*, London, UCL Press.

Crittenden, D. (2004), *amandawright@home*, London: Time Warner International.

Echols, A. (1989), 'The Taming of the Id: Feminist Sexual Politics, 1968–83', in C. Vance (ed.), *Pleasure and Danger*, London: Pandora, pp. 50–72.

Elliott, J. and Iredale, W. (2003), 'Housewives go Backwards in Status Race', *The Times*, 6 June: 6.

Faludi, S. (1992), *Backlash: The Undeclared War Against Women*, London: Vintage.

Fearnley-Whittingstall, H. (2001), *The River Cottage Cookbook*, London: HarperCollins.

—— (2003), *The River Cottage Year*, London: Hodder and Stoughton.

—— (2004), *The River Cottage Meat Book*, London: Hodder and Stoughton.

Felski, R. (2000), *Doing Time: Feminist Theory and Postmodern Culture*, New York: New York University Press.

Fish, R. (2005), 'Countryside Formats and Ordinary Lifestyles', in D. Bell and J. Hollows (eds), *Ordinary Lifestyles: Popular Media, Consumption and Taste*, Milton Keynes: Open University Press.

Friedan, B. (1963), *The Feminine Mystique*, New York: Dell.

Ghazi, P. and Jones, J. (2004), *Downshifting: The Bestselling Guide to Happier, Simpler Living*, London: Hodder and Stoughton.

Giddens, A. (1991), *Modernity and Self-identity: Self and Society in the Late Modern Age*, Cambridge: Polity.

Giles, J. (2004), *The Parlour and the Suburb: Domestic Identities, Class, Femininity and Modernity*, Oxford: Berg.

Glover, G. (2000), 'New Sex and Old Dusters', *Scotsman*, 20 September: 9.

Gregson, N. and Lowe, M. (1994), *Servicing the Middle Classes: Class, Gender and Waged Domestic Labour in Contemporary Britain*, London: Routledge.

Hakim, C. (2002), 'Lifestyle Preferences as Determinants of Women's Differentiated Labour Market Careers', *Work and Occupations*, 29: 428–59.

Hamilton, C. (2003), 'Downshifting in Britain: A Sea-change in the Pursuit of Happiness', Australia Institute Discussion Paper 58.

Hollows, J. (2000), *Feminism, Femininity and Popular Culture*, Manchester: Manchester University Press.

—— (2003), 'Feeling Like a Domestic Goddess: Postfeminism and Cooking', *European Journal of Cultural Studies*, 6, 2: 179–202.

Horsfield, M. (1997), *Biting the Dust: The Joys of Housework*, London: 4th Estate.

Jackson, S. and Moores, S. (eds), (1995), *The Politics of Domestic Consumption*, Hemel Hempstead: Harvester Wheatsheaf.

Johnson, L. and Lloyd, J. (2004), *Sentenced to Everyday Life: Feminism and the Housewife*, Oxford: Berg.

Lawson, N. (2000), *How to be a Domestic Goddess: Baking and the Art of Comfort Cooking*, London: Chatto and Windus.

Light, A. (1984), 'Returning to Manderley: Romantic Fiction, Female Sexuality and Class', *Feminist Review*, 16: 7–25.

Little, J. (2003), 'Riding the Rural Love Train: Heterosexuality and the Rural Community', *Sociologia Ruralis*, 43, 4: 401–17.

McRobbie, A. (1991), *Feminism and Youth Culture From Jackie to Just Seventeen*, Basingstoke: Macmillan.

—— (1994), *Postmodernism and Popular Culture*, London: Routledge.

—— (1996), '*More!*: New Sexualities in Girls' and Women's Magazines', in J. Curran *et al.* (eds), *Cultural Studies and Communication*, London: Arnold.

—— (2004), 'Post-feminism and Popular Culture: Bridget Jones and the "New Gender Regime"', paper presented at 'Interrogating Post-Feminism: Gender and the Politics of Popular Culture' conference, University of East Anglia, April.

Martens, L. and Scott, S. (2005), 'The Unbearable Lightness of Cleaning: Representations of Domestic Practice and Products, in *Good Housekeeping* Magazine (UK) 1951–2001', *Consumers, Markets and Culture*, 8, 3: page numbers not yet known.

Massey, D. (1994), *Space, Place and Gender*, Cambridge: Polity.

Mendelson, C. (2003), *Home Comforts: The Art and Science of Keeping House*, London: Weidenfeld and Nicolson.

Meyerowitz, J. (ed.) (1994), *Not June Cleaver: Women and Gender in Postwar America 1945–60*, Philadelphia: Temple University Press.

Mies, M. and Shiva, V. (1993), *Ecofeminism*, Halifax, Nova Scotia: Fernwood.

Miller, D. (1998), *A Theory of Shopping*, Cambridge: Polity.

Moore, S. (2000), 'Did we Fight for the Right to Bake?', *Mail on Sunday*, 22 October: 31.

Morley, D. (2000), *Home Territories: Media, Mobility and Identity*, London: Routledge.

Moseley, R. and Read, J. (2002), '"Having it Ally": Popular Television (Post)Feminism', *Feminist Media Studies*, 2, 2: 231–49.

Oakley, A. (1974a), *Housewife*, Harmondsworth: Penguin.

—— (1974b), *The Sociology of Housework*, London: Martin Robertson.

Odone, C. (2004), 'Christina Odone's Diary', *Observer*, 4 January, News: 25.

Pearson, A. (2003), *I Don't Know How She Does It*, London: Vintage.

Probyn, E. (1990), 'New Traditionalism and Post-Feminism: TV Does the Home', *Screen*, 31, 2: 147–59.

—— (1993), 'Choosing Choice; Winking Images of Sexuality in Popular Culture', in S. Fisher and K. Davis (eds), *Negotiating at the Margins: Gendered Discourses of Resistance*, New Brunswick: Rutgers University Press.

Probyn, E. (2005), 'Thinking Habits and the Ordering of Life', in D. Bell and J. Hollows (eds), *Ordinary Lifestyles: Popular Media, Consumption and Taste*, Milton Keynes: Open University Press.

Projansky, S. (2001), *Watching Rape: Film and Television in Postfeminist Culture*, New York: New York University Press.

Read, J. (2000), *The New Avengers: Feminism, Femininity and the Rape-Revenge Cycle*, Manchester: Manchester University Press.

Rowe, K. (1997), '"Roseanne": Unruly Woman as Domestic Goddess', in C. Brunsdon, J. D'Acci and L. Spigel (eds), *Feminist Television Criticism*, Oxford: Oxford University Press, pp. 74–83.

Skeggs, B. (1997), *Formations of Class and Gender: Becoming Respectable*, London: Sage.

—— (2004), *Class, Self, Culture*, London: Routledge.

Stacey, J. (1986), 'Are Feminists Afraid to Leave Home? The Challenge of Conservative Pro-Family Feminism', in A. Oakley and J. Mitchell (eds), *What is Feminism?*, Oxford: Blackwell, pp. 219–48.

Thornton, S. (1995), *Club Cultures: Media, Music and Subcultural Capital*, Cambridge: Polity.

Tyrer, N. (2000), 'Who wants to be a Domestic Goddess Anyway?', *Daily Mail*, 19 October: 47.

CHAPTER 7

Sex Workers Incorporated

Jane Arthurs

Debates over sex work and its representation are indicative of the deep divisions within feminism over sexuality and pornography. The 'sex wars' of the 1980s placed the censorship of pornography at the centre of the dispute, when 'sex-positive' radicals accused anti-pornography campaigners of allowing feminism to be appropriated by the conservative puritan agenda (Vance 1992). They, in their turn, have been criticized for colluding with the commercial sex industry in a capitulation to the values of entrepreneurial capitalism, and its structurally embedded sexism, racism, homophobia and class exploitation (McLaughlin 1991: 267). Since that time, and especially from the mid 1990s, there has been a proliferation of programmes about the sex industry, which have contributed substantially to the increase in explicit sexual talk and imagery on mainstream television. These have been condemned by some commentators as worthless voyeurism, a symptom of the decline in our public service broadcasting system as we move into the increasingly competitive commercial environment that characterizes television in the multichannel digital era (Millwood Hargrave 1999; Winston 2000). They have been viewed as simply one more example of the ways in which women's sexuality is objectified and exploited in the mainstream media. However, where these programmes include first-person accounts from the sex workers portrayed, allowing an insight into their subjective experience, they have also been welcomed as a means to overcome a long history of stigmatization of sex workers, not least from the women involved in the industry.

This chapter[1] will examine how these politically diverse perspectives over sex work have influenced television documentary and drama, with a focus on how feminist perspectives have been incorporated across a range of genres that have quite distinct aesthetic forms and purposes. Sex work as a legitimate career option, in line with calls from the sex worker unions to treat it as a job like any other, emerges not only in 'docu-porn' infotainment that trades on sexual display for its appeal, but also in 'serious' current affairs documentaries and 'quality' drama. The figure of the 'empowered' sex worker or the successful female sex entrepreneur reoccurs across these quality/trash boundaries. Feminist interventions have become entwined with a wider shift in attitudes to the sex industry brought about by the triumph of consumer capitalism – pleasure can be bought and sold without shame. Yet when it comes to the issue of 'trafficking in women' across national borders, an issue that has become a focal point for political intervention since 1998 and a recurring news story as a consequence, moral condemnation returns. Here feminist campaigners more often appear on screen to condemn the perpetrators and to advocate political responses to stem this tide of human misery from the impoverished countries of the world.

My analysis begins with an overview of the debates that have emerged within feminism about the politics of sex work and its representation, and the influence that these have had on television programmes about the sex industry. It then moves to a discussion of programmes that deal in particular with the trafficking of women to show how feminist perspectives have become incorporated into a wider struggle over the politics of immigration in an increasingly global labour market. What becomes clear in this analysis is that feminist perspectives have been mobilized, in different contexts, both as a source of legitimization as well as a critique of the commodification of sexuality within the dynamics of global capitalism.

FROM PROSTITUTION TO SEX WORK: A HISTORY OF FEMINIST INTERVENTION

The changing politics of sex work in feminist activism of the last twenty-five years can be traced across the transformations in Channel 4's approach to documentaries about the sex industry. Although it is Channel 5 that is famous for it, the majority of 'docu-porn' on British terrestrial television is shown on Channel 4, as a consequence, it can be argued, of its having shifted to selling its own advertising and the more commercial priorities that ensued. This highlights the enormous changes that have occurred on British terrestrial television, as well as in feminist cultural politics, since the launch of Channel 4. Its minority interest, public service remit led it to become the first channel to use documentary to explore the sex industry as a political issue for women. 'Pictures of Women' (Channel 4, 1982), an experimental series made by a women's collective, arose out of the women's movement and feminist film-making cultures of the 1970s.

It included programmes on prostitution and on pornography in which the dominant perspective was a feminist critique of these industries as forms of patriarchal exploitation. The book accompanying the series gives access to the ideological approach taken, although the programme was also formally innovative in an attempt to disrupt conventional forms of looking at women (Root 1984). Subsequent magazine programmes, which, amongst other items, occasionally addressed the sex industry as a political issue, continued through the 1980s, and first half of the 1990s (for instance 'Watch the Woman', 'First Sex' and 'Out on Tuesday'). These series were premised on an address to a politicized constituency of feminist women, or in the case of 'Out on Tuesday', gays and lesbians, an address that narrowed their appeal (Richardson 1995).

These overtly political series have disappeared and been replaced in the latter half of the 1990s by commercially successful, voyeuristic documentaries that fit seamlessly into an established culture of softcore porn reading practices. By this I mean that sexual arousal is stimulated by the display of female bodies in a structure of looking heavily coded as heterosexual. What we have now is a combination of traditional softcore pornography given new legitimacy by its association with a feminist discourse of empowerment. The turning point was Channel 4's late-night season of documentaries in 1995, the 'Red Light Zone', which offered an exploration of lesbian, gay male, transsexual as well as straight women's involvement in the sex industry. It was a diverse range of films, varying in quality, scheduled very late over several Saturday nights. The series attracted wide press coverage. The importance of this television 'event' was in announcing the channel's changing brand identity, distancing itself from the identity politics of the 1970s and 1980s and aligning itself with the more entrepreneurial, individualistic and hedonistic values of consumer culture. It also marked a recognition of the changing politics of sexuality, in which the transgressive politics of 'queer' had challenged the feminist antipathy to the sex industry and, alongside the sex workers' own campaigns, questioned the construction of women sex workers as 'victims'. The majority of the films were commissioned from women keen to counteract the male dominance of pornography production and the perceived puritanism of second-wave feminism.

The influence of 'sex-positive' strands of feminist and 'queer' politics and the rise of enterprise culture in the 1980s and 1990s enabled not only the emergence of these women film-makers, but also the rise of women as sex industry entrepreneurs. Documentaries about the sex industry often celebrate their economic success and their ability to explore their sexuality free from ignorance and shame. Taking 'Sex and Shopping' as an example, (Channel 5/Douglas

Chirnside Productions, 1998–2001), it is clear from the start that this 'frank look at the global pornography business' is intended to sexually arouse as well as to inform. Its first graphic extols us to TURN OFF OR TURN ON to SEX SEX SEX in bright neon letters, over a montage of sexual imagery and accompanied by brassy stripper-type music. For a British audience, it provides tantalizing glimpses of the hard-core porn available legally in Europe or illegally in Soho in London. 'What do you get for your money', asks a breezy voice-over discussing the videos available in German sex shops: '72 minutes of tape. 15 blow jobs, 14 scenes of vaginal sex, 13 anal, 12 come shots and an orgy from the 8 performers involved. Not bad for £20 even if the quality left something to be desired.'

A journalistic intention justifies the investigation; the series contests British laws censoring hard-core and looks to Europe as a model for more liberal regulation. Presenting the campaign for hard-core porn as a feminist goal provides further legitimation. The programme referred to above, for example, is structured as a hagiography of a German woman entrepreneur, Beatte Uhse, whose sex shop business has been highly successful. Her status as a feminist heroine is secured by picturing her in flying helmet, evoking memories of those other twentieth-century heroines who defied convention to take to the skies. She is presented as a post-war Marie Stopes, dispelling the suffering women experienced as a result of their ignorance about sex. Her business began as an illegal, mail-order contraceptive and advice service for unmarried women. She is shown as a role model for younger women entrepreneurs who aspire to her economic success.

The interviews with female sex workers in docu-porn often tell a story of independence born of economic rewards, and a sense of empowerment enabled by a more open attitude to sex. This one-sided perspective, designed not to disrupt the programmes' erotic appeal, cannot accommodate the more ambivalent feelings that are evident in other autobiographical accounts and ethnographic research with sex workers. This appropriation of the sex-positive agenda by television docu-porn has been seen as a cynical strategy to bring the sex industry into the mainstream. Television is now heavily involved through its marketing of the services available and in its provision of erotic programming. Women speaking out about their experiences to avoid being positioned as stereotypically helpless victims have merely served to produce (cheap) camera fodder. This is the view of the *Guardian*'s (male) television critic:

We've Seen it All Before
Is there a stripper in the entire country who hasn't been followed around by a camera crew intent on 'uncovering the real women' behind the lip gloss and titty tassels?

What with high-class erotic performers, private dancers – any old music will do – and lesbian strippers peek-a-booing out from television lately, it's a miracle that these working women actually manage to fling their g-string anywhere without it landing on a big furry mike. Strippers have replaced animals and airline employees as the docusoap-makers' subject of choice. The number of willing subjects comes as no surprise. After all, in what is quite literally showbusiness, it pays to advertise. (McLean 2001)

Gareth McLean's review of 'Strippers' (E4, 2001) pinpoints the problem women face in trying to produce 'feminist' documentaries about the sex industry, and he makes a convincing case:

'Strippers', implies the narrator, isn't your average exploitative tits'n'ass TV, designed to titillate its male post-pub audience. 'Strippers', she goes on, has been made by 'an all-female team'. Well dip me in honey and throw me to the lesbians. How feminist is that?...What the 'all-female team' fails to realise is that the audience doesn't care what these women think or say. Just as the customers in the pubs where the strippers dance treat them like a fruit machine or a juke box – they pop 50p into a pint glass for a brief distraction – so the camera does the same. (McLean 2001)

The power of speech is illusory when sandwiched between the erotic appeal of lingering shots of gyrating bodies on late-night television, turning the women's assertion of empowerment and pride into the familiar power relations of voyeurism. Support for this assessment is found in the Broadcasting Standards Commission's audience research. Reacting to a clip showing a stripper dancing and sitting on a man's lap, taken from 'Friday Night Fever', a late-night programme about a group of women from Essex on a hen night shown on ITV, a third of the sample of viewers thought it 'degrading' (Millwood Hargrave 1999). Whatever the intent, viewers' responses are regulated by the embedded cultural codes of pornography (Kuhn 1982). To disrupt these codes and to transform people's existing attitudes to sex workers takes more than changing the sex of the person behind the camera. Generic assumptions about what and whom these programmes are *for* ties them into a long history of institutionalized reading practices for pornography in which sexualized images of women are coded for men's masturbatory pleasure. The devaluing of the women involved is also linked to a history of stigmatization of sex workers that is tied to the power relations of patriarchy. It is to this history that I now turn.

The discursive construction of sex workers in the contemporary media has its roots in nineteenth-century conceptions of gender and sexuality, in which women were defined as 'other' to men. Women's 'purity' provided the necessary restraint to control men's sexual desires. The incitement to loss of control, symbolized in the figure of the prostitute, brought with it fears of chaos and disorder. Women who transgressed the feminine ideal of sexual restraint were branded as deviant and immoral. Female virtue was defined against the figure of the 'fallen woman', whose class or race identity often served to accentuate her 'otherness'. The binary division between respectable and disreputable women was also a division based on a spatial boundary between women's place in the privacy of the home and the dangers of the public street. As well as being defined as a threat to the moral order, prostitutes were also perceived as carriers of venereal disease. Soldiers were regarded as the most at risk from infection thus potentially weakening their ability to defend the interests of the British Empire. This exacerbated the sense of threat that prostitutes posed to the health and safety of the nation and justified state intervention to regulate their activities. Feminist interventions calling for the abolition of sexual 'slavery' originated in campaigns against this policy of imprisoning infected prostitutes. This was reinforced during the suffrage movement in the early 1900s when campaigners were concerned that the existence of prostitutes would undermine the status of all women at a time when they were campaigning for full rights to citizenship.

In the second wave of feminist activism in the 1970s a split emerged between feminists who opposed prostitution as a form of male exploitation, and those who wanted it revalued as a form of work from which women can benefit. Where some emphasized the danger and coercion, for others it was a pleasure and a choice (McLaughlin 1991: 251–2). Although there is agreement between these opposing camps on the overall aim, that is, to reduce the harm caused by the industry, there are deep divisions on how this might best be achieved. These disagreements are also reflected in government responses, which vary considerably. Even within the European Union there are diverse policies in place that range from abolition, to regulation and even legalization (Kilvington et al. 2001). But since the 1980s, the weight of opinion amongst feminist activists has shifted from condemnation and campaigns that favoured increased regulation and abolition, to an acceptance of commercial sex as a legitimate industry which is potentially beneficial to women if they are given more control over how it is run. Key to this transition has been the redefinition of the people involved as 'sex workers'.

The term 'sex worker' was coined by sex workers themselves to redefine commercial sex, not as a social or psychological characteristic of a class of women, but as an income generating activity or form of employment for women and men. Similarly, the use of the term 'sex industry' was aimed at inclusion of exotic dancers, masseurs, telephone sex operators, receptionists (maids) and a whole host of people (including men) who sell sex. (Rickard 2001: 112)

One important effect of this redefinition is that sex workers now have a voice to fight for their own rights rather than being subject to philanthropy. They have become involved in existing feminist organizations and set up their own unions, such as Call Off Your Old Tired Ethics (COYOTE) and the International Union for Sex Workers (IUSW). Amongst their demands in setting the agenda for reform are calls for an end to stereotypical portrayals in the media through recognition of the diversity amongst sex workers and their clients. These calls for positive representation are part of a more general campaign for legitimization. In particular, they question that women should always be perceived as passive victims rather than women who make choices to maximize their opportunities for economic security. They also want recognition that sex workers can actively enjoy their work. Negative portrayals are seen as the result of media producers projecting their own feelings about sex being dirty and seedy on to the situation. The resulting stigma provokes and permits violence against sex workers (Mistress L. 2001: 148–50). It also affects all women by contributing to the psychology of 'shame' that constrains their sexual freedom and prevents women having control over their own sexuality. In seeking to promote pride where once there was shame, the IUSW is using tactics developed by gay-rights activists. They are calling for decriminalization, campaigning against negative media portrayals and organizing celebratory carnivals to turn the secrecy of shame into the public display of pride (IUSW 2001: 151–3).

The problems posed by calls for positive representation are in many respects identical to those faced more generally by campaigners seeking to influence the representation of stigmatized social groups. One is the need to recognize diversity within the represented group so that a uniform negative stereotype isn't simply replaced by a uniform positive stereotype that is just as 'unreal'. This implies an acceptance of difficult and potentially damaging portrayals amongst the mix. Concern has been expressed over the incentive sex workers have to portray a falsely positive image of their work in order to encourage more custom. In portraying sex work as an attractive career option, ignorance of the more negative aspects of the job made it easier for women to make their debut selling sex. In effect, it lowers the entry barrier (Skibre 2001). It should instead be recognized that some aspects of the job are positive while others are negative, and that these will vary over time, just as with most jobs (Rickard 2001: 128; Liepe-Levinson 2002). Ambivalence towards the job they do is a recurring feature of sex workers' own writing about their experiences (Johnson

2002). This ambivalence needs to be recognized as existing within individuals rather than being distributed across a class hierarchy in which high-class escorts are glamourized while street workers are portrayed as helpless victims.

In the last few years, attention has turned to the global dimension of the sex industry and the flows of people and commodities that thrive on variations in national regulations and economic inequalities. The creation of an expanding European Union, the post-communist economic liberalization of Eastern Europe and the effects of the globalization of capital on the growing inequalities in the world economy have encouraged the movement of economic migrants into Western Europe with high hopes of improving their life chances. Yet impoverished young women keen to escape the constraints of their traditional role, enticed to migrate by the global image of the West as a utopia of individual freedom and material wealth that they see on commercial television and in magazines, find that they are largely excluded from sharing these benefits when they arrive as immigrants at the bottom of a casualized labour market (Mai 2004). This makes sex work one of the few options available.

The question of migrant women's vulnerability to sexual exploitation has therefore become part of a much wider political debate about controls over immigrant labour, with one side emphasizing border controls and the other the regulation of labour markets. Growing sensitivity to immigration has also been fuelled by a series of tabloid campaigns over asylum seekers and fears of international terrorism. The campaigns for strong border controls draw on pollution taboos, signalling the threat to the sexual health of the nation from foreigners, with even liberal newspapers running headlines reporting that 'Tories plan HIV tests for migrants' (Guardian, 15 February 2005) and 'Migrant women forced into cheap sex trade' (Guardian, 11 February 2005) alongside a picture and caption saying 'Street prostitution…the head of the vice squad says there is now a huge demand for unprotected sex.' A consultant doctor who challenged the accuracy of this report and the link made between foreign sex workers and disease is relegated to the final paragraph. The case for better regulation, on the other hand, to protect vulnerable, casualized migrant workers, became a political issue after the death of a group of twenty Chinese cockle-pickers in Morecambe Bay in 2004. The illegality of working without a permit undermines attempts to regulate this workforce for the benefit of the people involved. This leaves them prey to exploitation by organized crime, on the one hand, and criminalization by the authorities, on the other. Police raids on Soho in London in 2002 have been criticized as a politically driven attempt to increase the rate of deportation of illegal immigrants. Some of the women arrested were in fact asylum seekers with cases still pending, who turned to prostitution because they had no other source of income (Adams 2003: 136).

The failure to distinguish between those who have been forced into the trade and women working for themselves, has lead to all immigrant sex workers being labelled as victims of trafficking and liable to deportation.

Feminist organizations and academics campaigning on behalf of these women have been accused of legitimating such repressive responses from the state by stereotyping these women as victims of sexual exploitation rather than seeing them as women finding a way to earn money for themselves in a situation with few options. Jo Doezema (2001) has warned against the danger of 'Orientalism' in the interventions made by First World feminists to 'save' women from the poor countries of the world from exploitation. She argues that these interventions deny these women's right to self-representation, and produce them as helpless; their only hope is to be rescued by others in true colonial fashion, bringing the feminist values of a more civilized Western culture to bear on their situation (2001: 28). This works, she argues, to maintain the superiority of the 'saving western body' while the most likely outcome of legislation to protect women against trafficking (subsequently introduced in 2002 as part of the Nationality, Immigration and Asylum Bill) would be to restrict the freedom of movement of the women themselves (2001: 24–9). This view has been criticized in turn for colluding with the worst excesses of capitalist exploitation.

These debates over sex work and the trafficking of women are taken up in the following section in an analysis of television documentaries and drama from the late 1990s onwards. The analysis of these programmes will seek to foreground the ways that changing feminist perspectives on the representation of sex work, usually unmarked as such, have been incorporated into the discursive forms of these programmes. It also considers how what can or cannot be said is influenced by the embedded assumptions in the genre conventions deployed, and, in particular, the extent to which news conventions determine the presentational style and discursive structuring of current affairs documentaries. Although news stories also provide the background for the political thriller 'Sex Traffic', as a drama it has more freedom to develop alternative perspectives to the ideological mainstream, especially in the way that it avoids sensationalizing the trafficked women themselves.

CURRENT AFFAIRS DOCUMENTARY AND POLITICAL DEBATE

There are fears that the competitive pressures on television companies to retain audience share has led to a gradual decline of the kind of current affairs documentary that makes a genuine contribution to political debate in the public sphere. These changes have been termed 'tabloidization' in a comparison to the differences found between 'quality' and 'tabloid' newspapers. Tabloidization in newspapers is characterized by an increasing focus on personalities, sports, fashion, culture and consumer reporting over national and international politics. Even in quality newspapers there has been 'a greater stress on the personal and the private at the expense of the public and the structural' (McLachlan and Golding 2000: 35) in an attempt to attract a new readership, especially women and young people for whom reporting on political elites has had little perceived 'existential utility' (Sparks and Tulloch 2000: 32–5). There are also differences in the style of address with more concrete language, humour and melodramatic extremes replacing abstract, sober and measured reporting. Several writers in the defence of public service television have identified, and often regretted, the same trends in television as it has become more market-oriented (Langer 1998; Dovey 2000; Sparks and Tulloch 2000; Winston 2000). Jon Dovey (2000), for example, is suspicious that what he terms 'first person narrative' and 'true life melodrama', which are grounded in subjective experience, leave the underlying social and economic reasons for suffering and powerlessness unexamined and responsibility for change devolved to the 'empowered' individual.

These concerns are, however, entangled in questions of taste that have class and gender implications. The forms of rhetoric valued in 'serious' broadcast journalism with their emphasis on a detached impartiality, the balanced reporting of 'expert' opinion and the use of depersonalized, disembodied voiceover narration that positions the viewer in relation to the people and events portrayed have been criticized for their construction of an elite and masculine perspective masquerading as 'objectivity'. Myra McDonald (2000), however, cautions against drawing too rigid a dichotomy between the kind of analytic journalism that contributes to the public sphere and the entertainment values of popular culture because it works to reinforce a gendered hierarchy of values (mind/body, rational/emotional, public/private, fact/fiction). She makes a case for the use of personal testimonies to enhance our political understanding of an issue rather than to reinforce existing prejudice, and to mobilize affective involvement rather than simply satisfying our voyeuristic curiosity (McDonald 2000: 254). This coincides with the emphasis sex workers themselves place on self-representation to overcome the 'othering' effects of media discourse. Even so, she argues, personal testimony cannot substitute for meticulous research that draws on a variety of forms of evidence that go beyond the personal. I will be drawing on this evaluative framework to compare the examples discussed below.

The first is 'The Sex Trade' (1998), in the long-running BBC current affairs series 'The Money Programme' (BBC, 1966–). The second is 'Vice: The Sex

'Trade', a more populist, short run, current affairs series on the UK's mainstream commercial network channel, ITV. The comparison between these two examples will be used to consider whether the demands made by feminist activists and sex workers, for the recognition of diversity, ambivalence and self-representation, are being met by current affairs programmes. Do they work to encourage empathy with the women portrayed or does the generic imperative in current affairs to draw clear boundaries between the 'normal' and the 'deviant' work against this ideal? Moreover, do the rhetorical differences between 'quality' and 'tabloid' journalism affect the contribution each programme makes to political debate on matters of public importance arising from the sex industry?

'The Money Programme' is a current affairs documentary series that has been on BBC 2 for over thirty years. It has a journalistic interest in the speed of getting stories onto the screen, and it claims to be providing straightforward facts in order to contribute to the national debate on issues of concern. The 'long and distinguished history' of the series, as well as the reputation and prestige of the BBC as an organization, legitimates their claim to be uncovering the truth (BBCi 2001). 'The Sex Trade' demonstrates its impartiality by presenting a range of issues and perspectives without being tendentious. It recognizes a diversity of viewpoints, including those of the sex workers involved. It conveys the complexity of the issues posed by the expansion of the industry, largely without falling into predictable narrative patterns of victims and villains. It has carefully researched the scope and structure of the industry, and the range of political approaches taken to it. It contributes to public debate by setting out alternative perspectives. The (female) voice-over begins by signalling this range, while two sex workers conclude it with contrasting views on the question 'Would you recommend it as a job?' This is a well-researched contribution to the debate.

The first part of 'The Money Programme' looks at the sector as a story of business success, detailing the expansion of sexual services in the UK, especially their expansion into 'respectable' city centre and suburban areas. Here the language and agenda match those of the International Union of Sex Workers: 'It's just a job. Nothing more, nothing less. I work to support my family', says one street worker interviewed by the programme. It doesn't glamourize or demonize either the women or the job. The testimony of the sex workers helps to undermine any overgeneralized assumptions about the women who work in the industry and their motivations, while offering a map of its hierarchical structure. We encounter escort services in the West End of London that help middle-class girls pay for their education, and women with few other viable job options working to pay for a drug habit in the streets of Manchester. Moving beyond Britain we are told of the plight of exploited East European economic migrants in Western Europe in contrast to contented women working in legal brothels in Germany.

A diverse range of professionals also offer evidence to provide a wider context for understanding these experiences in economic and political terms, rather than offering moral approval or condemnation of the lives these women lead. Further statistical research evidence was commissioned by the programme to support their analysis in a context where facts are thin on the ground. We learn about how businesses make money, their choice of location, their marketing strategies, their customer base, the career opportunities and working conditions for staff, the regulatory environment and how to stay within the law. An interview with a rich entrepreneur explains how he made the business work. If the programme had finished here it would have resembled a guide to 'how to run a successful sex business', with some caution about the effects it might have on women caught up in the business at street level. It exemplifies the now legitimate view that for respectable, middle-class people the industry is an acceptable way to earn money. It then links the issues raised by all these forms of evidence to the policy initiatives being taken in Europe. It lays out the policy options without any prior assumption that the British way is best. Indeed, it rather suggests that the UK is failing to address the issues at all and that this programme's function is to draw their attention to them, thereby fulfilling its public service role.

There is, however, a caveat to my offering this documentary as exemplary investigative journalism, and this is the othering process that affects its approach to the 'trafficking of women'. The programme includes an investigation of the suffering caused by 'organized gangs tempted by easy profits', who are accused of the 'trafficking of women' into 'sexual slavery'. This became a news item in the wake of a United Nations report in 1998, followed by further policy initiatives in the European Union. It is significant that where the programme moves most clearly from a business to a news agenda, the generic imperative to draw boundaries between the 'normal' and the 'deviant' comes to the fore. This is a live political issue that the programme views from a dominant ideological perspective. It draws on the discursive conventions of news narratives, which, as previously discussed, associate prostitutes with death, disease, drugs and crime. They define prostitutes as victims in need of salvation and as a risk to social order who need to be controlled. They accentuate their difference from other women (McLaughlin 1991). The language expresses moral outrage and comparisons are drawn with the international drugs trade. In this section, expansion of trade is a sign of a lack of control over criminal activity, with the programme's role being to set out the options for political intervention.

Only when we move to consider foreign involvement is the criminality of
the business emphasized. Up to that point, the approach was to show how
loopholes in the law enabled legitimate business. Concern over the sexual
exploitation of women from poor countries becomes entangled in the politics
of immigration, and in the process provides the kind of disempowering,
Orientalist representations of the foreign men and women involved that
are criticized by Doezema (2001). In contrast to the first section of the
documentary, where everyone is treated with respect, here we are shown men
covering their faces in shame as police raid a London massage parlour. The
commentary tells us the owner is 'Maltese Charlie', who specializes in providing
under-age Thai girls. The voice-over tells us he was imprisoned, while some of
the girls were deported as illegal immigrants, but ten days later it is business
as usual at the massage parlour. It is implied that there is an unstoppable flood
of potential immigrants to replace the ones lost, an implication that feeds
into contemporary xenophobic discourses about immigration – the concern
to protect British borders from invasion by 'foreign hordes'. Nor are there any
direct interviews with any of the traffickers or the women being trafficked, so all
the information is provided in the third person. 'These women' are positioned
as voiceless victims and the 'extremely resourceful, clever gangs who make lots
of money' are faceless and powerful criminals whose desire to make money is
no longer a justification in itself as it was in the earlier, British section of the
documentary.

This example reveals, in my view, that the boundaries dividing the sexually
'respectable' from the 'disreputable' have been reset. No longer is the sexual
respectability of the British structured by a division between the private and
the public, between the home and the street, between the bourgeoisie and
the working woman. Instead, national borders are the spatial markers. It is
the ethnic others from whom we must be protected, or who are subject to
our philanthropic zeal. The fraught political question of maintaining British
national identity in the face of European integration and of protecting British
business from the effects of global markets is tied up here with issues of sexual
regulation. Feminist perspectives are mobilized to justify the need to put a
stop to the trade, with women from organizations like the Coalition against
the Trafficking of Women having achieved public visibility and influence over
the political agenda of the European Commission and the UN. The kind of
arguments put by Jo Doezema (2001), which question the effects of these well-
intentioned interventions, lack this kind of mainstream legitimacy.

The normalizing effect of this discourse, returning us to the historical link
between prostitution, deviance and crime, can be seen very clearly in an episode

of another, more populist, current affairs series broadcast on the UK's main commercial channel, 'Vice: The Sex Trade' (ITV, 1998, repeated in 2001). As in 'The Money Programme', critical perspectives were reserved for those foreign 'others' who invade national boundaries. This programme, entitled 'The New Slave Trade', positions prostitution within a discourse of scandal and deviance. It shares a vocabulary with anti-immigration rhetoric, with its emphasis on an uncontrollable increase in numbers: 'seventy per cent of off-street sex workers are not British'. The women from East Europe who are the focus of the investigation are helpless victims, at the mercy of the villains who are identified as 'the Red Mafia', a more vivid label for the Eastern European criminal gangs also referred to in 'The Money Programme'. The melodramatic, tabloid style of this programme allows for no ambivalence: this is corruption of innocence by evil. The women, we are told, are dehumanized by their suffering. Sensationalist language invites moral outrage, promising at the outset to 'expose the new slavery at the heart of Britain's sex trade', a rhetorical flourish often repeated with slight variations as the hook leading into each advertising break.

Sensationalism is the product of a fascination with stories of sexual trans-gression, in which the moral righteousness of exposing wrongdoing is entwined with an often unacknowledged pleasure of vicarious participation. The sensationalism is enhanced by lurid details in the voice-over of the women being stripped, gang-raped and imprisoned, so that we can imagine the degradation and humiliation of the scene. Undercover, secret reporting adds to this voyeuristic frisson, with grainy hand-held shots secretly capturing the women at work in dark, depressing rooms, which, we are told, they are seldom allowed to leave. None of these women would have been asked by the film-makers for their 'informed consent' to being shown in these humiliating circumstances, often naked but ignorant of the fact they were being filmed. None could complain, knowing that their position as illegal immigrants undermines their ability to do so. A British woman academic speaking for the International Organisation for Migration explains the women's plight on their behalf. The Orientalist relation this sets up is slightly offset by several interviews with women sex workers, but these are with a high-class escort service set up in Russia that flies young, educated, beautiful women to Western Europe for up to several nights with rich businessmen. It is not these women who are the problem the programme is exposing, however, It is the impoverished 'hordes of women' who have 'flooded' the massage parlours of London. It is these women who are positioned as the disempowered 'other' of our voyeuristic gaze.

Both of these programmes are engaged in normalization through the demarcation of deviance in ways that are generically driven. The same discursive boundaries dividing the normal from the deviant operate across quality and tabloid modes of address. This raises some doubt, in my view, about the stark difference that is often perceived in their relative contribution to public debate. It also shows that, in comparison with an analysis of the US media at the beginning of the 1990s (McLaughlin 1991), discourses about prostitution have changed substantially in response to the growing legitimization of the sex industry in advanced Western economies. It is one effect of the way that enterprise culture and consumerism have become hegemonic during the 1990s, a development that has influenced feminist as well as mainstream political norms. The boundary between respectable and disreputable women is still based on class differences, now, however, globally defined. Women's respectability no longer requires them to be sexually pure as long as they are rich and successful. It is the poverty and therefore the powerlessness of the foreign prostitutes that exposes them to the 'othering' process produced by news 'scandals'. In a context of global economic inequality, our ability to empathize takes on an ethnic and nationalist inflection.

SEX TRAFFIC: A GLOBAL DRAMA

Current affairs documentaries are a component in the public service output of UK television addressed to a national audience, an address that is likely to encourage the kind of boundary marking between the indigenous and the foreign that has been identified in the previous section. 'Sex Traffic' (Channel 4/Granada/Big Motion Pictures, 2004) on the other hand, a four-hour drama in two parts, relied on co-production finance between Channel 4 and the Canadian Broadcasting Company to make a programme that was calculated to have international appeal; the main characters and settings are drawn from across the globe. It invites us to share the perspective of two trafficked women from Moldova, Elena and Vara, who are taken to the UK by East European middlemen, at first voluntarily and then forcibly, via Serbia, Bosnia, Romania, Albania and Italy. In the same way as Michael Winterbottom's *In This World* (2002), a drama-documentary about Afghani illegal migrants, this strategy shifts the point of view away from a British perspective intent on defending national borders against invasion, to encouraging instead our empathy with the desperate circumstances of the individuals involved. This undermines any easy division here between 'us and them' in relation to the national identity of sex workers.

Its fictional form also overcomes the problems of access faced by documentary makers when investigating illegal activities, who often have to rely on police surveillance for their information and film footage. A carefully crafted visual script that controls the perspective from which the women's sexual exploitation is viewed replaces the voyeuristic aesthetics produced by hidden cameras. The focus is on the physical and emotional violence to which they are subjected by their capturers, rather than sex scenes with paying customers, thereby minimizing the promotion of pleasurable voyeurism. Our prior engagement with the women as protagonists aligns us with their suffering but also with their residual power to act as narrative agents rather than as powerless victims. They retain narrative agency at several key turning points in the drama, despite being subject to extreme violence and dependent on help from charitable organizations working to ameliorate the worst effects of the trade.

The difference between the two sisters helps to avoid any melodramatic divisions between vice and virtue, based on traditional stereotypes of women's moral superiority and sexual purity. The traffickers are driven by making money, but so is Vara; it was she who was first enticed by glossy magazine images of life in the West, and it is the material rewards of sex work, her flat and her fashionable clothes and hairstyle, that make her want to continue in that life. But neither are we encouraged to condemn her for her decision, to label her as the criminal 'other', because we have seen how she was lured into this 'choice'. Instead, it invites us to consider the individual stories that lie behind sensationalist headlines. Vara is not a 'positive image' designed to counteract the stigmatization of sex workers; instead we see her actions as morally ambivalent, driven by greed as well as by circumstances.

The pervasive individualism in the way the issues are portrayed is put in context by the parallel plot involving the Kernwell Corporation, a US security corporation supplying peace-keeping services in Bosnia and elsewhere, which is revealed as colluding with trafficking. The executives of this organization are shown to be as ruthlessly driven by the profit motive as the brutalized traffickers, thereby suggesting that it is the effects of a poorly regulated global market that allows free rein to greed.

This drama is able to eschew the stark moral choices and stereotypical characters of melodrama because it is told in the form of a political thriller, whose narrative conventions allow for the exploration of ambivalent and morally complex political situations. As a genre the political thriller takes news stories and contemporary political conflicts, often, as here, signalled within the diegesis through the use of newspaper and television headlines, and explores them in relation to individual characters as they get caught up in events. It is a genre with a history of ideological challenge to the power of the nation-state and its collusion with multinational corporations. The revelation of hypocrisy, the corruption that lies beneath the respectable veneer of the powerful, is a key generic theme, thereby disrupting any clear demarcation between the law and criminality (Elliot, Murdoch and Schlesinger 1983). The feminization of this genre on television, first seen in the BBC anti-nuclear drama 'Edge of Darkness' in 1985, enables a double critique in which the patriarchal values of global capitalism are as central to the analysis as the suspicion of state and corporate power.

This suspicion intensifies the sense of threat that engages our emotions, in that it removes the possibility of security being restored through 'official' forms of law enforcement. Thus 'Sex Traffic' is able to address the complexities of the issues raised by trafficking without sacrificing its appeal as highly engaging entertainment. Affective involvement enables rather than obscures an understanding of this complexity, because it secures the audience's interest across four hours of analysis in contrast to the 'sound-bite' format of news that inevitably simplifies and falsifies, and which works against any real engagement with the issues or people involved. This is a drama that challenges the gendered hierarchy of taste that values the rational, the objective and the factual over the emotional, the subjective and the fictional in debates over television as a public sphere. Indeed, its status as 'quality' television has been recognized by two BAFTA awards, for best drama serial and best actress (Anamaria Marinca), and by two awards from the Royal Television Society.

Engagement with the personal lives of individuals in fictional form does not inevitably obscure the economic and political structures within which these stories are played out; rather, it is in the metadiscursive narrative structure that these are conveyed. The safety of home and tradition are initially set against the risks of migration and modernity, with trusting innocence turning to cynical experience. As they travel across Eastern Europe the women's innocence and hope is stripped away, their warm clothing replaced by the skimpy attire of the sex worker. The drama ends with Elena returning to Moldova to be reunited with her mother and son. The warm glow of the setting sun replaces the stark cold blue/grey of the European winter that has characterized the rest of their journey. But the final scene undermines the sentimentality of this happy ending, when we are shown the cycle beginning again as a trafficker targets another young woman.

This trajectory is mirrored in the US where, at the beginning, the Kernwell Corporation is embodied in the warm tones of the plush interior of the family home of its chief executive. This idealized family life unravels as the corporation's self-seeking corruption is gradually exposed to his wife and son via information from the Internet and the news media. Their estrangement and the break up of their family home are marked by a final meeting in a cold, grey and white snow-covered car park. 'You'll lose everything' says his wife referring to the marriage break up. 'No we won't, we never do, we always win', he replies, thus affirming not only his primary loyalties but also the power of the capitalist system to survive a localized scandal. The profit motive is marked as the cause of cynical exploitation, overriding family bonds.

The drama offers a humanist message that only individual acts of kindness can function as a bulwark against the dehumanizing brutality of the market. But it also shows that these cannot change the structural inequalities that fuel this trade. In this respect, the drama is unusually reflexive in recognizing the limitations of its own textual politics, in acknowledging the way that the focus on individuals is necessarily limited in its perspective. It also questions the rhetoric of individual 'choice' for sex workers. In a speech made to an international conference on trafficking and sexual exploitation we are told, 'to say that all trafficked women are victims is I'm afraid naïve and ignorant and ignores the real truth, that many of the women may be better described as economic migrants eager to embrace the realities of life in the West. The real truth is that for some prostitution is a choice.'

The truth of this statement, however, is set against the brutal treatment of the women we have already seen, who did indeed 'choose' to leave their homes in search of a better life but who did not choose to be imprisoned, beaten and raped. Sympathy with this perspective is further undercut by the revelation that the seemingly concerned Kernwell executive giving this speech is himself secretly involved in the trade.

It is significant that 'Sex Traffic' does not define the traffic in women as being a matter of sexual exploitation specific to their position as powerless women. The moral issue is no longer presented as a puritan imperative to save 'fallen women' who must be helped back to respectability by a morally superior middle-class philanthropist in the tradition established by popular melodrama. Instead, this is a drama about human rights but with a clear-sighted view of the limitations to humanitarian responses. It locates itself in a political context where the International Labour Movement of the UN seeks to protect trafficked women as part of a wider campaign to prevent the forced or 'super exploited' migrant workers that a deregulated labour market allows and encourages (Raymond 2004). This international attempt at governance includes women in a larger category of the 'exploitable poor', thus incorporating the feminist agenda on this issue into a global class politics in the face of structural inequalities.

CONCLUSION

To return, then, to the debates introduced at the beginning of this chapter, these examples demonstrate that not all programmes about the sex industry are inevitably exploitative and voyeuristic, although some certainly are. In 'docu-porn', a spurious appeal to feminist legitimacy is undermined by the restricting codes of their limited erotic vocabulary, and the institutionalized relations of consumption that are characteristic of this type of sex industry documentary. Female authorship is no guarantee that these reading practices will be destabilized, nor that the inclusion of interviews will 'empower' the women portrayed. Feminist interventions into the politics of sex work and its representation have, however, had a marked influence on current affairs reporting on the industry. These have enabled new ways of understanding and relating to the issues and to the women involved. The reaction against the anti-porn feminism of the 1970s and 1980s has enabled a new public discourse of respect to emerge for women who do well in the business. The boundary between 'us' and 'them' is now more often a marker of national and ethnic difference in which migrant sex workers are associated with criminality and disease.

It is in drama that a more complex range of perspectives on the trafficking of women, within an analysis of the broader political and economic context, has been most fully realized. 'Sex Traffic' invites our empathy with women caught up in the trade, but also with other characters, who function as metonyms for a well-researched range of representative points of view. Feminist activists work alongside liberal do-gooders and corporate charities to stem the 'tide of human misery' that trafficking engenders. These are all positioned within a tight narrative structure, which functions as a metadiscursive critique of global capitalism. It is a powerful challenge to the commonly held hierarchy of values in debates over public service broadcasting that it is in a fictional, subjective and emotionally intense aesthetic form that we find the most convincing analysis of the political economy of trafficking. Moreover, it draws feminist perspectives into this analysis in recognition that the politics of capitalism and patriarchy cannot be disentangled.

NOTES

1.   This essay includes revised material from Arthurs (2004).

BIBLIOGRAPHY

Adams, N. (2003), 'Anti-trafficking Legislation: Protection or Deportation?', *Feminist Review* 73: 135–9.

Arthurs, J. (2004), *Television and Sexuality: Regulation and the Politics of Taste*, Maidenhead: Open University Press.

BBCi (2001), 'Money Programme', available online at http://news.bbc.co.uk (accessed 10 April 2001).

Doezema, J. (2001), 'Ouch! Western Feminists' Wounded Attachment to the Third World Prostitute', *Feminist Review*, 67,1: 16–29.

Dovey, J. (2000), *Freakshow: First Person Media and Factual Television*, London: Pluto Press.

Elliot, P., Murdoch, G. and Schlesinger, P. (1983), *Televising 'Terrorism': Political Violence in Popular Culture*, London: Comedia.

International Union of Sex Workers (2001), 'Sex Work Reassessed', *Feminist Review* 67,1: 151–3.

Johnson, M. L. (2002), *Jane Sexes It Up: True Confessions of Feminist Desire*, New York: Four Walls Eight Windows.

Kilvington, J., Day, S. and Ward, H. (2001), 'Prostitution Policy in Europe: A Time of Change', *Feminist Review*, 67,1: 78–93.

Kuhn, A. (1982), *Women's Pictures: Feminism and Cinema*, London: Routledge & Kegan Paul.

Langer, J. (1998), *Tabloid Television: Popular Journalism and the Other News*, London: Routledge.

Liepe-Levinson, K. (2002), *Strip Show*, London: Routledge.

Macdonald, M. (2000), 'Rethinking Personalisation in Current Affairs Journalism', in C. Sparks and J. Tulloch (eds), *Tabloid Tales: Global Debates Over Media Standards*, Lanham: Rowman and Littlefield.

McLachlan, S. and Golding, P. (2000), 'Tabloidisation in the British Press: A Quantitative Investigation into Changes in British Newspapers, 1952–1997', in C. Sparks and J. Tulloch (eds), *Tabloid Tales: Global Debates Over Media Standards*, Lanham: Rowman and Littlefield.

McLaughlin, L. (1991), 'Discourses of Prostitution/Discourses of Sexuality', *Critical Studies in Mass Communication*, 16, 3: 249–72.

McLean, G. (2001), 'We've Seen it All Before', *Guardian* (G2 Supplement), 17 April.

Mai, N. (2004), '"Looking for a More Modern Life…": The Role of Italian Television in the Albanian Migration to Italy', *Westminster Papers in Communication and Culture*, University of Westminster, London, 1,1: 3–22.

Millwood Hargrave, A. (1999), *Sex and Sensibility*, London: Broadcasting Standards Commission, available online at www.bsc.org (accessed 7 January 2000).

Mistress L. (2001), 'A Faustian Bargain: Speaking Out Against the Media', *Feminist Review*, 67,1: 145–50.

Raymond, J. (2004), *Guide to the New UN Trafficking Protocol*, Coalition Against Trafficking of Women, available online at http://catwinternational.org (accessed 12 August 2004).

Richardson, C. (1995), 'TVOD: The Never Bending Story', in P. Burston and C. Richardson, *A Queer Romance*, London: Routledge.

Rickard, W. (2001), '"Been there, seen it, done it, I've got the T-shirt": British Sex Workers Reflect on Jobs, Hopes, the Future and Retirement', *Feminist Review*, 67,1: 111–32.

Root, J. (1984), *Pictures of Women: Sexuality*, London: Pandora/C4.

Skibre, M. L. (2001), 'Norwegian Massage Parlours', *Feminist Review*, 67, I: 67–73.

Sparks, C. and Tulloch, J. (eds) (2000), *Tabloid Tales: Global Debates Over Media Standards*, Lanham: Rowman and Littlefield.

Vance, C. (ed.) (1992), *Pleasure and Danger: Exploring Female Sexuality*, London: Pandora.

Winston, B. (2000), *Lies, Damn Lies and Documentaries*, London: BFI.

Part III
Negotiating and Resisting Feminisms

Discipline and Pleasure: The Uneasy Relationship Between Feminism and the Beauty Industry

Paula Black

> Critics with a political understanding of beauty often condemn the market, but they do not live outside it.
>
> Peiss, *Hope in a Jar*

I have spent several years researching women's, and more recently men's, use of beauty salons and their relationship to the beauty industry more generally (Black 2004). This interest has been maintained for two reasons. First, beauty salons and the wider beauty industry are vast and expanding. In 2002, Mintel valued the UK beauty and spa business at £1.3 billion (Mintel 2002). In 2002 in the UK, there were almost 6.4 million users of beauty salons, which represented a 17 per cent increase on the previous year; this in turn followed increases in the years prior to that (Guild News 2002). This figure includes approximately 7 million male clients, and again, men form a growing market (Guild News 2001). In fact, men have been deliberately targeted in advertising, marketing and in the press as a relatively untapped source of revenue. The increase in the numbers of clients is mirrored by a 22 per cent growth in the number of businesses in the UK beauty sector between 2001 and 2002 (Guild News 2002). This means that the industry is an important site of employment for women. It is also an increasingly popular cultural practice, and one with which women, and some men, engage on a day-to-day basis. Second, the world of the beauty salon can serve as a microcosm within which to investigate wider social relations such as issues of class, gender, ethnicity, sexuality, embodiment, leisure activities and so on. In fact, I have developed a belief that most of human life may be observed directly or indirectly in the beauty salon.

The research upon which I base my arguments has involved interviews with eighteen teachers of beauty therapy, salon owners and beauty therapists in a large Northern English city, and in a smaller city in the English Midlands. In addition, twenty-three in-depth interviews were conducted with salon clients. These were recruited from the two cities across a range of different salon types. I have also interviewed key officials in professional organizations, studied trade publications and, in the name of research, received treatments in numerous different salons around the world. Not least, I have spent much time observing the work of salons, sometimes participating in a small way in the day-to-day routines within these spaces. I am happy to call myself a feminist, and set out with an avowedly feminist agenda, which entailed a deeply held suspicion of beauty salons and what they represent. During the course of the research I have held on to my criticism of what often drives women into beauty salons. However, my feminism has been modified to accommodate an understanding of the pleasurable aspects of the beauty industry, whilst maintaining a politically motivated rejection of the disciplinary practices involved. Feminist ethnography does entail a modification of pre-existing theory to take into account the empirical data generated from engaging with the lives of women (Skeggs 1995). I have done this to the extent that my preconceptions of the role of the beauty salon have been modified, but I do not claim to give an unmediated voice to the women in my study. Rather, I have interpreted their claims within a feminist sociological framework (Harding 1991). In this chapter, I outline how feminist work on the beauty industry has grappled with similar dilemmas. I then go on to discuss my research with women clients of beauty salons, and show how their understandings of their own body practices can be understood in relation to feminism.

PRISON OR PLAYTIME?

> The debate over cosmetics today veers noisily between the poles of victimization and self-invention, between the prison of beauty and the play of make-up.
>
> Peiss, *Hope in a Jar*

The beauty business today is thoroughly commodified, and women entrepreneurs were originally at its forefront. Some in the industry, such as Madam C. J. Walker, who became the first woman self-made millionaire in the USA (Peiss 1998), made fortunes from their entrepreneurship. This was important during a period in which employment opportunities for black women in particular were limited, and employment in the beauty industry offered a preferable alternative to domestic labour or other physically demanding and poorly paid occupations (Boyd 1996). Despite the commercialization and concentration of the beauty industry today, the sector remains an important source of female self-employment worldwide. Multinational conglomerates may now control a large sector of the industry, but women entrepreneurs and ordinary working women are still involved in the day-to-day delivery of services. It is important to bear in mind that the pattern of employment and commercial endeavours we see today are the product of a fragmented and complex history in which women have been the driving force in providing services, and in consuming them. This makes the industry doubly important for feminism to engage with.

Although a critique of cruder ideas concerning the beauty industry, particularly those based on Naomi Wolf's *The Beauty Myth* (1990), is now well documented it is worth briefly reminding ourselves of the basis of her arguments, and the criticisms that can be made. This is useful precisely because of the persuasiveness of her work, both among the popular press and in undergraduate work. In my own experience of teaching in the area of gender, the body and the beauty industry, I have found it is often difficult to shake students' attachment to the simplistic reasoning of *The Beauty Myth*, despite my attempts to do so.

Wolf (1990) describes how eating disorders, the appearance of women in the workplace and reproduction have become subject to the 'beauty myth'. This system of beauty has arisen as a part of a wider backlash against the social, economic and political advances made by women. Wolf dates the beginning of the contemporary Beauty Myth to the mid nineteenth century, and contends that 'The beauty myth is always actually prescribing behaviour and not appearance' (1990: 14). With the advent of industrialization, men went to work in productive units outside of the home, and the role of the 'homemaker' was invented for women, who were now confined to this domestic sphere. As the middle classes have expanded, the role of middle-class women has been constrained by social expectations as much as by material factors. Women became confined to the domestic sphere as mothers, homemakers and importantly as consumers, and the Beauty Myth emerged amongst a number of developments designed to enforce this control. The social mores around gender roles modified over the nineteenth and twentieth centuries, but post-war femininity was remodelled upon these earlier beliefs.

The picture painted by Wolf of the North American context is one of a backlash against feminism and the gains made by women in the public sphere. For example, as the influence on the women's press enjoyed by household product advertisers has declined, the influence of skin care and diet companies has dramatically increased. As feminism promoted the liberation of female sexuality, 'beauty pornography' (1990: 11) has commodified women's sexuality and linked it to beauty in the mainstream media. As health has become politicized around gender issues, cosmetic surgery has boomed as a specialism. And importantly, as feminism argued for women's rights over their own bodies, most notably in reproduction, eating disorders have vastly increased, and the average weight of fashion models has plummeted. Despite seeing the beauty system as all pervasive and damaging for women, Wolf does acknowledge the fact that often women desire to conform to this ideal. In this view, then, the role of the beauty industry is negative, even to the point of convincing women to become complicit in their own 'torture'.

Wolf's work has been important, as it has provoked debate and was successful in linking together women's economic, political and social position in contemporary society with topics as wide-ranging as eating disorders, cosmetic surgery, appearance in the workplace and the diet industry. However, I have several reservations about her view of the beauty industry and women's relationship to it. In the history she paints, and throughout her arguments, there is a clear focus upon middle-class women. Her description of the industrialization process ignores the fact that working-class women were drawn into work in factories, mills and middle-class homes. In the UK and the USA, working-class white and black women worked hard in industry and slaved in the homes of their middle- and upper-class employers. This view of the working world for a proportion of women sits uneasily with Wolf's view of the middle-class cult of domesticity and fragility that formed the basis of the Beauty Myth. Questions of 'race' are similarly underplayed; who was actually performing all the (domestic) labour that enabled the nineteenth-century woman to engage in her needlepoint? Bhavnani (1997) points out that the hard physical labour of working-class white and black women was crucial in allowing middle-class women the leisure and 'delicacy' inherent in this feminine ideal. Wolf fails to take into account class differences in women's relationship to the beauty industry, a serious failing given that my own and other research shows a complex set of practices and discourses at work which position women very differently in relation to femininity as a result of structural inequalities beyond gender (Skeggs 1997; Craig 2002; Black 2004).

Although Wolf denies the fact that her arguments require a conspiracy in order to operate ('this does not require a conspiracy; merely an atmosphere' [1990: 18]), her writing does hint at a type of conspiracy within patriarchy which produces the effects she eloquently describes. This is partially because she fails to engage with underlying questions of women's relationship to ideals of 'beauty'. Because she does not deal with issues of class or race in any significant way, and also fails to theorize the nature of her category of 'women', she is unable to account for women's complicity in the Beauty Myth. As a result she must resort to unsatisfactory discussions of the role of the media and advertising in somehow encouraging women to 'internalize' the Beauty Myth. However, more recent work has shown how despite some level of ambivalence, it is women's desire to actively make the best of the resources they find themselves with which can better account for this process. What is also lacking from her account is a theoretical framework which links structure with subjectivity (Davis 1995; Black 2004).

In contrast, Sandra Lee Bartky's work (1997) is useful in helping to understand the expansion of the beauty industry without resorting to conspiracy. She attempts to incorporate Foucault's work on the micropolitics of power into her analytical schema, but adds gender as an important factor lacking from his work. She describes three categories of practice which bring about the transformation of male and female bodies into masculine and feminine modes of being: practices which bring about a certain size and shape to masculine and feminine bodies; practices which create specific postures and modes of movement; and practices aimed towards the external surface of the body (1997: 65).

In a discussion of the beauty industry, it is the idea of the external body as a surface for display which is most interesting. Women's bodies can be viewed as a canvas, the basis of which must be smooth and hairless in order for the cosmetic paint that is applied to achieve its required aim. The fashion, cosmetic and advertising industries market a vast array of products designed to prepare the skin, to remove hair and to achieve a desired look with cosmetics. Sometimes, the discourses of medicine and science are drawn upon in order to convince women of their efficacy. These labours upon the body do not indicate simply sexual difference, but rather sexual inequality. The disciplinary practices described by Bartky are seen by her as producing a 'practiced and subjected' body (1997: 100). In their endeavours to achieve the idealized look of femininity, women are destined to failure; this introduces shame and insecurity into the equation of dominance. The audience for such a performance is men, and Bartky explicitly states that the disciplines of femininity are not class or race specific. Whilst she does acknowledge that women with limited incomes may suffer additional shame at their inability to consume and display the products of the beauty industry, in general she states that in an environment of institutionalized heterosexuality, all women become 'object and prey for men' (1997: 101).

Women find themselves in a no-win situation. In order to appear fully feminine and reap the rewards of male approval (or at least avoid male disapproval) they must learn the skill of feminine bodily comportment and appearance. However, by being associated with such trivialities, women are unable to achieve power or status (Grosz 1994). The constant negotiation of this double bind was a key theme in the narratives of beauty salon clients in my own research.

Why then do women submit to the 'fashion-beauty complex'? As with Wolf who argues that women internalize the Beauty Myth to such an extent that they become complicit in their own 'torture', Bartky argues that the needs of the fashion-beauty complex are internalized. In a more convincing argument than that offered by Wolf however, she draws upon Foucault's concept of discipline to explain how such a process occurs. Although the beauty expert, the parent, the teacher and other agents of authority may have some effect on this internalization process, by far the most important factor is the role that femininity plays in the woman's own subjectivity. In this sense her subjectivity as a woman is created and ensured by attention to these disciplinary practices. In a society that genders its subjects into binary categories, there is no other way of being outside of masculine and feminine. In order to achieve an integrated sense of self, and to avoid both formal and informal sanctions attached to any disruption of this gender order, the woman must achieve both an internal and external femininity:

> To have a body felt to be 'feminine' – a body socially constructed through the appropriate practices – is in most cases crucial to a woman's sense of herself as female and, since persons currently can be only as male and female, to her sense of herself as an existing individual. To possess such a body may also be essential to her sense of herself as a sexually desiring and desirable subject. Hence, any political project that aims to dismantle the machinery that turns a female body into a feminine one may well be apprehended by a woman as something that threatens her with desexualisation, if not outright annihilation. (Bartky 1997: 105)

Bartky here hits upon the crux of the question regarding feminist approaches to the beauty industry. All seem to agree that women internalize certain standards of feminine appearance and bodily being. There is also some consensus over the ambiguity of this process. It is potentially damaging, and at the same time pleasurable. However, around the potential for resistance to these bodily disciplines, and the very desirability of rejecting the ideals themselves, there is fragmentation and disagreement. Bartky, whilst strong in outlining her analytical position and in understanding the ambiguity of this 'pleasure and danger', is much less convincing in the political project she proposes. If the fashion-beauty complex is tied up with the very creation of our notion of the individual, and with the disciplining of those individuals, then how are we to resist such microscopic power? Bartky's first hope is that the contradictions women experience between their own increasing liberation and freedom, as compared to bodily discipline, may give rise to political change. She also mentions 'oppositional discourses' as a source of hope, and cites women body builders and moves within lesbian communities as examples. Finally, she points to the fact that a mass-based women's movement still exists which can campaign around these issues and begin a radical questioning of the meaning of femininity. However, the women in my own research were already both more ambivalent and potentially critical of the beauty industry than Bartky allows, whilst at the same time less engaged with these potential sources of resistance than she might hope.

I have chosen to contrast these two writers as they hold very different views of the contemporary beauty industry, but they share a deeply critical position on women's engagement with it. They are also similar in their insistence that such body practices are primarily to do with gender. Although I have found Bartky's arguments offer much in understanding the gendered nature of the disciplined body, the fundamental flaw in both her and Wolf's arguments is the overriding focus on gender at the expense of other differences between women. Two very different approaches, which tackle these issues, come from Kathy Davis (1995) and Maxine Leeds Craig (2002).

Cosmetic surgery may be seen as an 'extreme' manifestation of the contemporary beauty industry, and, as such, reactions amongst feminist writers have ranged from outright rejection, through a guarded defence, to embracing technology as creating the potential to challenge essentialized beliefs around the female body. In a series of books and articles Kathy Davis (1991, 1995, 1997, 2002, 2003) has set out her argument, which succeeds in attributing agency to the women who undergo surgery. When we begin from women's everyday lives, cosmetic surgery cannot be seen simplistically as an oppressive outpost of patriarchy working through the medical profession to inflict pain on women's bodies in the name of femininity (Davis 1991: 33). Similarly, women themselves cannot be seen as deluded 'cultural dopes', subject to an all-pervasive system of inequality and oppression. Their actions must not simply be read off as 'false consciousness'. Instead, Davis shows how within the constraints facing them, women act to make the best of the situation with which they are faced. In common with the beauty salon clients I spoke to, the women in her study were often highly critical of the emphasis on feminine beauty in Western societies. However, they did not see themselves as unthinkingly conforming to such ideals, rather they argued that they were acting to bring their bodies in line with their own self-image, often against the wishes of male partners. For these women, cosmetic surgery, Davis argues, is actually an act of empowerment where they have taken control of their lives in the one area open to them. For Kathy Davis, then, cosmetic surgery is about women actively negotiating their own identity, albeit within constrained potentials (Davis 1995).

This emphasis on agency in relation to the beauty industry has inevitably attracted criticism. Negrin (2002), for example, points out that Davis's emphasis on women's solution to their problems avoids addressing the very reasons for their initial dissatisfaction, and effectively individualizes women's issues with their bodies (Negrin 2002: 24). She argues that by undertaking cosmetic surgery, women may actually be hampering any potential for political challenge to these underlying causes, as they may be less inclined to engage in critique of wider social and cultural factors. In this way, cosmetic surgery can be seen to reinforce the problem, rather than to offer a limited solution to gender oppression. In undertaking surgery, the ultimate control over the body, and the aesthetic outcome achieved, lies in the hands of cosmetic surgeons themselves. Certainly, in the UK and the USA, this group of medical professionals has been shown to hold ideals of appearance based on white Western hegemonic standards (Gilman 1999). In underplaying such factors, Davis emphasizes the potential feminism inherent in decisions to undergo cosmetic surgery at the expense of a feminist critique that focuses more on wider structural questions. Although sympathizing with these criticisms, it is easy to see how Davis presents the analysis she does. Her research was an ethnographic study, explicitly taking the 'everyday social practices of women as its starting point' (1991: 33). After having spent an extended period of time with clients and workers within the beauty industry, I can identify with an account that aims to present these women as active social agents. In my own work, I have struggled to balance the everyday with the structural, and the world of active choices with the wider context of constrained options. Any critique of Davis should take into account this methodological issue.

Maxine Leeds Craig (2002) fills a significant gap in the available literature by applying a sociological analysis to the politics of race articulated through the body and through everyday culture. Her focus is on the 1960s and 1970s, thus placing an inevitable spotlight on the implications of the Civil Rights Movement and its aftermath. In attempting to understand the phrase 'black is beautiful', both through a political discourse and the everyday practices of black men and women themselves, Craig grounds her discussion in beauty salons and beauty contests, again illustrating how the general political level may be usefully analyzed through the specifics of women's bodies.

She sets out her theoretical preoccupation as being the 'multidimensionality of racial rearticulation' (2002: 14). In so doing, she is at pains to incorporate an analysis of class and gender into her theoretical framework, whilst always foregrounding her understandings of race. Craig points to four key elements that formed the context within which new standards of beauty emerged: 'the disparagement of black women in dominant cultural images; an African-American discourse of race and respectability; the broad acceptance of theories of black self-hatred; and the close connection between social class and skin tone within black communities' (2002: 18). These elements led to often complex and contradictory cultural practices. So, for example, whilst the 1968 Miss America contest drew protests from members of Women's Liberation, at the same time the first Miss Black America competition was staged in order to promote a positive image of black female beauty. A black woman at the Miss America protest expressed her own ambivalence in trying to hold together a gender politics cross-cut by awareness of racism, sometimes within the feminist movement itself (2002: 5). What Craig succeeds in doing is to show how a racial politics fought over women's bodies and how the Civil Rights movement built on and incorporated aspects of earlier political struggles. It also integrated class and gender issues, sometimes challenging traditional structures, and sometimes simply reproducing inequalities along these lines. For Craig there is no simple critique to be made from a privileged position outside. All cultural and political practices are caught within a web of historical relations and social structures, which allow some potential for rearticulation, whilst also at times entrenching other unequal social relations. Beauty practices can also be understood within this framework: 'Black men and, I would argue, all women live in what might be considered "marked" or stigmatized bodies. Only the unmarked can trivialize the fleeting, joyous, cultural victory experienced when dominant meaning is subverted and what was formerly ridiculed is finally celebrated' (Craig 2002: 14). More complex arguments, such as this, go some way to helping us understand women's (and men's) relationship to an expanding beauty industry.

'YOU CAN DO WHATEVER YOU WANT WITH YOUR LIFE'

Once the empirical findings of research with women who are engaging with the fashion and beauty industry are taken into account, it becomes clear that a host of practices and discourses intersect (see, for example, Furman 1997; Willett 2000; Gimlin 2002). There is no monolithic industry that can be simplistically criticized, and no single set of explanations or experiences which women put forward. In my research, I categorize women's body practices into four types: health treatments; pampering; routine grooming; and corrective treatments

(Black 2002, 2004). Each of these categorizations relates to different types of treatments, and also to the varying roles that are serviced in a woman's life. Feminist critique has generally focused on what I have labelled 'pampering' and 'corrective' treatments, with less interest and criticism shown in/for other treatments, for example, those related to health. Corrective treatments are those such as facial hair removal, which most obviously relate to the performance of gender within tightly prescribed boundaries. 'Pampering' is utilized by the salon client as a means of claiming time for herself, and removing herself from the multiple demands experienced in her everyday life. As specific practices and the discourses associated with them are linked to social position, including categories such as class and ethnicity, there is a danger that the practices most closely associated with marginalized positions are those most easily criticized.

Amongst the interviewees in my study, it was generally agreed that beauty salon visits were something that had become more common amongst women in recent times. Women in their twenties and thirties especially felt that their own beauty routines were significantly different from those of an earlier generation. In terms of the amount of time spent on beauty routines, on the products consumed and salon visits, these women believed that they devoted more time, effort and disposable income to their own beauty routines than their mothers had done. These changes were explained in terms of women's freedoms to spend both time and money on themselves. Beauty salon visits were seen as part of a leisure and service industry catering to the needs of women independent in both their financial and personal decisions. Beauty therapists, too, explain the increase in their business in these terms. The expanding leisure industry and the extensive commodification of beauty rituals have contributed to the professionalization of the salon, which has in turn altered the behaviour of women from one generation to the next. Women also felt that they were increasingly subject to pressure to appear groomed, and to maintain certain levels of appearance. This pressure is filtered through the media and other cultural forms, as well as being one of the regulations operating in the workplace. The requirement for regulated and 'groomed' appearance in the workplace is one of the demands of the service industries, and women who invest in their bodies in this way are reacting to understandable workplace pressures (Adkins 2001; Wellington and Bryson 2001). However, with freedom comes the pressure to succeed. By being part of the 'can have it all' generation, women felt that they were expected to 'have it all', and that appearance was a key indicator of success in important, if limited, terms. Although not widespread, there was some reflection on these changes in the context of feminist beliefs:

I think that there is a generation of women who are university educated, who were brought up not directly by their mothers but the generation above, to have certain opinions of what women should be, and they were quite strongly ingrained opinions, which is where my thing came from; constantly reading feminist type novels gave me strongly ingrained views. I am a teacher, and I don't think any of my pupils have it. And I think there is not one girl in my sixth form who isn't absolutely plastered in make-up. I don't think there is one girl who says you shouldn't shave your legs, that is conforming to the particular type of femininity. They would just laugh at you. (Laura)

When I later questioned Laura about the effects she thought this had on these young women, she replied that they would 'probably be happier and less angst ridden than our generation'.

A far more common experience of this pressure was expressed by slightly younger women such as Clare:

> *Clare*: My mum always said to me 'oh you can do whatever you want with your life'. But that is like a massive pressure isn't it? Because I could have done anything and look what I have done. I haven't done anything. Oh God, I am such a failure! Do you know what I mean? But I think lots of our generation are like that, like we are really miserable because like beating our heads against a brick wall, because we are not something that we should be, but are not really sure what it is because we don't know what we want.
>
> *Paula*: Do you think having that ideal of what we should start off as is part of the whole problem?
>
> *Clare*: Yes because you have got the house, the apartment, the career, you have got to be gorgeous because we can have it all.

Clare's anxieties are expressed here in terms of what might be termed 'post-feminism'. The gains made by feminism, such as access to free and safe contraception and a commitment to equality in the workplace, at least in the affluent industrial world, mean that young women have been freed to make choices regarding occupation and sexuality within less rigid restrictions than their mothers. However, this freedom has also been experienced as responsibility and fear of failure. This group of women has also rejected the strict dichotomy between feminism and femininity, which characterized popular understandings of feminism in the 1970s and 1980s (Moseley and Read 2002). Moseley and Read argue that the choices made by young women in the UK and USA are drawn from an agenda set by feminism, but that the rejection of beauty culture and femininity previously associated with the feminist movement has been reworked. Young women believe, therefore, that they can 'have it all', and that this entails career, economic independence, property owning, sexual freedom and investment in a feminine appearance. The freedom and fun to be had by gaining these rewards is also a pressure to succeed with all of them. What I think is missing from Moseley and Read's discussion, however, is an acknowledgement that the desire to achieve a feminized body is the product of a commodified system. For the new 'career woman', the services of the beauty industry facilitate the achievement of an appropriate femininity, but at a cost. The desire to have it all is fostered within a Liberal market economy. With sufficient levels of disposable income, the young woman buys leisure and pleasure from industries geared up to convince her that she has failed without them.

In a similar way to beauty, sex has become both a leisure pastime and a commodified arena where the woman is expected to excel. In her study of Ann Summers parties,[1] Storr points out the pleasure to be gained from such activities, as well as the price to be paid for enjoying these 'freedoms':

> post-feminist values combine an emphasis on individual empowerment (rather than collective power) with a sense of *entitlement* to pleasure: and further this pleasure is regarded not as a right gained by social struggle or feminist argument, but simply as a consumer good. In the case of my research with Ann Summers this sense of entitlement was evident in the oft-repeated phrase 'it's the nineties'. Party organisers would often tell their guests not to feel embarrassed about buying vibrators because 'it's the nineties', a phrase which encapsulates both the sense of consumerism (you have a right to buy the product) and the sense that social change is not the goal of ongoing struggle but has already been achieved. (Storr 2003: 32)

The clients of a beauty salon share much in common with the Ann Summers party hosts and guests, and the legitimating discourses drawn on to explain their behaviour also share echoes of this 'post-feminist' strategy. Both are worlds where women may indulge in time for themselves in the company of other women. They are able, and encouraged, to spend their disposable income on themselves. They engage in sensual pleasure that does not include men. The spaces in which these activities occur are either permanently feminized spaces, or are occupied as such for a specific period of time. All these factors contribute to the claims made by these women that what they are doing can be interpreted as the result of freedoms arising from the changing position of women in general. In this sense, Ann Summers parties and beauty salon visits might be seen as either pro-feminist activities, or practices engaged in as a result of changes brought about by feminism. However, as Storr points out, the pleasure and freedom is only available within carefully policed boundaries. In her research, those boundaries concerned heterosexuality and gender based on a specific type of femininity. In the beauty salon, women certainly claim time and pleasure for themselves, but the means whereby they indulge this claim does little to liberate or challenge heterosexism or sexism per se.

AMBIVALENT PLEASURES

All the women I spoke to in my research had some reservations about their engagement with the beauty industry, partly because of their scepticism about its more extravagant claims, but also because of the associations with shallowness or vanity, which a focus on the body entails. Women themselves are fully aware of the double bind they are caught in – ridicule and disapproval for failing to produce the 'disciplined and subjected body', but overtones of the 'bimbo' if they do. Unsurprisingly, this ambivalence is dealt with by recourse to claims about the positive choice to engage in body practices for pleasurable reasons, or for the instrumental necessity to maintain the body in a healthy and well-groomed state. Feminism, where it was acknowledged at all, simply heightened this tension:

> I suppose it's all part of the beauty industry thing. Ten years ago, I wouldn't have considered doing it, for feminist reasons… It's like something else that I have done, that I kind of didn't do for a long time, was to lose weight, and it's like that in a way. I always knew that I would be pressured by society to lose weight, and I was the shape I was, but nevertheless two or three years ago I thought, 'I'll lose weight and see what it is like', and I did. But it's the same kind of dichotomy, is that the right word? On the one side I know I shouldn't be pressurized into that and I know it's the fault of society and all that kind of thing, but on the other hand I do it anyway. (Laura)

Given this ambivalence felt by clients, and to some extent by beauty therapists as well, why do women continue to engage with the beauty industry on such a wide scale and intimate level? Bartky (1997) can partly answer this question with her argument that rejection of femininity as a woman can lead to the sense of annihilation of self. However, as I point out above, her arguments in themselves are inadequate. I have understood the complex and sometimes contradictory positions women occupy as a product of a striving for appropriateness. This 'getting it right' is the key to understanding not only beauty salon visits or the operation of the wider beauty industry, but also for making sense of women's relationship to ideals of femininity.

The understanding of the ambivalent femininities being striven for in the beauty salon must arise from the sense that all women inhabit a society based on gendered and unequal objective social structures. These external social structures are paralleled by internalized mental structures, which lead to particular ways of seeing the world. This psychological framework has been described by Bourdieu as the habitus, or, in his words, 'a mental structure which, having been inculcated into all minds socialized in a particular way, is both individual and collective' (Bourdieu 1998: 66). Through the habitus, women come to make choices that are constrained by their gendered identity (Mottier 2002). This explains why women can make what seem to be individual choices based on tastes and preferences, but also why in any particular society we see patterns which relate to gender identity. For Bourdieu, the process of becoming a woman involves 'symbolic violence', what he calls a 'gentle violence' (Krais 1993; Bourdieu 2001: 1), whereby the alignment of the habitus with objective social structures is realized. This alignment is accepted as 'natural', and as such remains both commonsensical and difficult to resist. What we come to see as taken-for-granted ways of being a woman or a man are actually the result of a very social process of learning to see the gender differences in our society as 'natural', rather than the result of social and political processes. Despite this inevitably gendered position, the woman also inhabits objective social structures that are hierarchical in relation to class, ethnicity and sexuality. These are also incorporated into the habitus. In this way, gender identity always intersects with a range of other categories relating to a variety of unequal social locations.

Whilst agreeing with the power of symbolic violence, and the power exerted when the habitus and objective structures align to produce this domination, what I find interesting are the spaces allowed where habitus and social structures are imperfectly aligned. In fact, it could be argued that a perfect alignment is never possible. Psychoanalytical work has shown how femininity is not an easy role to adopt, nor one that is ever fully achieved (Rose 1983). Neither objective structures nor the habitus can ever form a unified monolithic totality; contradictions exist both within and between them. The tensions between the internalized standards of female gender and their expression through the body are one example, and the ambivalence exhibited by the women in my study to their own investment in feminized bodily capital illustrates such spaces. Spaces for critique can emerge, for example, from class position, from a feminist-inspired criticism of the gender order, from a sense of racial politics, or from a non-heterosexual identity. For all these reasons, the woman is able both to embrace and reject an idealized femininity (Skeggs 1997; Craig 2002).

How then can we understand the role of feminism in making sense of contemporary cultural practices that involve engagement with the beauty industry? Feminist writers have begun to grasp the ambiguities and potential pleasures inherent in the fashion and beauty industries. However, they have also, rightly, on the whole remained sceptical of the disciplining of women's bodies to conform to an idealized femininity moulded by sexism, heterosexism, racism and class inequalities. The commodification of the body inherent in beauty practices has also come under scrutiny. However, particularly where research is grounded in the empirical evidence of women's everyday lives, a more nuanced understanding can be advanced. A key question is the extent to which feminism must reject femininity as it is currently coded in Western capitalist society. For women themselves undertaking cosmetic surgery, visiting a beauty salon or entering beauty contests, a deep ambivalence lies at the heart of their activities. They are often all too clearly aware that they are 'damned if they do and damned if they don't'. An investment in bodily capital makes particular sense where other capitals and opportunities, such as educational qualifications, are limited (Skeggs 1997). However, this investment is risky, and is one that does not produce capital which is easily converted. However, failure to invest in the body at all leads to the potential annihilation of female identity. Given this impossible position, it is important to bear in mind both that women are acting to make the best of their situation within a field of limited potentials, but also that the beauty industry cannot be abstracted from wider social structures and relationships. The investments made and the bodies produced will have different value according to the position of the woman who makes them; however, none can afford to disinvest completely.

NOTES

1. Ann Summers parties are organized through a company which sells erotic games, toys and clothing through parties held in womens' homes.

BIBLIOGRAPHY

Adkins, L. (2001), 'Cultural Feminization: "Money, Sex and Power" for Women', *Signs*, 26, 3: 669–95.

Bartky, S. L. (1997), *Femininity and Domination: Studies in the Phenomenology of Oppression*, London: Routledge.

Bhavnani, K. (1997), 'Women's Studies and its Interconnection with "Race", Ethnicity and Sexuality', in V. Robinson and D. Richardson (eds), *Introducing Women's Studies*, second edition, Basingstoke: Palgrave.

Black, P. (2002), '"Ordinary People Come Through Here": Locating the Beauty Salon in Women's Lives', *Feminist Review*, 71: 2–17.

—— (2004), *The Beauty Industry: Gender, Culture, Pleasure*, London: Routledge.

Bourdieu, P. (1998), *Practical Reason: On the Theory of Action*, Cambridge: Polity.

—— (2001), *Masculine Domination*, Cambridge: Polity.

Boyd, R. L. (1996), 'The Great Migration To The North and the Rise of Ethnic Niches for African American Women in Beauty Culture and Hairdressing, 1910–1920', *Sociological Focus*, 29,1: 33–45.

Craig, M. L. (2002), *Ain't I a Beauty Queen? Black Women, Beauty, and the Politics of Race*, Oxford: Oxford University Press.

Davis, K. (1991), 'Re-making the She Devil: A Critical Look at Feminist Approaches to Beauty', *Hypatia*, 6, 2: 21–43.

—— (1995), *Reshaping the Female Body: The Dilemma of Cosmetic Surgery*, London: Routledge.

—— (ed.) (1997), *Embodied Practices: Feminist Perspectives on the Body*, London: Sage.

—— (2002), 'A Dubious Equality: Men, Women and Cosmetic Surgery', *Body and Society*, 8,1: 49–65.

—— (2003), *Dubious Equalities, Embodied Differences: Cultural Studies on Cosmetic Surgery*, Lanham: Rowman and Littlefield.

Furman, F. K. (1997), *Facing the Mirror: Older Women and Beauty Shop Culture*, London: Routledge.

Gilman, S. L. (1999), *Making the Body Beautiful: A Cultural History of Aesthetic Surgery*, Princeton: Princeton University Press.

Gimlin, D. (2002), *Body Work: Beauty and Self-Image in American Culture*, Berkeley: University of California Press.

Grosz, E. (1994), *Volatile Bodies: Toward a Corporeal Feminism*, Bloomington: Indiana University Press.

Guild News (2001), 'Beauty Index 2001', *Journal of the Guild of Professional Beauty Therapists*.

—— (2002), 'Beauty Index 2003', *Journal of the Guild of Professional Beauty Therapists*.

Harding, S. (1991), *Whose Science? Whose Knowledge? Thinking from Women's Lives*, Milton Keynes: Open University Press.

Krais, B. (1993), 'Gender and Symbolic Violence: Female Oppression in the Light of Pierre Bourdieu's Theory of Social Practice', in C. Calhoun, E. LiPuma and M. Postone (eds), *Bourdieu: Critical Perspectives*, Cambridge: Polity.

Mintel (2002), www.timesonline.co.uk (accessed 31 July 2004).

Moseley, R. and Read, J. (2002), '"Having it Ally": Popular Television (Post-) Feminism', *Feminist Media Studies*, 2, 2: 231–49.

Mottier, V. (2002), 'Masculine Domination: Gender and Power in Bourdieu's Writings', *Feminist Theory*, 3, 3: 345–59.

Negrin, L. (2002), 'Cosmetic Surgery and the Eclipse of Identity', *Body and Society*, 8, 4: 21–42.

Peiss, K. (1998), *Hope in a Jar: The Making of America's Beauty Culture*, New York: Metropolitan Books.

Rose, J. (1983), 'Femininity and its Discontents', *Feminist Review*, 14: 5–21.

Skeggs, B. (1995), 'Situating the Product of Feminist Ethnography', in M. Maynard and J. Purvis (eds), *Researching Women's Lives From a Feminist Perspective*, London: Taylor and Francis.

—— (1997), *Formations of Class and Gender: Becoming Respectable*, London: Sage.

Storr, M. (2003), *Latex and Lingerie: Shopping for Pleasure at Ann Summers Parties*, Oxford: Berg.

Wellington, C. A. and Bryson, J. R. (2001), 'At Face Value? Image Consultancy, Emotional Labour and Professional Work', *Sociology*, 35, 4: 933–46.

Willett, J. A. (2000), *Permanent Waves: The Making of the American Beauty Shop*, New York: New York University Press.

Wolf, N. (1990), *The Beauty Myth: How Images of Beauty are Used Against Women*, London: Vintage.

CHAPTER 9

Learning from B-Girls

Charla Ogaz

INTRODUCTIONS

Charla: OK, so if you all could tell me your names, and you can tell me your given name, if you want, and your hip hop name. What is that name and where does it come from?

Rockafella: My real name is Anita Garcia, my maiden name. No, not really, it's been two years already [since she got married]. And my dance name is Rockafella. Two reasons for that: one is that it became a job description: to rock fellas, but originally, it was because I was dancing in this place called Rockefeller Center in New York, and this cop was like, 'Move on.' At first I was really defiant, and the cop was like, 'You're trespassing.' And I was like, 'You don't even know; I could be the illegitimate daughter Rockefeller; you don't know.' Whatever; I gave them that story. So to make a long story short, the cop was like, 'This is your personal invitation, Lady Rockafella: you gotta vacate.' It had nothing to do with the Rockefellers, the family, the money, the corruption, or the capitalism; nothing like that. Those people, the socially conscious ones are like, 'Oh, he was a capitalist pig' and all that. Or on the other side, 'Yo, JayZ! Oh!' It has something to do with breaking. I didn't mean to get that elaborate; I'll pass it. OK, that's it.

Aiko: My name is Aiko Shirakawa. I have no dance name, just Aiko.

Rockafella: It's exotic enough, Ms. Thang.

Aiko: It's different enough, I guess. And that's about it. My name came from my grandfather, who was a little Japanese man. He gave my mom ten names to pick when I was born, and she picked Aiko.

All of us are girls/women named by/after men. My first name, 'Charla' comes from my mother naming me after her ob/gyn who delivered me into this world and whose first name was Charles. Like many other Latinas, my mother believes doctors walk on water. As a budding-feminist undergraduate, I changed my last name to my mother's maiden name, and gave up my mother's married name, to which I had no biological ties. In taking the surname, 'Ogaz', however, I too inadvertently took the name of my mother's father, the uncontested patriarch of the clan, with whom my mother was overidentified, bringing the female/femme masculine out in my gender lineage: *Yo soy la macha* – a lot like b-girls. B-girls are young women who breakdance, in particular, and who participate in hip hop culture, in general. And that's really how my naming practices connect with Rockafella's and Aiko's; I see us as *femmes masculines*, for want of better words: girls who are 'tough', not biologically, but by choice, and then by training.

Rockafella's narrative about her entrance/initiation via the name as a complex signifier references three things: rockin' fellas, her job description, an off-take of 'rockin' the circle', what every breakdancer hopes to do; her claiming of public space via her play on the invisibility of reproduction legitimation practices (reminiscent for me of Hortense Spillers' 'Mama's Baby, Papa's Maybe' [1987]), naming herself possibly the illegitimate Rockefeller; and, by erasure and appropriation, contradicting the Rockefellers' patriarchy and appropriating the signifier as her own. Nevertheless, as is also true for the three of us, it seems, 'The expressions of resistance and opposition which characterise this relation (of naming) are fraught with contradiction' (McRobbie 1980: 38). In our naming practices, however chosen or given, the commonality is that male power is inherited, or in the best (feminist) scenario even usurped.

Exploring the (seeming) contradictions within women's lives is a contemporary development in feminist discourse, and one, I would suggest, that establishes one of multiple third waves. Though many of us fight the tendency in our work – while simultaneously being inspired by the fantasy – this fight is against what Sherrie Tucker calls her 'second wave feminist hopes for unearthing historical utopian women's communities' (2000: 2–3). Tucker's point is important: one of the main ways the second wave is distinguished from any third is by this utopianism that has historically guided feminist narratives. By acknowledging the 'quotidian expressions of feminist consciousness' (Davis 1998: xvii) that appear to be contradictory from a utopian perspective, we can, rather, understand these experiences in women's lives as 'antagonistic relationships' that are 'noncontradictory oppositions' (Davis 1998: xv). Chandra Mohanty refers to these non-oppositional tensions or the third spaces beyond binary oppositions, arguing that:

> The relations of power I am referring to are not reducible to binary oppositions or oppressor/oppressed relations. I want to suggest that it is possible to retain the

idea of multiple, fluid structures of domination which intersect to locate women differently at particular historical conjunctures, while at the same time insisting on the dynamic oppositional agency of individuals and collectives and their engagement in 'daily life.' (1991: 13)

Joan Morgan, a hip hop critic, offers a similar perspective in her essay, 'Hip-Hop Feminist' (2004). Referring to the historical struggle in the US between a white middle-class feminist movement and the alternative formations made by women of colour, she says that 'White women's racism and the Feminist Movement may explain the justifiable bad taste the f-word leaves in the mouths of women who are over thirty-five, but for my generation they are abstractions drawn from someone else's history' (2004: 278). Morgan speaks of a generational difference here, but clearly her claim does not read as an essentializing statement locking women over thirty-five into a second-wave (ideological) position. Her point, as I read it, is that the oppositional ideology from those fights within feminism does not necessarily determine the ideology of all feminists in the US. Arguing for a feminism 'brave enough to fuck with the grays', Joan Morgan suggests that the opposition between '"victim" (read women)' and '"oppressor" (read men)' cannot capture the complexity of contemporary lived experiences and identities (Morgan 2004: 280).

Reorienting our ideologies to consider the space between seemingly opposing positions allows us to enter discussions about living with men and masculinity in ways that are sometimes both pleasurable and painful. Rather than seeing one as complicit in patriarchy if one chooses to work with men in male-dominated contexts or to perform masculinity as an individual choice, a third-wave discourse can sustain the dialogue about these third spaces, the in-between experiences all of us have that are complex, politically confusing and sometimes rewarding. In many ways, I see this opportunity to enter the third spaces between opposing positions as a necessary step towards understanding feminism within heterosexuality, and thus within dominant, mainstream popular culture. (Third spaces are also important in understanding various positions outside of the white-black racial dichotomy that pervades so much popular and academic discourse.) This work with girls who breakdance is my attempt to continue in this vein, and it is the articulation of such third spaces within the culture and practices of b-girls that this essay seeks to explore.

In particular, breakdancing and masculinity are often understood by popular-culture historians as one and the same. Sally Banes says that 'breaking is a way of claiming the streets with physical presence, using your body to publicly inscribe your identity on the surfaces of the city, to flaunt a unique personal style within a conventional format' (Banes 2004: 14). Similarly, Hazzard-Donald says

Hip hop dance is clearly masculine in style, with postures assertive in their own right as well as in relation to a female partner. In its early stages ... the dance did not allow for female partnering; it was purely male expression and rarely performed by females. Particularly in early hip hop the male does not assume the easygoing, cool, confident polish characteristic of earlier popular-dance expression. Even in its early stages hip hop dancing aggressively asserted male dominance. (Hazzard-Donald 2004: 509)

So, is it a contradiction to ask questions about women in hip hop, which is such a highly masculinized culture? Can we only expect contradictions in their answers? If breakdancing is understood as a male and masculine art/sport, then how do women survive when they enter this world as participants aiming for equal power?

THE FIELD/THE DANCE

In this essay, 'the field' is an event produced by 5th Element: International Women's Day. 5th Element is a collective of women artists, producers and fans of hip hop in San Jose, California, which works to produce hip hop events centred on women. The afternoon before the event on 8 March 2003, I was allowed to document a conversation that Aiko helped coordinate and pull together: Rockafella and herself would have a conversation about women in hip hop based on interview questions presented by me. Generally, I suggested that we start with their b-girl names, how they took these names, and, by extension, how they first entered hip hop. I told them I was also interested in how their entries into hip hop communities related to their lives at school and at home. Although we ended up being guided by these preliminary questions, and the more exact and nuanced interview questions fell by the wayside, the discussion ended up ferreting out many dynamics of sex/gender, race/ethnicity, social class, nationality and age, which are all issues that I believe define third-wave feminist struggle, analysis and the contradictions and/or third spaces of living in 'democratic' centres. In my initial interview design, I assumed that I would have to ask specific questions about experiences of social stratification in order to garner the data for an analysis of what women of colour in the US call 'multiple subjectivities' (Alarcon 1990) or 'intersectionalities' (Crenshaw 1991).

My main theoretical impetus as a scholar is to find and record experiences of these simultaneous, co-constitutive social stratification practices that construct individuals in complex identity locations in society and culture. US women of colour feminist theory gives me this conceptual framework, and building upon this theory is what I consider to be my own work in the larger formation of third-wave feminisms in the US. Following my conversation with these two old-school b-girls, I am now convinced that after building rapport and asking questions about life and larger social structures in general, the stories of social stratification and how they survived these experiences necessarily rear their ugly heads.

Charla: OK, so how long have you been dancing, or more specifically, how long have you been breakdancing – or whatever kind of hip hop dancing you do?

Aiko: OK, let me start because mine's shorter.

Asia: Nooo!

Rockafella: Yours is longer!

Aiko: OK, so I started popping when I was eleven in 1979. I first saw popping when I was eight at my elementary school in San Jose, but nobody would teach me. So I started popping when I was eleven, and up until about when I was fifteen when I got introduced to some lockers from LA who taught me how to lock and taught me boogaloo, which I didn't know anything about until they came and told me that that style was an LA style of popping, which actually came down from Fresno, but it's all good. From fifteen to twenty, I was in their group, Quick Style. So I was introduced to that, and then I started trying to learn to break when I was around thirteen or fourteen, but nobody would teach me, so I just learned a little bit of basics, and then nobody would teach me anymore, and breaking started to fade in the mid 80s. Then by the late 80s, Quick Style was still locking and doing shows, but nobody else was dancing. No one was dancing until the early 1990s, and I began to start to pop and lock because of people like Rockafella and Asia who inspired me to get back into it. And some dope b-boys also. So I continued to get into that, and then into emceeing, hosting shows, competitions, break competitions, popping competitions, and helping Asia with the B-Boy Summit. That's pretty much my history, in a nutshell, without all of the details.

Here, Aiko explains her first and repeated exclusion from breakdancing, when she tried to begin and no one would teach her: an exclusion because of gender that Rockafella also reflects later in the discussion. As Guevara argues, this is a typical experience: 'when girls do get involved in breaking, they are often patronized by boyfriends or big brothers who decide which steps are sufficiently safe or feminine for them to do' (1996: 58). It is also interesting to note how Aiko's re-entry to hip hop dancing was empowered by adult female support, now forming a bi-coastal b-girl community.

Rockafella: I've been dancing forever. I was also always in Sweet Sixteens [usually formal parties for girls 'coming-out' on their sixteenth birthdays], weddings; I was always performing or doing something with salsa. And then I was always attracted by the hip hop vibe because of my African background. I was like, 'Ew, what are the black people doing?' So I would check it out and try to emulate, imitate what the guys were doing. So, you know, if it was the wop or whatever, I was trying to jump in. And when I was sixteen, I went to my first club and just fell in love: the loudspeakers, the sounds, the people, the circles. I was like, 'I gotta do this.' And there were a couple of females who were jumpin' in there, but again, we were caddy because, you know, we're women, what do you expect, we're trying to fight for crumbs. So, I couldn't get nothing in that sense, but I did like to go clubbing, and I made a real name for myself being so young and being able to get into clubs without IDs and stuff like that. So I was able to get into the club dances and all that vibe. And then when I was nineteen, I met my boyfriend when I was sixteen, and I ran away with him, and he was a dancer so he brought all the dance stuff, too. But when I was nineteen, we started to dance on the street with the breakers who were breaking on the street, and breaking wasn't popular at that time at all, but these heads were doing it to make money. So I fell back in love with it. I was like, 'Yeah, I wanna do this.' But then again, like they just said, no one ever teaches — I mean even now, people do teach but it's a whole different vibe. I couldn't learn it that way, so whatever they were doing, I'd try to do it, and because I was a girl, everybody was clapping. So I did feel that ... I didn't count it as breaking cuz it was like a knee spin, or chopped up footwork, or really buggin' on the top rock, so I didn't count it. When I was twenty-three, I met Quick Step who is my husband now, and he was like, 'OK, that's great and all, but this is a six step; this is a freeze. If you want it, I think you'd be good. I think you could make a difference.' Cuz I was so tired of being played by guys: jumpin' in circles and getting' humped, you know what I'm saying? So I was like, 'I want somethin' that's gonna stand, not be knocked down by a guy.' So I was like, 'I want it.' And he was like, 'Well, this is how you gotta do it. Three times a week, four times a week, you gotta come here and just do this over and over again.' Bruises and cuts and all that. So I really started breaking when I was twenty-three, and I'm thirty-one now, so that's eight or nine years or something like that... Yeah, from them I learned waves, the hit. I had no idea about California; I had no idea what was going on like that, so it was like blind. So we pretty much had the same mission: 'I have something I can hold.' Yeah, not based on my titties or my bootie.

Rockafella's dance autobiography reflects the co-constitutive nature of racialized, sexist and economic forces in her everyday experience, and clearly she points to how her developing aesthetic for (break)dancing was a kinetic force propelling her towards solutions. She locates herself in the diasporic hip hop continuum from Africa, though this gets complicated later by the exclusion practices of African-Americans towards Puerto Ricans within hip hop. She then quickly suggests some girlfighting, but reflects on the internalized sexism demonstrated in 'fighting for crumbs'. This clear reflection of how women are held in the bottom rungs to compete with each other for the lesser (paying) jobs is illustrative of a feminist critique of male institutionalized hierarchical power structures in all other social institutions. Women succumb to the sexist order and fight each other at the bottom for limited power/attention.

Rockafella also talks about her legal transgressions to get into public dance spaces, in pursuit of the social pleasure in dance. I don't get the impression she comes to (break)dance through men, as much as accompanied by them. At some point, however, it becomes a job. The ending is a sharp critique of the gender dynamics in her experiences. She's clear that part of the applause is because she's a girl, doing boy things well. The underlying, implied assumption is that the moves are more difficult for women, and that these difficulties have static biological foundations that need special talent to overcome. This is confirmed in several other conversations I've had with b-boys. From here, she quickly moves to the boys' sexualization of her in the circles, and points to what I call her strategic resistance to this, by dedicating herself to educating herself and building skills she 'can hold'.

THE METHOD

I'm an interdisciplinary scholar by training, so my approach to this project has been multiple, to say the least. Because my relationships with Aiko and Rockafella are growing over time, I have chosen 'ethnographic' conversations to document these b-girls' work. I had been telling Aiko about my project to document b-girls' participation in breakdancing culture for over a year, at various 5th Element: Women in Hip Hop events, by the time we sat down to talk at length. Aiko and I had worked together on three of 5th Element's shows. Rockafella and I had not met until the day before our discussion, but Aiko had told her about my project, so I had the 'in', so to speak, through her. Thus, by the time of the interview, I'd like to say that we were more of a community than not, and by that I mean that we shared some common values about women in hip hop, having come together through 5th Element.

Discussing conventional social science research practice and the positioning of the researcher, Angela McRobbie has argued that 'The point is that this absence of self (this is quite different from the authorial "I" or "we") and the invalidating of personal experience in the name of the more objective social sciences goes hand in hand with the silencing of other areas, which are for feminists of the greatest importance' (1980: 39). Ann Oakley's 1981 essay 'Interviewing Women' offers another academic context for understanding the methodology I used to build this discussion. Documenting a long line of feminist critique of traditional social scientific practices, Oakley offers a feminist ethic for establishing relationships with informants in which 'the relationship of interviewer and interviewee is non-hierarchical' and where 'the interviewer is prepared to invest his or her own personal identity in the relationship' (Oakley 1981: 41). Therefore, just as some feminists have challenged the utilitarian ethics of social scientific research, they have turned the role of the interviewer on its head, and this, in turn, not only makes the interviewer less of a colonizing force but also potentially aligns her with the research subjects. In some ways, my relationship with my research subjects is hierarchical because I look up to them so much as a fan and non-hierarchical because we're the same age and I'd chosen to be a partial participant in the local culture of 5th Element.

I chose this project as much as it chose me. Because of my effort, the efforts of women in 5th Element, the b-girls who have chosen to participate in my research, the b-boys, even, who have come to office hours to tell me they support my work and invited me into their practice sessions, I've begun a project that has challenged me to articulate the politics of male dominant culture in relation to female subcultural manifestation. Throughout my research, I've definitely coded myself 'b-girl' in order to be accepted as a 'participant' and not just an 'observer'; however, in this process, what I've found deeper below the surface is that there's a b-girl inside of me! My research remains 'hygienic', so to speak, because the difference between research subject and researcher cannot really be crossed (except in fantasy) because I do not breakdance.

Perhaps, as Oakley suggests, this deepens the ethics of the research towards greater equality between researcher and research subject. Perhaps, ironically, coming to understand the reality, needs and desires of b-girls, is first begun by acknowledging and identifying with the reality, needs and desires of the b-girl within. At the least, self-reflexivity allows us to begin to understand how and why the field is fenced, the community framed, the subjects subjected and the objects of study objectified: this sense of the personal as political is a particular mode and content of research that, in my opinion, is inherent in feminism and beyond generational chronologies – whether figured as waves, movements or other historical processes. What I think the third waves can add to this aspect of feminist research, however, is the self-reflexivity that great post-colonial theory can bring. Mohanty (1991) asks us to consider our own 'Western eyes' and though Oakley sees feminism as the great equalizer, this perspective, too, can be charged with a blinding utopianism. The third waves must continue not simply to claim one's sex as an equalizer, nor simply one's feminism, but to interrogate all of the researcher's colonial investments.

I am a fan of, if overidentified with, the old-school b-girls. When I see b-girls take the circle, I'm not only deeply impressed, but also pleasantly enraptured with the sense that females can overcome seemingly all-pervasive, personality-saturating fear of male arenas and deliver the beauty of the dance for their own sake, against almost all odds. They do all this while inhabiting their bodies in ways many women find hard to achieve: with consciousness, diligence and commitment to shine against the odds. Judith Lynne Hanna writes of the power of dance as a form of communication between dancer and audience: 'Dance performance is immediate, emotionally charging the performer and audience in sporadic or continuous interchange if both are receptive. However, dancing often generates electricity and reflection about the performance that linger long afterward' (Hanna 1988: 18). As Hanna suggests, the b-girls produce a metaphor for me to think about feminism in popular culture and how my own motivations as a feminist figure into my ability to perform in the arena of the patriarchal academy. As a feminist, I am motivated by the daring, fluency and success of the b-girls who enter the circle after painstaking years of exclusion from, yet deliberate mastery of, b-boy rules and codes. As much as I am a dancer and enjoy watching popular dancing, the gender politics that I perceive to be active in breakdancing inform my chasing this story, and my research. As someone who often feels alienated by the national politics of the US both domestically and internationally, I appreciate hip hop and cultural resistance generally, and b-girls specifically, for their 'collective expressions of disaffiliation from Authority and the hegemony of the dominant classes (by either sex)' which, also for me, as for McRobbie have 'sent shivers of excitement down my spine' (1980: 48).

THE SOCIAL/HISTORICAL CONTEXT

My larger project is an ethnography of women in hip hop culture, especially within breakdancing. Given that breakdancing is one of the only male-dominated Western dance forms, I became fascinated with how women became assimilated into the culture by being schooled by men, learning, practising and perfecting the heightened masculine roles associated with hip hop, and then by both competing against and innovating among males. I saw this as a potentially positive example of successful cultural cross-gender, or transgender, code-switching and I see the advanced female breakdancers as political activists who have entered an institutionalized art form (even if the institution is/was the street), l/earned its rules and languages and then established the power to innovate and change the practice of dominant masculinity by changing both the codes and the rules of its performance. Thus, in this research context, I've completed interviews with old-school b-girls – women now over thirty – who have the value as interviewees of clear hindsight of their adolescent attempts to build stable identities within breakdancing communities.

For Guevara, the contemporary cultural politics of hip hop are underpinned by a consistent attempt to repackage 'black or Latino aesthetic innovations' to sell as entertainment to white America, so that 'the contextual and traditional meanings of those innovations have been airbrushed out. Cooptation by the dominant culture invariably involves repression' (Guevara 1996: 51). In seemingly direct response to Guevara, Rockafella speaks to this in our conversation, naming the appropriation, but denying, in her community's experience, the repression:

> Rockafella: And that's true how the media can brainwash you, 'Oh, this is passed; nobody does this anymore.' That's the one thing I love about hip hop is we're defiant in all respects, you know? I don't care if you think you're going to outdo or take it out, we're going to keep doing it, and we're going to keep it going. It's very defiant, and I think that's a quality I like and that I identify with. That's why it's going so left, you know, because we were really resisting having no identity, having nothing.

The co-optation of hip hop by the mainstream which Rockafella recognizes, and speaks of actively resisting, also works to represent it as a cultural form which is gendered in conventional, hierarchical ways. Mainstream representations of hip hop, like many other pop music forms, work to marginalize and silence women's contribution leaving them 'depicted in secondary roles as cheerleaders or bystanders rather than as producers and active participants' (Guevara 1996: 57). To counter this still popular notion that even I've witnessed in b-boy culture, Guevara corrects the record, and observes that while breakdancing is often seen as having developed as competition between men, it may also draw upon female dance practices:

The speedy footwork and acrobatic tricks of freestyle double-Dutch, for instance, are no less impressive than those of breakdancing. Like most breaking moves, this energetic female street game depends on how well the jumper balances her body weight, the swiftness of leg and feet movements, and the gracefulness of her performance. (Guevara 1996: 58)

I hesitate to fully align my own observations with those of Guevara, however, because I sense a strong competitive force in some b-girls, and it is this appropriation of traditional masculinity I find remarkable and engaging.

In the conversation with b-girls recorded here, I am interested not just in the contradictions, but also in the processes of social stratification that gather around discourses of race, class, sexuality, age and gender. These processes of social stratification sometimes create contradictions in human lives – or even non-contradictory antagonisms – but always create a complexity that requires the consideration and analysis of power relations, and almost always direct address and action. Griffin has pointed to the way that critical youth studies have contested the tendency to represent young people as either 'troubled or troubling' (2001: 148), and instead looks at 'cultural transformations (and stasis) in specific local, national and international contexts' (2001: 159–60). In the extract that follows, Aiko's account of the place and function of hip hop in her neighbourhood speaks precisely of this kind of grounded context in which youth cultural practices can be understood:

Charla: But you think both the popping and the gangs came from low-income environments?

Aiko: No, the gangs sprouted. They were always around, but they sprouted in what we call the hip hop communities, and popping came from that. Because, you know, they didn't have nothin' else to do. They weren't selling drugs. If they weren't doin' drugs, if they weren't doin' bad things, stealing, whatever, then they were dancing. You know what I'm saying?

Charla: So you see the dance as an alternative to these other things?

Aiko: Totally. That's exactly what I'm saying. And for me, coming from the neighbourhood I came from, and from this area in California, San Jose, this area was one of the worst areas you could live in. One of them. There's a few.

Charla: Why? What was so bad about it?

Aiko: There was drugs. There was hookers. There was people with knives, back when knives was the thing. Not really guns. [laughs] They couldn't afford those. So, you know what I'm saying? So it was really kinda a bad area, but we had, we supported each other in dance. You could go to Eastridge Mall and see the best dancers or groups going against each other. And that was our way out. Not to get involved with the negative. It saved me; totally saved me. Dance saved me.

Again, in my estimation, these moments and liminal, complex third spaces which sit between directly opposing parts, become the focus of my third-wave feminism. As representative of these socially fraught moments, we see Aiko illustrate the creative way in which dance became the resolution of the tension, the middle path, so to speak. Dance became the method to create a third space, the spaces momentarily outside of the antagonisms of poverty, crime, violence and the more destructive modes of dominant masculinity.

INSTITUTIONS AND RESISTANCE: NEGOTIATING HIP HOP, FAMILY AND SCHOOL

Charla:	OK, so I'm curious about several things. First of all, so you talked a little bit about what dancing was for you, but I'm curious what kind of family environments you all came from, and if the dancing was part of that, part of what you got at home?
Aiko:	I'm from a single-parented family. Mother with three kids. Didn't have a clue as to jobs, and security, and how to get a home. She so happened to come by really good people who allowed us to have a home, and happened to go back to school, to be able to earn enough to keep a home for us, to keep clothes on our backs, food in our mouths. And we were still really poor, and we didn't even know. We didn't know.
Rockafella:	Was there dancing in your house or music?
Aiko:	There was definitely music, because me and my brothers had a love for music, and soul was the music. Funk; you know what I mean?
Charla:	Just you and brothers? Sisters?
Aiko:	Just brothers. I was the baby, and I had two older brothers. And um, it was really hard. We grew up. It was really hard. But dance saved me. I love music; it was my get-away. It was like my fantasy … being able to …
Charla:	Your escape?
Aiko:	Yeah, my escape. Totally my escape. And I can't thank God enough for this escape.
Rockafella:	Wow! That's a deep story.
Aiko:	For real.
Charla:	Did your brothers dance?
Aiko:	[laughs] They tried. But they didn't dance like me. When my era came up, it was the late 70s and 80s when breaking was coming to its fullest, and

	locking was at its fullest, and popping had just come in, and breaking, you know what I mean? It was really the inner-city thing to do. You know, our only outlet. We can do it by ourselves. We don't need anybody else, you know what I'm saying? We don't need nothing. But maybe a radio. And if we don't have that, then we can practice on our own.
Charla:	So you said the schools were friendly to it?
Aiko:	Oh yeah, totally in the 80s.
Charla:	Were the teachers?
Aiko:	The teachers?
Charla:	Did they give you the space, or was it just tolerated?
Aiko:	No, it was outside. Always outside, and always tolerated. And we also were given a lunchtime kinda thing with turntables and a little stage. So they allowed us our vent. They knew that we needed to vent some way, somehow. And instead of letting the gangs build and fight after school, then they allowed this to happen.
Charla:	Do you think it's different now?
Aiko:	Yeah, because they don't feel it like we felt it then. It wasn't an alternative. Now it's a choice. You can be like, 'You know what, I can be in a gang, maybe hang out with my boys, and then if I wanna go over here and dance and get my props from the dances.' You know, now it's a luxury, whereas before, then, it was like, uh … an out.

What reveals itself clearly here is how central dance was to what Aiko sees as survival in situations of poverty. When asked about her family, she first talks about the urban blight and the rise of gangs in low-income, of-colour ghettos in San Jose. The surprising part is how easily the usual dichotomy between home and street in sub/cultural studies is disrupted by consideration of the school. At least in Aiko's experience in public schools in San Jose, California, hip hop artistic practice was given public space and licence in the late 1970s and early 1980s. This was, as Aiko believes, a conscious practice by school officials to create an 'outlet' for youth dealing with the oppression of poverty. If McRobbie (1980: 39) has noted how home and family is a 'structured absence' in subcultural analysis, so is the school. However, as my interviewees demonstrate, these are central to understanding hip hop.

Aiko's social analysis is profound. In her testimony, extra-curricular activity made or broke young people subjected to the same social conditions of poverty. From the picture she draws, I get an image of young innocent children trying to adapt to and simultaneously avoid hellacious social conditions. And I, personally, do not believe that drugs (legal or illegal) or sex work are inherently negative, but when these options show up in situations of economic hardship, they take on other meanings of dependency and dis-ease, even a menace to the people responsible, not to mention the children who do not choose the models of human life in front of them. In this sense, I find that the real value of a feminist cultural studies/interdisciplinary approach (both US- and British-based) is its scholars' willingness to deal with the gaps, absences, and contradictions that exist between social oppression, on the one hand, and resistance, on the other. In this sense, asking questions about the dancing, perhaps the most seemingly inane aspect of youth culture, brings a remembrance of both the social context around the dancing, as well as a consciousness that the individual decision to dance was a resistance practice of the most crucial kind.

In a 1996 study by Kum-Kum Bhavnani and Angela Y. Davis, 'Incarcerated Women: Transformative Strategies', they conduct interviews that they call 'conversations with a purpose', and upon which I've modelled my own conversations. Though not interested in ranking oppression, Bhavnani and Davis's claim that 'Imprisoned populations are more vulnerable than any other – both in respect to technologies of power used to control the body and to discursive processes that rectify the human being as prisoner' (1996: 149) can be compared to the situation of youth attempting to grow up healthfully in situations of social oppression. While practices of control are heightened in prison, one must wonder if humans aren't more vulnerable as children in the chaos of social oppression in ghetto life. And again, what I find so hopeful is how these two young women in particular, and others who end up straight in situations of social deprivation, actually re-'appropriate and discipline the body' (1996: 149), their own bodies. For these old-school b-girls, dance became their technique for contesting the destructive social forces around them and controlling their own bodies, and through this, their social status.

Finally, the girls' narratives of their family lives and how their participation in hip hop culture dis/connected them from/to their families' homes reflect the intersectionality that youth experience as they cross from the private to the public spheres. Aiko points out the clear economic oppression in her neighbourhood, and in what follows, Rockafella narrates her search for a stable identity amidst the competing demands of affiliations based on race and ethnicity, class, religion, gender and sexuality both within and outside of the family home:

Aiko: What was the year?

Rockafella: Well, that was seventh grade. High school – I went to an all girls school, so that was really different. The girls were not trying to break or anything like that. They did have their cliques, you know, the popular girls, the pretty girls, the butch girls.

Aiko: Was there hip hop in the girls' school?

Rockafella: There was. You always had like, maybe five. But I think the girls who did it in parochial schools were like the ones who had bad grades, who had problems, who got pregnant but had the abortion and everybody talked about her. You know, she was runnin' the line, she was the one tightening up in the bathroom. That religious family … or in that school, I had help to pay my tuition. A lot of poor people could apply to a fellowship thing, and they'd pay your tuition. But it seemed to me it was more the troublemaking girls who were into hip hop, and I thought that was cool, because as I was telling you before, my family moved around so much that I was always breaking friendships, making new friends, breaking that, going here, trying to fit in. You know, the new girl, again. So I was always having a little fight here, a little argument there. So when I got with these hip hop people girls, I was like, 'Oh, I can fit in because I can do this. I know this is the way it is.' The Mike Tyson dance, or whatever. [laughs] Yeah. That's the way I built an identity cuz I used to play ball, but again, that was a whole different part of me, so, in order to navigate the new school and the new girl thing, I was always like, 'Oh, hip hop, I can do this, and I can throw a wave, and I'm going to this party, and I got this fake ID; what's up?' So yeah, I ran away at sixteen and I went to live with my boyfriend, and he knew everybody in Queens, all the dancers from Washington Heights. He was just popular. He introduced me to the scene.

Charla: He was a b-boy?

Rockafella: Um, he could pop. He couldn't do much floor stuff, but I think my family really frowned on the whole hip hop thing… My parents did not like the breaking; they didn't like me running away; they didn't like the idea I was going to clubs. At that time I was exploring my sexuality; I was exploring how to smoke a cigarette, and all that, so it was banned – all that was contraband. 'Why can't you just be home? Be a good girl?' Religious, you know, I mean, 'You're being indecent. You're going out at what time? What time you coming back?' So hip hop was just evil; it was just negative.

Aiko: You were in a Catholic home?

Rockafella: Yeah, very, and very Latin. But even like Latin, like salsa, if I said I wanted to go to a party and wear a dress: 'No, you can't do that. Your skirt has to be past the knee, and you've gotta be a little more covered, and don't move your hips so much.' So even in that respect, it could have been Latin dance, but it still would have been like, 'Damn, you're too sexual.' Yeah, 'What are you asking for there?' But I think as I got older and more into breaking – well, when they knew I was breaking on the street for money, that was the biggest mortification for them. They were like, 'My daughter dancing on the street, with a bunch of guys? Oh my God!'

Besides this, their stories of growing up girls deeply resonated with my own. As bell hooks has written in her book, *Bone Black: Memories of Girlhood* (1996), young people are in the midst of grounding 'the foundation of selfhood and identity' as 'distinct from and yet inclusive of the world around' them (1996: xi). In particular, she says that we should see 'the significance of girlhood as a time when females feel free and powerful' (1996: xii). hooks points to the contradiction that young females must sustain, however, between feeling free and powerful and being treated and represented as domestic and powerless. She documents the relief and affirmation she found in Toni Morrison's stories:

> It wasn't simply that Morrison focused on black girls but that she gave us girls confronting issues of class, race, identity, girls who were struggling to confront and cope with pain. And most of all she gave us black girls who were critical thinkers, theorizing their lives, telling the story, and by so doing making themselves subjects of history. (1996: xii)

As Guevara says, 'Women obviously experience an even more intense opposition for their involvement in hip hop than do men. On top of official harassment come family and peer demands for composure in the name of femininity... as cheerleaders, bystanders, and exotic outsiders ... its supposedly masculine rituals threaten still another haven of male hegemony' (Guevara 1996: 61). Though breakdancing is largely done indoors now, both in studios and on stages, Rockafella, as an East Coast b-girl, had to contend with the complications rising out of working by dancing on the street for tips, because 'the street remains in some ways taboo for women' (McRobbie 1980: 46–7).

All women struggle to maintain a positive self-image and social identity, however, the struggle seems greater when gender differences are complicated by race and ethnicity differences, sexuality differences and class oppression. For these women in breakdancing, transgendering oneself in order to dance reminds us of other tomboys and the severe social punishment for girls who persist with these 'other' gender identities. Judith Halberstam explains that 'Tomboyism is punished, however, when it appears to be the sign of extreme male identification (taking a boy's name or refusing girl clothing of any type) and when it threatens to extend beyond childhood and into adolescence (1998: 6). The contradiction here is that while the family, culture and society may be punishing the girls for gender transgression, among their peers, Hazzard-Donald testifies that she 'knew that dance could help me to belong with my peers and garner admiration from within my community, and it could open an entire new realm of being, self-definition, and socialization' (Hazzard-Donald 2004: 513). Clearly, walking the fine line between youth culture's acceptance and society's rejection and punishment is an old story in American popular culture arising most fully in the rebel-without-a-cause figure. More sociologically, though, and particularly in the case of young women, 'the categories available to women for racial, gendered, and sexual identification are simply inadequate' (Halberstam 1998: 7). In this sense, 'For many of us too, escaping from the family and its pressures to act like a real girl remains the first political experience. For us the objective is to make this flight possible for all girls, and on a long-term basis' (McRobbie 1980: 44).

TRANSGENDERING: RESISTANCE TO SEXUALIZATION

Nevertheless, in breakdancing subcultures, the situation for girls has changed. In discussing the clothing and style choices females used to make in hip hop culture, I asked:

Charla: You used to wear baggy pants?

Rockafella and Aiko: Oh hell yeah. Yeah.

Aiko: Since I was nineteen, I was wearing big pants, and back then, nobody was wearing big pants. We'd wear um for dancing. It gave us more room to move.

Rockafella: We wore um cuz that's how everybody else was dressing. And it was the way to be. Honestly, women ... well even in the breaking times, we were over in tight pants, like with tight knees and stuff when breaking was out. And I don't think that women had their own way. Women just wore what the guys wore. So if they were wearing the tight Lees, and the Kangol, then so was I, even though I had braids, lipstick and big doorknocker earrings, but I had to do what they were doing. So when the guys went to big pants, the girls went to big pants. Because we had no real say. I mean this is recently that Ecko and FUBU are doing women's lines, but it was just whatever the guys were wearing, I was wearing.

Aiko: But that's also just part of hip hop. That was our scene; that was our thing. And it wasn't being told to us, 'Well this is hip hop, this is what you do.' It was the people we were around, and the type of music.

Rockafella: Yeah, we chose it. We reflected what was happening ... You know, though, we wore what the guys were wearing, and I had to change eventually, and I kept the baggy pants, but I changed my mannerisms, and my mouth. I was cussing so much ... But I think I felt like, I didn't wanna show my booty; I didn't wanna show my titties; I just wanted to be one of the guys, cuz dancing on the street, guys are always trying to get it. You know? So I think if I could just be like a man, you know, then maybe

	they'd respect me or just be afraid I'd pop 'em in the face or somethin', you know? So it was just a way to be…
Charla:	So how did you get your safety, with the clothes?
Rockafella:	Ummm…
Charla:	Or what's that like being around so many men in their world? Would you call breakdancing a man's world?
Rockafella:	Yeah, it is… It's just part of it. You just expect it. You just know that that's what they're gonna do, and instead, I'm either gonna write in my book, or get into my music, or dance, or be surface with them. You don't want to get too deep either, because you know I'm gonna be like, 'Why are you doing that?' [laughs]
Aiko:	[laughs] I'll turn into a nag, you know? Back in the day, though, there were so few females doin' anything, so I was in a group with all guys. And I always hung out with a bunch of guys, mostly dancers, emcees, you know, that thing called rappers. And I've always been who I was because I had two older brothers, and my mom's very strong, very strong woman, very outspoken, the mom-dad in one. So I ended up being the same way, and kinda' rough around the edges, and whatever, but I hung with the best of 'em, you know, not only because I was strong, because of how I grew up and because I had to. Like Rockafella said, 'Cuz you had to.' You had to. Otherwise, they catch you slippin', something's gonna happen. So you had to hold your own. So um, so, the girls in the scene definitely had to be…
Rockafella:	Rougher.
Aiko:	Yeah, rougher, to hold their own. But now days it's not really like that.
Rockafella:	No, it's not like that at all. They're safe. They're totally safe.
Aiko:	Yeah, because we have more numbers of girls and times have changed… You're not the only girl.
Charla:	You mean at a practice session or something?
Aiko:	Yeah, at a jam, at a competition.

McRobbie notes that while subcultures appear to offer boys 'a (temporary?) escape' from normative gender roles, the relative lack of girl subcultures affirms the relative lack of opportunity for girls to escape gendered expectations. In particular, for McRobbie, ideologies of heterosexual romance illustrate how '[f]or working-class girls especially, the road to 'straight' sexuality still permits few deviations' (1980: 45). McRobbie's analysis is both confirmed and refuted by the conversation documented here. In the new school, in a few cases, b-girls do have their own crews, females-only. And even in the old school, our conversation shows that females are both sticking together and supporting each other across the continent. As for compulsory heterosexuality, Rockafella's story illustrates the gender norming over and again both in her family, the schools she attended and in the subculture of hip hop she ran to in order to escape the family, school structures and restrictions against – and offences on – her blooming sexuality. Ironically, she ends up transgendering herself to hide her sexuality and its dangers on the street in male circles. In this sense, we see here how 'female masculinity is generally received by hetero- and homo-normative cultures as a pathological sign of misidentification and maladjustment, as a longing to be and to have a power that is always just out of reach' (Halberstam 1998: 9). Halberstam contends, however, and b-girls show us that 'what we understand as heroic masculinity has been produced by and across both male and female bodies' (1998: 2).

So while her escape into the subculture of breakdancing did not liberate her immediately, the b-girl has, over time, defeated the sexism through her skills and resolved the tensions that her transgendering created. Thus, in this case, Hebdige's (1979) notion of 'style' as practised by these b-girls was used to resist sexualization within the subculture, at the same time that it signified a challenge to the dominant culture. Mostly, though, taking on the style of breakdancing amounts to transgendering practices for sure, but in the end, to being a 'dope' b-girl. Sally Banes says that 'breaking began as a public showcase for the flamboyant triumph of virility, wit, and skill. In short, of style' (2004: 14). Thus, if Hebdige in a schema similar to Banes's considered style to be male, then in this case, it makes sense that style and 'masculinity must not and cannot and should not reduce down to the male body and its effects' (Halberstam 1998: xv). Either way, I've learned from these b-girls that dancing in a male-dominated subculture requires skill, but rocking the circle with full confidence in one's own stable identity comes with time and maturity:

Aiko: You know, it's also about a woman's maturity. What age are we when we finally say, 'I don't care what anybody thinks, I'm doing this for me, and I'm loving it.' And that's like what you said, maybe twenty, maybe later; it takes a lot.

Charla: It was twenty-three (Rockafella), and you too (Aiko)?

Aiko: I was twenty-five when I got back into it, but when I started doing it, I was way younger.

Tricia Rose offers a poignant reflection of women who participate in rap music that carries over to what I've found to be true with women in breakdancing. She says that by paying close attention to the genre and its creation, we can see how women 'provide for themselves a relatively safe free-play zone where they creatively address questions of sexual power, the reality of truncated economic opportunity, the pain of racism and sexism and, through physical expressions of freedom, relieve the anxieties of day-to-day oppression' (2004: 294). For the b-girls whose accounts are given here, breakdancing suggests a powerful third space of play, resistance and creative achievement.

BIBLIOGRAPHY

Alarcon, N. (1990), 'The Theoretical Subject(s) of This Bridge Called My Back and Anglo-American Feminism', in G. Anzaldua (ed.), *Haciendo Caras*, San Francisco: Aunt Lute Press.

Banes, S. (2004), 'Breaking', in M. Forman and M. A. Neal (eds), *That's the Joint: The Hip-Hop Studies Reader*, New York: Routledge.

Bhavnani, K and Davis, A. (1996), 'Incarcerated Women: Transformative Strategies', in I. Parker and R. Spears (eds), *Psychology and Society: Radical Theory and Practice*, London: Pluto Press.

Crenshaw, K. (1991), 'Mapping the Margins: Intersectionality, Identity Politics, and the Violence Against Women of Color', *Stanford Law Review*, 43, 6: 1241–99.

Davis, A. (1998), *Blues Legacies and Black Feminism*, New York: Pantheon Books.

Griffin, C. (2001), 'Imagining New Narratives of Youth: Youth Research, the "New Europe" and Global Youth Culture', *Childhood: A Global Journal of Child Research*, 8, 2: 147–66.

Guevara, N. (1996), 'Women Writin, Rappin, Breakin', in W. E. Perkins (ed.), *Dropping Science: Critical Essays on Rap Music and Hip Hop Culture*, Philadelphia: Temple University Press.

Halberstam, J. (1998), *Female Masculinity*, Durham, NC: Duke University Press.

Hanna, J. (1988), *Dance, Sex and Gender: Signs of Identity, Dominance, Defiance, and Desire*, Chicago: The University of Chicago Press.

Hazzard-Donald, K. (2004), 'Dance in Hip-Hop Culture', in M. Forman and M. A. Neal (eds), *That's the Joint: The Hip-Hop Studies Reader*, New York: Routledge.

Hebdige, D. (1979), *Subculture: The Meaning of Style*, London: Methuen.

hooks, b. (1996), *Bone Black: Memories of Girlhood*, New York: Henry Holt and Company.

McRobbie, A. (1980), 'Settling Accounts with Subcultures: A Feminist Critique', in S. Frith and A. Goodwin (eds), *On Record: Rock, Pop, and the Written Word*, New York: Pantheon Books.

Mohanty, C. (1991), 'Introduction', *Cartographies of Struggle: Third World Women and the Politics of Feminism*, Bloomington: Indiana University Press.

Morgan, J. (2004), 'Hip-Hop Feminist', in M. Forman and M. A. Neal (eds), *That's the Joint: The Hip-Hop Studies Reader*, New York: Routledge.

Oakley, A. (1981), 'Interviewing Women: A Contradiction in Terms,' in H. Roberts (ed.), *Doing Feminist Research*, London: Routledge & Kegan Paul.

Rose, T. (2004), 'Never Trust a Big Butt and a Smile', in M. Forman and M. A. Neal (eds), *That's the Joint: The Hip-Hop Studies Reader*, New York: Routledge.

Spillers, H. (1987), 'Mama's Baby, Papa's Maybe: An American Grammar Book', *Diacritics*, 17, 2: 65–81.

Tucker, S. (2000), *Swing Shift: 'All-Girl' Bands of the 1940s*, Durham, NC: Duke University Press.

CHAPTER 10

Illegitimate, Monstrous and Out There: Female *Quake* Players and Inappropriate Pleasures

Helen W. Kennedy

There have been relatively few explicitly feminist analyses of popular computer games playing as a cultural practice, and very few which engage positively with existing female players, their pleasures and their communities. The Cassell and Jenkins edited collection *From Barbie to Mortal Kombat* (1998) is still the only volume focusing on the issue of gender and computer game culture, and it largely deals with the issues of how to make better games for girls and how to improve female access to games playing, rather than engaging with the games and players that already exist (or existed then). T. L. Taylor's (1999, 2003) research into female players of the highly popular, massively multiplayer online role-playing game (MMORPG) *Everquest* (Sony Online, 1999) is a significant exception to this general tendency. The feminist response to female players of First-Person Shooter games (FPS) has been either to condemn them for their adoption of masculine values (as evidenced by hooks in Marriott 2003) or largely to dismiss these players as of little interest to feminism, and to privilege instead the creative practices of female game artists (Flanagan 2003). However, by locating these female play practices within a technofeminist framework, and by drawing on play and performance theory, it is possible to see that computer games can afford many moments for the creation of oppositional meanings, and further can allow for the elaboration of an oppositional identity. Computer game playing is a specific cultural practice where the popular meanings of technology, play and gender converge. Although one can never see games as anything but reflective of, and embedded within, capitalism, patriarchy or technoculture, they can at the same time provide the materials for the enunciation and exploration of alternative pleasures, practices, politics and subjectivities.

In the discussion that follows, I draw upon a case study which focuses on the consumption and production practices of individual female *Quake* players, female

Quake playing clans and the ways in which they have separately and collectively represented themselves to the rest of the online games playing community which has formed around *Quake*. This case study is part of an ongoing study of female games players, and the communities that have developed through their play and play-related practices. Here I will be drawing upon the online material produced by individual players and particular play communities (web pages, websites and other more specifically game-related creative practices), and interviews and correspondence with individual players. This research began in 2000 and the interviews were conducted over an eighteen-month period between 2001 and 2003, during which time I also learned to play the games in single-player mode, and played with other female players online. I also draw from earlier online archive material on specific female gamer websites such as www.grrlgamer.com. First, however, it is necessary to sketch out the specific context of these practices in order to better understand the ways in which these players and producers are required to negotiate and subvert particular meanings around appropriate feminine behaviour and appropriate feminine pleasures.

Quake (and its sequels) is an enduringly popular example of the 3D first-person shooter genre, making use of an innovative game engine that offered new possibilities in terms of the 3D representation space of the game and the speed of gameplay. *Quake* also offered multiplayer capabilities and eventually the possibility for it to be played online via dedicated game servers ('Quake 3: Arena' and 'Quake 3 Gold' are the latest iterations offering this online facility). *Quake* was initially released on 24 June 1996 as a shareware version, with the release of the official version following a few months later in August. The shareware ethos and the possibility of making changes to the game allowed fans unique access to the production and distribution of new game content for others to share (this process is known as modding – short for 'modifying') and in the process spawned an online community based around these practices. These fan activities have also enabled new forms of relationship between producers and consumers, where power relationships between them may become less fixed, less predictable and less easy to control.

Not all computer games have allowed for this degree of code manipulation on the part of the player, but as a result of this *Quake* has been extraordinarily successful in gaining and maintaining a devout network of committed players. The producers of *Quake* have actively fostered this range of cultural practices and have sought to facilitate the development of the community and the space for the exchange of material. This has made good economic sense for the producers of *Quake*, as it is this community of passionate players that can help to secure the success of a game. 'Disappointment tinged reviews of "Quake III", while often nonplussed with the actual content of the game proper, insisted it was worth buying for the support it would inevitably receive from the mod community' (*Edge*, #126, July 2003: 58). These factors have allowed for the emergence of highly visible participatory cultures in which there is a collapse of distinction between the dominant culture (the games industry) and the subculture (games players and modders) not typically associated with cinema going or television viewing (see Giddings and Kennedy 2005). There are two critical aspects of this fan/subcultural activity which are important for the following discussion of female *Quake* players: playing computer games involves an engagement and proficiency with computer technology, and computer game practices, competences and pleasures are highly gendered.

To play a computer game you have to master the interface in order to engage with the game at any level, from loading it through to making the settings suit your play style (at the very least analogous with setting up and operating a video recorder, for example). This means that at a very basic level you have to be able to make use of a mouse, and operate a keyboard simultaneously – these games require that you are adept at the handling of these controls and are incredibly unforgiving of the absolute novice. The moment that you click the mouse to signal your readiness for play, you are immediately thrown into a noisy, chaotic, confusing 3D environment filled with computer-generated characters whose sole function is to destroy your avatar as quickly and as efficiently as possible – even on the easiest setting in the game (there are several levels of difficulty available ranging from the novice, through hardcore to the hardest level 'nightmare'). The speed and pace of the game has to be adapted to very quickly in order to make any progress, and is quite distinct from the gentler more contemplative pace of strategy or role-playing games. This description provided by one female player neatly captures some of this complexity:

> You have to be able to use the mouse for more than just point and click – you have to sort of be able to use it around in space which is a bit different and it's easy to end up looking at the ceiling or getting stuck in corners and becoming frag bait. Oh, yeah, and your left and right hands are doing totally different things, you've got to really know where all the keys are. At first I couldn't get it all sorted out, changing weapons, jumping, moving around and shooting – it was all a bit much and my mouse hand would be doing one thing and I'd have to look at the keyboard to try and find the right keys... then after a while it all sort of clicks and you're just staring at the screen and your hands are going like crazy and you just sort of do it all on automatic and you feel like its you in there, sneaking round corners and fragging[1] that poor little eyeball on legs to bits... (Xena)

This can be extended to the processes of modification, which will require some facility with operating sub-programmes, understanding game code and operating graphics packages. Even without engaging in modding practices, in order to play online you will have to be able to navigate through the Web to find a server and choose a level to play that is active, each step requiring you to operate the computer with some skill and proficiency. Understanding computer games as an entry point for familiarity with computers has underpinned the politically motivated 'games for girls' movement. This movement, which began in 1995, was underpinned by the understanding that 'getting playful' early with technology is crucial in helping to gain access to jobs involving technology as adults. Games are seen, in this context, as a means of training users in particular skills that are deemed socially and culturally valuable. In this way, the development of technical competence and familiarity through gaming is seen as a valuable means to an end. Many others who are actively engaged with trying to improve female access to technology have focused on computer games as a critical means through which to foster technological competence (Cassell and Jenkins 1998; Laurel 2001; Graner-Ray 2004). A similar discourse of access operates amongst the key figures actively involved in the female *Quake* community. Vangie 'Aurora' Beal, who ran the 'gamegirlz' online resource and played in Clan PMS (Psycho Men Slayers), here makes a fairly typical statement enunciating a firm belief in this set of connections between play, technology and technological competence: 'Girls will start off working with computers by playing fun games, and will end up being able to fully compete with men in tech skills. Now that's something I like to be encouraging' (Cassell and Jenkins 1998: 328).[2]

The computer game thus emerges as the dominant playful medium for experience and pleasure, as well as the most profitable commodification of the potentials of computer processing. Importantly, computers and computer proficiency are symbolically coded as masculine. Coyle argues that 'to question the masculinity of computers is tantamount to questioning our image of masculinity itself: computers are power, and power, in our world, must be the realm of men' (1996: 43). Cockburn (1992: 39) also emphasizes the way in which technology forms a crucial part of our gendered identity. Not all men are adept with computers (or other highly valued forms of technology) and 'what is experienced as failure by individual men may not affect the general image of hegemonic masculinity. [However, t]hose who are masters demonstrate not only that they are "real men" themselves, but they demonstrate a phenomenon recognized as masculinity and confirm the meaning of the concept' (Lie 1995: 391). Computer games emerged fully bound up in this gendered symbology.

Game design, content, packaging and marketing all serve to demarcate games playing as a specifically masculine activity. This remains as true today as it was in the early 1980s, and this is despite the numerous attempts, both commercially and politically motivated, to undermine this notion. Brenda Laurel is one of the few female games designers to be recognized in the wider culture, and she was one of the key players in the 'games for girls' movement. Laurel confirms this gendered lineage of the computer game and computer game culture:

Computer games as we know them were invented by young men around the time of the invention of graphical displays. They were enjoyed by young men, and young men soon made a very profitable business of them, dovetailing to a certain extent with the existing pinball business. Arcade computer games were sold into male-gendered spaces, and when home computer consoles were invented, they were sold through male-oriented consumer electronics channels to more young men. The whole industry consolidated very quickly around a young male demographic – all the way from the gameplay design to the arcade environment to the retail world. (Keynote address given at Computer Human Interaction 98 conference, April 1998)[3]

To date, the majority of research and writing around female computer game players has tended to suggest that there exists a 'feminine' set of computer game pleasures and preferences – something which is vehemently resisted by many female players:

I keep reading about articles and studies where experts say girls don't like shooting and blasting games but instead prefer quiet, contemplative games with well-rounded characters and storylines that stimulate their imagination. I'd venture to say, however, that these studies are a reflection of how we condition girls to be passive. The image of a woman with a gun is too shocking, too disruptive and threatening to the male dominant order of things. (Aliza Sherman, Cybergrrrl, in Cassell and Jenkins 1998: 335)

'The notion that some forms of activity and entertainment are more appropriate to men and some to women, that some genres can be called "masculine" whilst others are labelled "feminine", has a long history' (Tasker 1993: 136). Whatever the intention, these studies of 'feminine' play styles and play preferences contribute to the construction of appropriate feminine tastes and behaviours, which cannot help but inform the ways individuals understand their preferences as either 'normal' or 'abnormal'. Female *Quake* players have to live with and reconcile the fact that their pleasures will be deemed unfeminine and inappropriate. In her feminist analysis of women's leisure, Betsy Wearing has drawn on Foucault's notion of heterotopias: '[i]n contrast to 'utopias' which are fictional critiques of society, without any actual locality, "heterotopias" for Foucault can be "real" existing places of difference which act as counter-sites or compensatory sites to those of everyday activity' (1998: 146). Wearing argues the importance of these 'counter-sites' as a means of experiencing alternative subjectivities and forms of self-empowerment not readily available in other aspects of daily experience, and suggests that they 'provide spaces for rewriting the script of what it is to be a woman, beyond definitions provided by powerful males and the discourses propagated as truth in contemporary societies' (1998: 147). The players themselves are quick to articulate a critique of normative femininity: 'People say it's not ladylike to sit in front of a computer or want to play a game where you run around with a shotgun, but why not? I get insulted a lot and told I'm like a boy, but I'm not. I'm just a different kind of girl' (Stephanie Bergman).

THE COMPUTER GAMES PLAYER AS CYBORG

To understand the specificity of computer games as a distinct cultural practice through which we engage with technology, it is useful to draw on theories of cyberculture. These theories seek to understand the ways in which technologies (particularly, but not exclusively, computer technologies and biotechnology) contribute to social relationships, cultural practices and subjectivity (Haraway 1990; Plant 1993; Featherstone and Burrows 1995; Stone 1995). Whilst such approaches must be addressed critically, they raise compelling issues that help to account for the experience of playing computer games as both material technologies and as a critical aspect of the technological imaginary. Computer games, like most computer applications, work through feedback between user and software. It has been argued that these games, or, more precisely, the circuit of game and player in the act of playing, are literally (for the duration of the game at least) cybernetic:

> We do not see here two complete and sealed-off entities: the player on the one hand and the game on the other. Rather there is an interchange of information and energy, forming a new circuit... Through the tactile and visual interface with the machine, the entire body is determined to move by being part of the circuit of the game, being, as it were, *in the loop*. (Lister *et al.* 2003: 370)

Computer games are not only populated by 'cyborgs' in the form of technologized superbeings and monstrous hybrids, but also produce the game player *as* cyborg. The figure of the cyborg (as developed by Haraway [1990]) offered us the idea that our new intimate connection with machines could create a space for identity affiliation and agency which would destabilize conventional relationships between body, machine and nature, challenging the 'command, control and conquer' logic of state/corporate digital domination. Instead of critiquing technology solely on the basis of its embeddedness in both a colonialist, teleological and capitalist set of processes, the dawning of the cyber age was met with a sense of new opportunities; the figure of the cyborg was offered by Haraway as a way to move beyond the potentially essentializing association of women with nature. Haraway (1990) offered the cyborg as a new metaphor for subjectivity, which could potentially avoid the problematic and pervasive binaries nature/culture, female/male. In so doing, she promoted the cyborg as a 'site of possible resignifications ... to expand the possibilities [of subjectivity] ... to enable an enhanced sense of agency' (Butler 1992: 16).

Crucial to this new sense of agency was a rally call for those who were deemed to be marginalized by technoculture to embrace their affinity with technology and to offer new symbols, new uses and practices through which to 'code' this new subjectivity. Female *Quake* players, their creative practices and the community they have developed should be understood as relevant to a technofeminist agenda that seeks both to offer new images of technologized embodiment, and to foster an active engagement with technology amongst women. Haraway argues, 'Cyborg imagery can suggest a way out of the maze of dualisms in which we have explained our bodies and our tools to ourselves ... [and provide] a powerful infidel heteroglossia. It is an imagination of a feminist speaking in tongues to strike fear... It means both building and destroying machines, identities, categories, relationships, spaces, stories' (1990: 223).

CYBORGIAN PLEASURES

Playing *Quake* is therefore a means for displaying or performing technological competence and a form of technological embodiment, but it is also the means through which technological competence can develop further beyond the game itself, as we shall see. When describing what they enjoy about *Quake*, women use terms such as 'athleticism', 'balance', 'coordination' and 'taking risks', in a way that suggests that the cyborgian nature of game play is experienced as a set of embodied pleasures. Although it is the avatar that performs these feats of athleticism or coordination within the game space, it is the player's skill in controlling the interface that shapes this performance. The sense of agency the players experience is doubled, and the player experiences a freedom of movement and sense of authority and mastery within the game alongside a sense of empowerment, through their skill in mastering the technology. These two responses indicate the double nature of their pleasure:

> I really like the way the other bots in the game respond to how well you are doing – they get really narked if you win and say things like let's all gang up and kill 'tankgirl' next time, or the machine says 'excellent' when you frag a couple of bots in a row. I know it sounds a bit, I don't know, but it makes me feel really good and I feel like I'm really there. (tankgirl)

> I loved the challenge with Hunter – she's so beautiful, and she says all this sort of spiritual stuff and she's really hard to beat one on one, and I felt really proud when I won when playing on 'hurt me plenty' mode which is quite hard. (Supergirl)

Many of these women articulate a strong sense of pleasure in surprising male players with their competence and skill when playing online or over LAN connections (local area networks such as those found in Internet cafes). They are aware that they are not expected to be good at these games, and gain enormous satisfaction in flouting convention. In this typical response, the player has first encountered *Quake* with a group of male friends at a cybercafe, became hooked, bought the game to practice at home and then subsequently had the opportunity to play against the same group of male players. 'Next time we played together over a LAN connection I held up my end and I could see that the blokes were really surprised and even a bit fed up that I was 'fragging' them so successfully… I LOVED IT!' (Amanda/Xena). These female players – who take pleasure in their mastery of a game seen as requiring skills which are clearly demarcated as masculine – are aware of the transgressive nature of their pleasure.

FROM PLAYER TO PRODUCER – FIRST YOU HAVE TO SLAY A KING

Considering the extent to which first-person shooter games are deeply steeped in masculine culture, it is no surprise that it created quite a stir when Stevie Case/ KillCreek – a young female game player from Kansas – defeated John

Romero (co-creator of *Quake*) in a series of *Quake* Death Matches in 1998. He was so impressed by her that he created a web shrine to celebrate her prowess – http://members.tripod.com/~heimstadt/stevie.com – 'The Temple of Stevie KillCreek Case and other "Quake" Goddesses'. KillCreek's skill and renown attracted a great deal of attention within the *Quake* community as well as outside – including a feature on Case in *Rolling Stone* and a feature in *Playboy*. KillCreek was subsequently involved in the beta testing for later versions of *Quake*, eventually worked with John Romero and continues to pursue a career in the games industry. Mastering the strategic and technical skills necessary to beat the designer of a game as popular as *Quake* is a significant achievement, and KillCreek remains an icon for other female 'Quakers'. Zoe Flower describes what it was like to have Case getting so much attention in the late 1990s:

> Case was getting all sorts of press and was the basic representative of women in games. I felt that it was a shame that the only woman in the spotlight was a gamer, and not a developer or someone with more influence in the world of game creation. But Stevie Case demonstrated just what it meant to be a woman gamer at the time. It was like she was from outer space, as if aliens had landed. (Zoe Flower)[4]

KillCreek's success led her to be approached by Angel Munoz, who was the founder of the Cyberathlete Professional League. She was signed up as the first member and competed for eighteen months, during which she was hailed as a 'torchbearer' for other female gamers and particularly for those interested in professional competitive gaming. 'Women are starting to realize that they have the same abilities in sports – and things like sport – as men', said Leann Pomaville, a 38-year-old former school teacher who runs the girl gaming sites 'Da Valkyries' and 'Quake Women's Forum'. 'Quake is a game where your own personal skill makes all the difference, like in a sport.' Further serving to undermine the notion of 'masculine' competences, these competitive *Quake* players destabilize the normative construction of 'masculinity' whilst also demonstrating its 'performative' nature. There are now highly competitive international all-female games tournaments that take place around the world.

SKINNING THE MONSTROUS FEMININE

Skinning is the art of creating the images that get wrapped around 3D player character models in 3D games. These images are what give the 'mesh' a solid, realistic look. A good analogy is if you think of the skin as the paper that goes around the bamboo frame (mesh) of a chinese lantern. You paint what you want on the paper and the game wraps it around the frame for you based on the mapping the model has with it. (Chiq/Milla, female *Quake* player and skin artist)[5]

A particularly adept skinner may eventually see her skin being included in the range of characters on offer to other players through online communities, and may receive prizes and acclaim for her art.[6] Skinning is not an easy process – some taking as much as sixty hours to complete; like other art forms, it is a process requiring a great deal of commitment and engagement. Camilla Bennett is a skin artist whose consumption/play practices have developed into more professional/creative activities.[7] A self-taught skinner since 2000, Milla has developed a high degree of competence and has moved on from designing her own skins to a professional role as a texture artist in the development of the skin for the heroine of Betty Bad (WildTangent), a web-based game, and has developed skins for 'Unreal Tournament' and produced art work for the company Liquid Development. Milla has also won a number of awards for her skins, and features prominently on the key website which operates as a trading post for 'skinners' and players (Polycount). Milla also operates as a role model for other female *Quake* players:

> I found this one skin artist 'Milla' and I thought – 'I want to do that'. Her website is the most beautiful and has this lovely front page with this line 'skin is armor' which I just loved I don't know why and she's really doing stuff and even getting awards and things for her skins. I like spent ages following all the links and there was like this whole community out there of other women producing really great images, and I followed up all the links on the 'Quake' sites and taught myself how to download different 'skins' for me to play around with and I even tried to make some of my own – not successfully though… (buff-e-girl)

This player is just one among many, for whom their game play becomes the jumping off point for a greater engagement with technology in general:

> It really made me want to learn how to use graphics on the computer – I had never thought that I could or that I would ever be interested, I'd done some online chatting, used the computer for emails and played some free web games and stuff but I hadn't thought of myself as any good with computers… A friend is teaching me how to use Photoshop on his computer and when I'm okay I'm going to try to do a really good skin and stick it up on the web. (Supergirl)

Chiq/Milla describes her own personal skin: 'Woods woman/warrior in a post-apocalyptic context. She's flaking rust, greasy and has these damn pesky hoverblades stuck to her feet.' The imagery used draws heavily from fantasy/science fiction as well as closely resembling the type of female subject that often crops up in feminist cyber punk literature. 'Female skinners sample elements from the pre-existing female character lexicon and add new flavours into the mix, resulting in fem monsters better suited to their female inhabitants' (Schleiner 1999). Such fantasy constructions of identity offer an exploration of alternative subjectivities in which being feminine does not necessarily equal being a victim or needing rescuing. Producing skins for their own use or to 'pimp' out to others allows players to engage in the production of images and symbols through which to articulate their own identity, tastes and agency. The skins often become the means through which a player will express aspects of her identity to other members of the community, either through its inclusion in a web page or during online tournaments.

As indicated above, it is clear that some feminist critics do not approve of women engaging with games like *Quake* and see little to celebrate in the creation of images of tough 'warrior women'. In an article which focused on both the recent increase in the number of active heroines in film, television and computer games and the rise in the number of women enjoying shooter games, bell hooks offered a dismayed response: 'Most disturbingly ... the female protagonists who engage in physical combat in popular movies, television programs and video games encourage women not to challenge patriarchy ... The effect is especially potent in video games ... because the games' fantasies are so immersive' (cited in Marriott 2003). I have encountered a very similar response when I have discussed female *Quake* players at conferences and in seminars. Very often, there is an anxiety that these women are merely playing at being like men; a more extreme response was that within the current climate of terrorism and acts of random violence, women enjoying playing violent shooter games was symptomatic of the final decline of civilization. Here we see a notion of appropriate womanhood as 'nurturing' and peace-loving, alongside an uneasy slippage between 'fantasy' and reality. What happens within this critique is that women who do engage in these practices or take pleasure in them are ascribed a 'false consciousness'. The claim that they encourage women 'not to challenge patriarchy' suggests that these women are willing dupes in their own oppression – their pleasure is pleasure only in their own subjugation. This would suggest that we could establish a specifically feminist game pleasure and a correlative set of appropriate images that could be decided in advance. What is needed is a recognition of the heterogeneity of play practices and pleasures, and their role in providing experiences of empowerment – both within the game and as an engagement with technology.

FEMALE QUAKE COMMUNITIES

The online capability of these games has allowed for the emergence of 'clans' (teams of players who compete against other teams in tournaments) who may also develop their own particular clan 'skins'.[8] A number of communities have formed through these play practices – some are clan specific, while others are more open.[9] 'Network shooters like "Quake" and "Unreal" enable social grouping into clans that coalesce both locally among friends, workers and family, and also long distance over the Internet. The female clan offers a powerful support structure to female gamers, a place where knowledge can be shared and friendship bonds strengthened that extend outside the scope of the game' (Schleiner 1999). This is particularly significant in relation to the 'offline' representations and constructions of computer game culture, whether television programmes, which may feature a female presenter but clearly address a male audience, to the numerous magazines – official and unofficial – which through their style, layout, content and tone indicate their address directly to a male (and frequently adolescent) audience. Scantily clad female bodies are used in advertising promotions for many games; games industry gatherings feature a preponderance of booth babes who are there to entice the 'putatively' male professional (developers, designers, writers, reviewers). As a financially significant player in popular culture, computer games remain the most resolutely sexist in their advertising, marketing and promotions. Yet in the heterotopic world of online game culture, female gamers and game reviewers have found a context that enables them to enunciate their identity, declare their existence and to find others of their kind. Through the creation of web pages, websites and webrings, these women are able to recognize and affirm each other's identity as 'gamer' in opposition to an offline context where they are invisible, marginalized and frequently demeaned. This is of particular significance to players who may feel isolated as a female:

> I was the only female I knew who played and then one day I went on the Web and discovered all these sites and women and art and chat about games and I just thought 'wow' – there weren't just loads of other women out there playing 'Quake' but they were making stuff with the game as well, new 'skins' for the female game characters, sharing them out with other women and even playing together online in what they called 'clans'. (Xena)

The female *Quake* playing community demonstrates a playful use of names to demarcate a specifically oppositional female identity within the online community. This is true both of the naming of individuals and the naming of clans or communities such as Chiq, Hellchick, Supergirl, Geekgirl, Clan PMS (Psycho Men Slayers), Da Valkyries and The Women of Quake, Clan Crack Whore, Nimble Little Minxes, The Coven, Hell's Warehouse. The names appropriate female subjectivities and identities that are drawn from real or mythical monstrous female identities (these names are also evocative of the kinds of radical feminist re/mis-appropriation of previously pejorative terms). In so doing, they demonstrate their perception of themselves as countering hegemonic representations of femininity as well as the masculine representation of games culture and games players in general. Female *Quake* playing personae are chimeric, cyborgian and disruptive; they appropriate the demarcation of the female body as already always monstrous and redeploy these images as a 'tactical assault' on the normative construction of this identity. The images and names clearly draw from a long history of transgressive feminist informed femininity, countering notions of femininity as passive or nurturing. By foregrounding both their 'femaleness' and their skill in the game, they offer a different set of meanings for computers, computer games and technological competence. By bringing their own bodies or their fantasized bodies to the play arena, they disrupt the assumption of a white male heterosexual player and avatar. They also problematize the dominant image of games playing as a masculine retreat from the 'feminized' body, and make the female body figure as an agent in this relationship with technology. In so doing, they offer compelling representations of cyborg subjectivity.

> Lethal female body architecture, deft combat moves and an organized female affront in the form of female gamer clans are shifting the gender topography of the shooter. Working the keyboard and mouse behind these female fighting machines are the women players who have dared to cross a rigid gender boundary into a violent gamer culture often understood by men and women alike as a boys' world (embraced by men affirmatively, often disparaged by women). (Schleiner 1999)

This celebration and reappropriation of the monstrous feminine cannot be dismissed as simply 'aping' masculinity; as already suggested, their performance of skills which have been deemed masculine can be read as undermining the assumption of a 'male body' as the site of these competences (Butler 1992).

Recourse to performance theory enables us to understand the relationship between play, ritual and performance, but also to understand the cultural signific-ance of play as a kind of performance. Victor Turner offers an account of both the individual significance of play and performance, but also their significance in the formation of communities and the enunciation of community identity. Turner describes various types of play, both traditional and modern, and seeks to understand their personal and social significance. Like Bakhtin, he understands rituals, festivals and play as sites both of the affirmation of cultural norms and standards, and also of potential cultural critique. The special time and space of play is described as liminal or liminoid – they have a different character and are positioned differently in relation to the dominant meanings of the culture within which they are located. The liminal is characterized as a type of play or ritual that is often compulsory in some sense – either a community gathering or an essential 'rite of passage'. Whilst these activities may contain within them either the 'abrogation or negation' of existing power structures and subjectivities, they are seen as a means of more securely anchoring their participants to the status quo. Liminoid phenomena, on the other hand, are much more individualized and commodified; they 'develop apart from the central economic and political processes, along the margins, in the interfaces and interstices of central and servicing institutions – they are plural, fragmentary and experimental in their character' (Turner 1982: 58). Liminal and liminoid are both for Turner the 'seedbeds of cultural creativity', but it is the liminoid which has the power to transform through radical 'manifestos' and critique.

Turner's notion of the liminoid thus not only gives us the notion of play as a source of creativity, but also the possibility to consider play as a site of political meanings and interventions: play has both a hegemonic function and a critical one. This understanding of these liminoid 'situations as settings in which new models, symbols, paradigms arise' (Turner 1982: 28) provides us with a means of acknowledging the role that play can have in allowing individuals and groups to subvert dominant meanings, and is an appropriate framework through which to understand the heterogeneous practices of individual female players and the communities that have formed around these practices. Turner also offers us a further useful analytical tool – the notion of *communitas*; this is relevant to the ways in which members of the female games community enunciate their identity in relation to the dominant masculine games community, but also to how 'communities of players' in general position themselves as 'other' to ideas of work-based communities. For Turner *communitas* 'does not represent the erasure of structural norms from the consciousness of those participating in it; rather its own style, in a given community, might be said to depend upon the ways in which it symbolises the abrogation, negation or inversion of the normative structures in which its participants are quotidianly involved' (1982: 58).

These feisty, fearless and transgressing female gamers taking up space and answering back are performing a kind of gender insubordination which may not be feminist in its intentions, but may be feminist in its effect upon themselves as subjects and within the wider community. These online personas or avatars provide us with representations of performed subjectivities, where the boundaries of what is acceptable are potentially different from those experienced in the offline setting. The web pages, websites and online personas can be viewed as enunciations of identity that are directed at particular discourses important to them. These performative spaces enable the living out (however temporarily) of imaginative heterotopian identities or playful representations of self, which may be limited and constrained, but in very different ways to the offline context they regularly inhabit.[10] Certainly, the successful repetition of these performances appears to have direct consequences on the offline subjectivity in that in the examples given here, the games players also achieve a different status within the culture as they access a producerly mode of engagement with technology.

FEMINISM 'IN' AND 'AT' PLAY: FEMALE QUAKE PLAYERS AND THE POLITICS OF SUBVERSION

The female *Quake* playing community makes no specific claims to a feminist agenda or a feminist politics, yet it is clear from the practices of the community that their activities are at least implicitly informed by issues which have been central to feminist critiques of technology and of popular culture. They have often deployed a (sometimes contradictory) feminist discourse in the articulation of their relationship to the game culture in general. On the one hand, they have produced websites, web pages and formed clans through which to enunciate their outsider status by means of naming and the imagery that inspires their skins. Their activities are analogous to other kinds of feminist practice, where separate space is deemed important for the critical work of developing a network and supporting other women. They make use of language derived from feminist debates, through which they describe their experiences and critique the representation and treatment of women in computer games and computer games culture. More recently, Stephanie Brail (a prominent player and spokesperson in the female games community) has made more explicit reference to feminism in an interview that celebrated the success of female websites in helping to foster a more inclusive community for female players online. She also, however, bemoaned the continued sexism and sexist imagery in games content and in the games industry in general:

A lot of women want to hide their heads in the sand these days. Out of some sort of bizarre denial, they want to believe that anything slightly related to feminism is just a bunch of radical, bitter, (heaven forbid) lesbian hoo-ha that doesn't really apply to them... How does this relate to computer and video gaming? If you think women have equality in this arena, then all you need to do is pick up a game magazine or read the credits at the end of a video game. How many women play vital roles in reporting on video and computer games? How many women programmers or designers do you see?

Brail makes the connection between the role of women in the industry and the representation of women in computer games:

> It's obvious when playing most video games who's in charge here: men. Many titles are the video game equivalent of beer commercials. I mean, c'mon, let's take a recent game release, 'Dead or Alive Beach Volleyball', in which there is a bunch of women in bikinis with big fake boobs bouncing up and down in virtual sand.
>
> Some women look at skimpily clad, big breasted women in games and yawn, saying that men in video games are often similarly attired in next to nothing and also have good bodies. Sure, but there's a huge difference between a man with no shirt on and a man showing off his huge throbbing manhood through tight underwear. Have you ever seen *that* in a video game? Or how about a guy in a thong? I sure haven't. Men in games are not portrayed sexually: women are. (Brail, 2005)

In Mary Flanagan's analysis of women artists creating games, she emphasizes the critical aspect that women are using the medium of games as a means of 'self-discovery' (2003: 371). Flanagan stresses that her interest is in 'women making games for themselves, using the tools of this system, countering them, and making new meaning with them' (2003: 380). She argues:

> [w]omen game artists are in some ways the embodiment of the cyborg 'weaver' imaged by cyberfemininsts such as Haraway and Plant, though in an unpredictable and unromantic way ... these game makers are technically proficient women who have chosen to incorporate cyberfeminist and political ideas into their work while remaining conscious of the limitations imposed by their male-constructed and -dominated artistic platform. With their clear evaluation of social experiences such as discrimination, violence, the representation of women ... as well as their unique notions about the body, homeland, landscapes, and social constructions as they relate to the body and to identity, women's games celebrate the act of playing as a means of self-discovery. (2003: 381)

Despite their lack of specific feminist intentions, the female *Quake* players, skinners and their community make precisely this kind of intervention. Many of the websites which function to service and maintain the female gaming community offer critiques of the representation of women in games, share experiences of sexist behaviour, debate the efficacy of creating games specifically for girls and women and provide a valuable, highly participatory space for other female gamers to contribute to these debates. Simultaneously, they offer positive images, experiences and role models for other female players as well as frequently offering technical support and instruction in how to create their own web pages, websites or how to use particular software.

Flanagan distinguishes the female artists from the 'women in games' community or grrrlgamer community: 'they are not seeking to create new gaming paradigms. Rather, they work to get women "accepted" by the male gaming communities playing male games and offer camp-like readings of popular existing games' (2003: 380). It is not necessary to dismiss the everyday practices of those who lack the critical or technical knowledge required to make the kind of explicitly feminist and theoretically informed work which Flanagan privileges; these works would potentially be opaque to those without the necessary skills to decode and decipher their meanings and their politics. Whilst these female game artists are making a valuable and potent contribution to the meaning and understanding of computer games (as is Flanagan in her valuable celebration of their work), we need not dismiss the pleasures and practices of those who do actively engage with and take pleasure in popular games culture. As Yvonne Tasker has pointed out in relation to a similar trend within feminist film criticism, 'this critical trajectory reveals the operation within feminist criticism of a class-based, high cultural, attitude towards the popular ... an attitude familiar from other forms of criticism' (1993: 136). Flanagan's use of quotation marks around the word 'accepted' also suggests that this is somehow both easier and less meaningful.

I would argue that these women who take pleasure in and contribute to popular games culture contribute significantly to the democratization of technology and technological competence in a way that elitist/artist interventions can rarely hope to achieve. Popular games culture is made up of a range of heterogeneous players, practices and pleasures and it is the crucial site where dominant notions of technology, gender and technological competence are constructed, negotiated and contested. Sustained feminist engagement with computer games as a site of pleasure and as a form of active engagement with technoculture is long overdue.

NOTES

1. Fragging is the term given to killing another character (or bot as they are sometimes described) in the game.

2. All quotations from this edited collection are taken from the end section of the book, where prominent figures in the female games community respond to the issues raised by the essays in the volume.
3. http://www.tauzero.com/Brenda_Laurel/Recent_Talks/Technological_Humanism.html.
4. 1999 http://www.gamegal.com/zoeflower/zoe5.html.
5. www.chiq.net.
6. http://www.planetquake.com/polycount is a site that monitors and nominates particular skins, as well as providing guides and downloads of recommended skins and mods.
7. See her work online at www.chiq.net.
8. An amusing example is The Partridge Family Quake Clan viewable at http://www.geocities.com/Area51/Cavern/2690
9. Planet Quake (http://www.planetquake.com) is perhaps the most important example of the latter.
10. See Taylor (2003) for a discussion of this in relation to Everquest players.

BIBLIOGRAPHY

Brail, S. (2005), 'Why Games Need Grrrl Power', available online at http://www.grrlgamer.com/fragem/grrlpower.html (accessed February 2005).

Butler, J. (1992), 'Contingent Foundations: Feminism and the Question of "Postmodernism"', in J. Butler and S. Joan (eds), *Feminists Theorize the Political*, London: Routledge.

Cassell J. and Jenkins, H. (eds) (1998), *From Barbie to Mortal Kombat: Gender and Computer Games*, Cambridge, MA: MIT Press.

Cockburn, C. (1992), 'The Circuit of Technology: Gender, Identity and Power', in R. Silverstone and E. Hirsch (eds), *Consuming Technologies: Media Information and Domestic Spaces*, London: Routledge.

Coyle, K. (1996), 'How Hard Can it Be?', in L. Cherny and E. R. Weise (eds), *Wired_Women: Gender and New Realities in Cyberspace*, Washington: Seal Press.

Featherstone, M. and Burrows, R. (eds) (1995), *Body and Society* Special Issue 'Cyberspace/Cyberbodies/Cyberpunk: Cultures of Technological Embodiment', 1, 3–4 November.

Flanagan, M. (2003), '"Next Level": Women's Digital Activism through Gaming', in G. Liestol, A. Morrison and T. Rasmussen (eds), *Digital Media*

Revisited: Theoretical and Conceptual Innovations in Digital Domains, Cambridge, MA: MIT Press.

Giddings, S. and Kennedy, H. W. (forthcoming 2005), 'Digital Games as New Media', in J. Rutter and J. Bryce (eds), *Understanding Digital Games*, London: Sage.

Graner-Ray, S. (2004), *Gender Inclusive Game Design: Expanding the Market*, Hingham: Charles River Media.

Haraway, D. (1990), 'A Manifesto for Cyborgs: Science, Technology, and Socialist Feminism in the 1980s', in L. J. Nicholson (ed.), *Feminism/Postmodernism*, London: Routledge.

Laurel, B. (2001), 'New Players, New Games', available online at www.Tauzero.com (accessed 20 March 2004).

Lie, M. (1995), 'Technology and Masculinity: The Case of the Computer', *The European Journal of Women's Studies* (Special Issue on Technology), 2, 3: 379–94.

Lister, M., Kelly, K., Dovey, J., Giddings, S. and Grant, I. (2003), *New Media: A Critical Introduction*, London: Routledge.

Marriott, M. (2003), 'Fighting Women Enter the Arena, No Holds Barred', *New York Times*, 15 May.

Plant, S. (1993), 'The Future Looms: Weaving, Women and Cybernetics', *Broad Sheet*, 22, 3: 12–16.

Schleiner, A.-M. (1999), 'An Underworld Game Patch Router to Female Monsters, Frag Queens and Bobs whose First Name is Betty', available online at http://www.opensorcery.net/mutetext.html (accessed 11 September 2003).

Stone, A. R. (1995), *The War of Desire and Technology at the Close of the Mechanical Age*, Cambridge, MA: MIT Press.

Tasker, Y. (1993), *Spectacular Bodies: Gender, Genre and the Action Cinema*, London: Routledge.

Taylor, T. L. (1999), 'Life in Virtual Worlds: Plural Existence, Multimodalities, and Other Online Research Challenges', *American Behavioral Scientist*, 43, 3: 436–49.

—— (2003), 'Multiple Pleasures: Women and Online Gaming', *Convergence*, 9,1: 21–46.

Turner, V. (1982), *From Ritual to Theatre: The Human Seriousness of Play*, New York: Performing Arts Journal Publications.

Wearing, B. (1998), *Leisure and Feminist Theory*, London: Sage.

WEBSITES

www.chiq.net
www.elspa.com
www.gamegirladvance.com
www.gamegirlz.com
www.grrlgamer.com
www.caligirl.net
www.planetquake.com/qwf/resources.htm (Quake Woman's Forum)
www.riotgrrl.com
www.womengamers.com
Http://members.tripod.com/~heimstadt/stevie.com 'The Temple of Stevie
    KillCreek Case and other Quake Goddesses'

Index

abortion, 31, 87
Adams, N., 126
Adkins, L., 152
Adorno, T., 98
Advertiser, The, 29
Age, The, 33, 35
Akass, K., 13, 80, 81, 83
Akhavan-Majid, R., 33
Alarcon, N., 164
Albrechtson, J., 35
Alcott, L., 102
'Alias', 60
Alice Doesn't Live Here Anymore, 44
'Ally McBeal', 8, 12, 16, 44, 60, 79–93, 104
Alther, L., 1
Ang, I., 6
Angelou, M., 60
Anthony, S. B., 60
Appleyard, D., 107
Arch of Triumph, 18
Arndt, B., 35
Art of Cooking, The, 54n.3
Arthurs, J., 11, 79, 92
Australian, The, 35

b-girls, 161–81
Baby Boom, 105, 108
backlash, 7–8, 43, 59, 84, 102–3, 105, 111, 145–6
Bakhtin, M., 196
Banes, S., 163, 179
Barker-Plumber, B., 30
Barthes, R., 42
Bartky, S. L., 147–9, 155
Baumgartner, J., 62, 71n.10
Beal, Vangie 'Aurora', 186
beauty, 6, 17, 64, 143–59
Beck, D. B., 71n.5

Bell, D., 55n.13, 97, 110, 112
Bellafante, G., 60
Benning, S., 66
Berggren, H., 28
Bergman, I., 18
'Beyond River Cottage', 115n.5
Bhavnani, K., 146, 174
body, the, 145–57
Bourdieu, P., 156–7
Bowlby, R., 102
Boyd, R. L., 145
Bradley, P., 27–9
Braidotti, R., 83
Brail, S., 197–8
Braunstein, R., 28
breakdancing, 17, 161–81
Brewis, J., 112–13
Bridget Jones's Diary, 58, 60, 69, 80, 84
Broadcasting Standards Council, 123
Brumberg, J. J., 66
Brunsdon, C., 4–5, 6, 8–9, 100–1, 104, 105, 106
Bryson, J. R., 152
'Buffy the Vampire Slayer', 18, 44, 60, 64, 69, 99, 104
Burnside, A., 106
Burrows, R., 188
Bush, G., 36
Bush, G. W., 46
Butler, J., 2, 189, 195
Byron, C. M., 53n.2

Call Off Your Old Tired Ethics (COYOTE), 125
Carlip, H., 71n.10
Carr, K., 107
Casey, E., 11, 97
Cassell, J., 183, 186
'Changing Rooms', 41
'Charlie's Angels', 2, 6

Chesterton, G. K., 55n.14
Child, J., 55n.16
Chocano, C., 84
Clarke, A. J., 97
class, 9, 11, 14, 32, 47–8, 59, 99, 109, 111–13,
    136, 145–7, 147, 164, 167, 171, 174
CNN, 33
Coalition Against the Trafficking of Women, 131
Cobb, S., 70n.3
Cockburn, C., 186
Cole, A., 71n.5
comedy, 79–81, 82–3, 85, 90–3
computer gaming, 17, 183–202
consumption, 10–11, 14, 50–1, 62, 64, 97–8,
    109–10, 120, 145–6, 152, 154
cooking, 41–2, 46–8, 51–2, 101, 105–7
cosmetic surgery, 146, 149–50
Cosmopolitan, 1
Costain, A. N., 28
Country Life, 108
Coyle, K., 186
Craig, M. L., 146, 149–51, 156
Craven, W., 16, 57, 58
Craddock, F., 55n.16
Craddock, L., 70n.3
Crenshaw, K., 164
Crittenden, D., 107
Curthoys, A., 31
cyberfeminism, 61, 189–90, 195, 198

D'Acci, J., 54n.4
Daily Mail, The, 107
Davis, A., 71n.5, 162, 174
Davis, K., 147, 149–50
'Delia's How to Cook', 54n.11
Denfield, R., 59
Depp, J., 42
Di Franco, A., 60
Dicker, R., 71n.10
Dillon, M. J., 91
documentary, 119–33
Doezema, J., 127, 131
domestic violence, 34–5
domesticity, 17, 41–65, 97–115, 145
Douglas, S. J., 72n.15
Dovey, J., 128
Dow, B. J., 13, 79
downshifting, 106, 109–13
Drake, J., 14, 62, 71n.5, 71n.10, 63–4

'ER', 18
eating disorders, 86, 89–90, 145–6
ecofeminism, 109–10
Echols, A., 102
Edge, 185
'Edge of Darkness', 135
education, 172–6
'Ellen', 18
Elliot, P., 135
Elliott, J., 112
Elshtain, J. B., 103
Equal Pay Act (1975), 43
Equal Rights Amendment, 32
'Escape to River Cottage', 115n.5
'Escape to the County', 108
Espenson, J., 18
ethnography, 144, 167–9
Everquest, 183, 200

Faludi, S., 7–8, 59, 84, 103, 111
fandom, 85–90, 185
fashion, 6, 147–8
Faust, B., 30
Fearnley-Whittingstall, H., 108, 115n.5
Featherstone, M., 188
Felski, R., 98, 100
film, 4–5, 42–5, 66–7
'First Sex', 121
First Stone, The, 35
Fish, R., 108
Flanagan, M., 183, 198–9
Fleming, V., 18
Forster, L., 11
Foucault, M., 89, 147–8, 188
Fox-Genovese, E., 59
Fraser, N., 37–8
'Frasier', 91
French, M., 106
'Friday Night Fever', 123
Friedan, B., 4, 6, 8, 101–2, 103, 107, 109
'Friends', 91
Furman, F. K., 151

Gamman, L., 9, 10, 11
Garner, H., 35
Garrett, R., 70n.3
Garrison, E., 14–15, 71n.10
Gay, 82, 90, 92, 121
Gaynor, G., 2

generational politics of feminism, 1–2, 13–15,
    43–5, 57–72, 163, 168–9
Genovese, A., 34, 35, 37
genre, 44–5, 67, 81, 90–3, 119–20, 123, 127,
    133–7, 187–8
'Get A New Life', 108
Ghazi, P., 107–8, 109
Giddens, A., 100
Giddings, S., 185
Giles, J., 98, 100, 101, 102
Gilligan, C., 57
Gillis, S., 12–14
Gilman, S. L., 150
Gimlin, D., 151
girl power, 57, 64
Global Taste, 54n.3
Globalization, 62, 97, 120, 126–7, 129–33,
    136–7
Glover, G., 106
Gold Diggers, The, 5
'Golden Girls, The', 79
Golding, P., 128
Good, G. E., 91
Gottlieb, J., 10–11
Goward, P., 35
Gramsci, A., 38
Graner-Ray, S., 186
Green, K., 71n.10
Greer, G., 16, 27, 29–30, 103, 106
Gregson, N., 112
Greven, D., 92
Griffin, C., 171
Grosz, E., 148
Guardian, The, 122–3, 126
Guevara, N., 165, 170–1, 176

Habermas, J., 36–7
Hakim, C., 99–100
Halberstam, J., 176, 177, 179
Hall, E. J., 8
Hallam, J., 8, 106
Hamilton, C., 108
Hanna, J. L., 169
Hanson, P., 36
'Happy Days', 93n.3
Haraway, D., 188, 189, 198
Harding, S., 144
Hardwicke, C., 66
Hargrave, A. M., 119, 123

Harry, D., 2
Hartley, J., 36–8, 82
Haskell, M., 4
Hays, C. L., 46
Hazzard-Donald, K., 163–4, 176
Hebdige, D., 179
Henry, A., 10, 79
heterosexuality, 11, 60, 62, 63–4, 86, 90–1, 109,
    178, 155, 163, 178–9
Heywood, L., 14, 62, 71n.5, 71n.10, 63–4
Hinds, H., 2–3, 54n.6
hip-hop, 9, 162, 163–4, 167, 169, 170–1, 172–7
Hollows, J. 55n.15
'Home Front', 41
'Home Improvements', 91
hooks, b., 71n.5, 61, 176, 183, 193
Horsfield, M., 98
How to Be a Domestic Goddess, 46, 52, 105–7
How to Cheat at Cooking, 54n.11
How to Eat, 51
Howell, J. 33
Huddy, L., 27
Hughes, J., 66
Humphries, J., 112

I Don't Know How She Does It, 105
immigration, 17, 34, 36, 120, 126–7, 131–2
In This World, 133
Inn of the Sixth Happiness, The, 18
International Organisation for Migration, 132
International Union for Sex Workers (IUSW),
    125, 129
Iredale, W., 112

Jackie, 2
Jackson, S., 97
Jameson, F., 14, 62–3
Jancovich, M., 79
Jenkins, H., 11, 72n.15, 183, 186
Jensen, S., 84
Joan of Arc, 18
Johnson, L., 100, 114n.2
Johnson, M. L., 126–6
Johnston, C., 5
Jones, J., 107–8, 109
Jones, L., 64, 72n.14
Jong, E., 106
Just Seventeen, 2
'Jump-the-Shark', 85–91

Karlyn, K. Rowe, 9, 104
Kennedy, H. W., 185
Keyes, M., 45, 53
Kilvington, J., 124
Kinflicks, 1
Krais, B., 156
Kuhn, A., 123

'L Word, The', 18
'L. A. Law', 12, 18
labour, domestic, 49–50, 98, 99, 101, 106, 112, 146
labour, paid, 119–37, 143–5, 152
Langer, J., 128
Laurel, B., 186, 187
Lawson, N., 41–2, 46, 51–2, 105–7
Lee, J., 9, 11
leisure, 49–50, 55n.14, 112, 152, 154, 188
lesbian sexuality, 18, 34, 62, 82–3, 84, 86, 90, 121
Levin, M., 32
Levine, E., 6
Lewis, L., 11
liberal feminism, 4–5, 7, 13, 16, 101–2, 113
Lie, M., 186
Liepe-Levinson, K., 125
Light, A., 106
Light Reading, 42
Lister, M., 188
Little, J., 109
Lloyd, J., 100, 114n.2
Lotz, A., 13, 54n.4, 71n.10, 79
Lowe, L., 61
Lowe, M., 112
Lucy Sullivan is Getting Married, 45
Lumby, C., 36, 61
Lury, C., 11
Lyons, J., 79

McCabe, J., 13, 80, 81, 83
McDonald, M., 128
McKee, A., 37
McLachlan, S., 128
McLaughlin, L., 119, 124, 130, 133
McLean, G., 122–3
McRobbie, A., 5, 9, 10, 15, 43, 70n.3, 104, 105, 162, 168, 169, 173, 176, 178
'Mad About You', 89
Madonna, 2, 44, 60
magazines, 6, 10, 41, 46, 48–9, 108

Maglin, N. B., 63, 71n.5, 71n.9
Maguire, S., 58, 80
Man Who Cried, The, 42
Marc, D., 80
Martha Stewart Living, 48–50
Marshall, G., 9, 44
Marshment, M., 9, 10, 11
Martens, L., 11, 97, 98
Marxist-feminism, 101
Mason, A., 48–9, 53n.1, 53n.2
Massey, D., 97
Mazursky, P., 44
Memoirs of an Ex-Prom Queen, 1
Mendelson, C., 107
Merck, M., 83
Meyers, M., 48–9, 53n.1, 53n.2
Meyrowitz, J., 6, 102
Mies, M., 109
Milestone, L., 18
Miller, D., 11, 97
Min Ha, T., 61
Mintel, 143
Mistress L, 125
Mitchell, J., 30, 38n.1, 71n.5
modernity, 97–8, 100, 110
Modleski, T., 92
Mohanty, C., 61, 162–3, 169
'Money Programme, The', 128–33
Moore, K., 31
Moore, S., 106
Moores, S., 97
Moraga, C., 61
Morgan, J., 163
Morgan, R., 6
Morley, D., 97
Morrison, T., 176
Moseley, R., 79–80, 83, 104, 153–4
Mottier, V., 156
MTV, 63, 72n.12
Mulvey, L., 5
Munford, R., 12–14
Murdoch, G., 135
'Murphy Brown', 12, 79, 89

nation, 33, 47–8, 131, 132, 133
National Organisation of Women (NOW), 30
National Women's Studies Association, 60, 71n.6
Nationality, Immigration and Asylum Bill (2002), 127
'Native New Yorker', 1

Negrin, L., 150
Neisel, J., 63
news media, 8, 16, 25–40, 83–5, 106–7, 127–33
Nichols, M., 9, 44
'Nigella Bites', 51–2
'No Going Back', 108
Nolan, S., 30

'O.C., The', 18
Oakley, A., 71n.5, 101, 104, 168
Observer, The, 107
Odone, C., 107
One Nation Party, 36
Orientalism, 127, 131, 132
Orlando, 42
Orr, C. M., 61
O'Shane, P., 30
'Out on Tuesday', 121

Paglia, C., 59
Parker, R., 103
Patten, M., 55n.16
Pearson, A., 105, 108
pedagogy, feminist, 16, 43, 57–72
Peiss, K., 143, 144
Perry, D., 63, 71n.5, 71n.9
'Pictures of Women', 120
Piepmeier, A., 71n.10
Pipher, M., 57
Plant, S., 188, 198
Playboy, 191
Pleasance, H., 10
Pollock, G., 103
Popular feminism, 1–2, 7–12
pornography, 119, 120, 122, 123, 137
Porter, M. J., 91
Potter, S., 5, 42
post-feminism, 1–2, 7–15, 16–17, 41–55, 43–5,
    46, 51, 59, 61, 71n.10, 79–80, 81, 83–5, 86,
    88–9, 91–2, 97–115, 153–4
Powers, A., 64
Poynton, B., 82
Probyn, E., 89, 100, 103, 111
Projansky, S., 12, 71n.7, 71n.10, 102
Pretty in Pink, 66–7, 68
Pretty Woman, 9, 44, 99, 104

Quake, 183–99
queer politics, 61, 121

'race', 9, 11, 30, 32, 36, 59–60, 61, 62, 63,
    71n.4, 71n.6, 72n.12, 82, 126–7, 144–5,
    146–7, 150–51, 156, 163, 164, 167, 171,
    173, 174, 176
Rachel's Holiday, 45
radical feminism, 8, 12–13, 15, 102
Radner, H., 11
Radway, J., 6, 93
Ramaprasad, J., 33
Rapping, E., 28
Raymond, J., 136
Read, J., 8, 13, 79–80, 83, 104, 153–4
Reagan, R., 7, 102
'Red Light Zone', 121
Rée, J., 101
Reid, E., 31, 37
'Relocation, Relocation', 108
'Return to River Cottage', 115n.5
Reviving Ophelia, 57
Rhode, D., 27–8
Rhodes, L., 42
Richards, A., 62, 71n.10
Rickard, W., 125
Riddles of the Sphinx, 5
Riley, D., 89
River Cottage Cook Book, The, 115n.5
'River Cottage Forever', 115n.5
River Cottage Meat Book, The, 115n.5
River Cottage Year, The, 115n.5
Robson, M., 18
Rodriguez, M. S., 8
Roiphe, K., 35, 59, 62
Rolling Stone, 191
Root, J., 121
'Roseanne', 9, 79
Rosen, M., 4
Rose, J., 156
Rose, T., 9, 179
Rosler, M., 42, 46, 51, 53, 54n.3
Royal Television Society, 135
Russell, B., 55n.14
Ryan, Senator S., 32
Rybczynski, W., 50

Sandoval, C., 61, 71n.6, 71n.8
Schafly, P., 32
Schleiner, A-M., 193, 194, 195
Schlesinger, P., 135
Scorsese, M., 44

Scott, R., 58
Scott, S., 98
Scream, 16, 58, 60, 63, 67, 68, 72n.16
Scream 3, 57
Second-wave feminism, 2–8, 14–15, 25–7, 42–4, 45–6, 53, 57–8, 59–61, 63, 65, 68, 69, 70n.2, 84, 100–2, 104, 111, 124, 151, 153, 162–3
Semiotics of the Kitchen, The, 42
'Sex and Shopping', 121–2
'Sex and the City', 10–11, 13, 16, 44, 60, 79–93, 104
Sex Discrimination Act, 1984 (Australia), 31, 32
'Sex Traffic', 127, 133–6
sex workers, 17, 119–39, 173
sexual abuse, 64
sexuality, 11, 18, 34, 35, 36, 60–1, 62, 63–4, 67, 82–3, 87, 89, 119–39, 146
Shalit, W., 85
Shanahan, A., 35
Shiva, V., 109
Shulman, A. Kates, 1
Shyer, C., 105
Siegel, C., 60–1
Skeggs, B., 11, 110, 112, 144, 146, 156, 157
Skibre, M. L., 125
Smith, D., 41–2, 46–8, 51–3, 53, 54n.11, 54n.12
Sommers, C. Hoff, 35, 59
Spare Rib, 1
Sparks, C., 128
Spencer, J., 14
Spice Girls, The, 57, 60, 64
Spigel, L., 43
Spillers, H., 162
Spin, 64
'Spin City', 91
Spivak, G., 60
Sreberny, A., 28, 37
Stabile, C. A., 54n.9
Stacey, Jackie, 2–3, 54n.6
Stacey, Judith, 103–4, 113
Stanley, A., 46
Stewart, M., 41–2, 46–51, 52–3
Stoller, D., 13–14
Stone, A. R., 188
Storr, M., 154
Strange, N., 55n.13
'Strippers', 122–3
Suu Kyi, A., 33
Sydney Morning Herald, 33

Talbot, M., 53n.1
'Tales from River Cottage', 115n.5
Taormino, T., 71n.10
Tasker, Y., 187, 199
Taylor, T. L., 183, 200
television, 10–11, 12–13, 41–2, 44–5, 46–8, 51–2, 79–93, 108, 119–39
Thelma and Louise, 58
Third-wave feminism, 1–2, 7, 13–15, 57–8, 61–4, 69, 70n.2, 71n10, 99, 162–3, 165, 169
Thirteen, 66, 68
'thirtysomething', 12, 87, 102
Thornton, S., 100
Thriller, 5, 42
Time, 59, 60
Times, The, 107, 112
transgender, 170, 179
transsexual, 121
Tuchman, G., 4
Tucker, S., 162
Tulloch, J., 11, 128
Turner, V., 195–6
'Two Fat Ladies', 41
Tyrer, N., 106

Uhse, B., 122
United Nations, 16, 27, 31–3, 130, 131, 136
Unmarried Woman, An, 44
US Third World Feminism, 60, 61

van Erp, B., 85
van Zoonen, L., 27–8, 35, 37
Vance, C., 119
Veblen, T., 50
'Vice: The Sex Trade', 128–33
Vogue, 51

Wald, G., 10–11
Walker, A., 71n.5
Walker, Madam C. J., 144
Walker, R., 61–2, 64, 71n.5
Walters, S. D., 8, 9
'Watch the Woman', 5, 121
Wearing, B., 188
Wellington, C. A., 152
Whelehan, I., 36
Wicke, J., 8
'Will and Grace', 91
Willett, J., 151

Williams, R., 38
Williamson, J., 5
Willis, S., 82
Wilson, E., 11
Winship, J., 6, 49–50
Winston, B., 119, 128
Winterbottom, M., 133
Wolf, N., 36, 59, 145–7, 149

Wollen, P., 5
Women's Day, 49
Women's Electoral Lobby (WEL), 30–2
Women Who Want Be Women, 32
'Wonder Woman', 2
Working Girl, 9, 44, 104

Zeiger, S., 10